Who's Who in Dancing

Who's Who in Dancing
1932

Arnold Haskell
and
P. J. S. Richardson

Noverre Press

First published in 1932

This facsimile reprint published in 2010 by

The Noverre Press
Southwold House
Isington Road
Binsted
Hampshire
GU34 4PH

© 2010 The Noverre Press

ISBN 978-1-906830-30-4

A CIP catalogue record for this book is available from the British Library

SANTOS CASANI
Britain's Recognised Leading Authority on Ballroom Dancing and Principal of the World Famous
CASANI SCHOOL of DANCING, 90 Regent Street, Piccadilly Circus, LONDON, England.

UNITY IS STRENGTH.
Learn the **CASANI METHOD,** work together and be successful.

For full particulars apply :—THE SECRETARY, 90 Regent St., London, W.1.

Special facilities for Foreign and Provincial Teachers.

See pages xiii and xvi.   Telephone : REGENT **4438-9.**

SPOTLIGHTS
FLOODLIGHTS
BATTENS
FOOTLIGHTS

and all kinds of LIGHTING EFFECTS
for the Dance Hall, Ballroom and Rink.

Makers of the

PATENT "SELF-CONTAINED"

.. **PRISMATIC BOWL** ..

Non-Burnable Colours for Spotlights, etc.
May we send you a sample?

Please write for our Catalogue.

CINEMA TRADERS, Ltd.
26 Church Street, Charing Cross Road,
LONDON, W.1.

TO SCOTTISH READERS

ALEX McINTOSH

Private Studio : 3 Lansdowne Crescent,
GLASGOW, N.W.

HIGHEST CERTIFICATED MALE TEACHER OF DANCING IN THE WEST OF SCOTLAND. (ALL STYLES).

Specializes in the training of students for the Stage or as Teachers. Students are given an individual and personal training, and not only is the true technique taught, but how to impart it to others, is also taught and studied.

Every encouragement is given to bring out the best in each student, and when they are proficient, they are introduced into one of the best Societies of Dancing in Great Britain.

Interest does not stop at the end of the training of the young teacher, but they are helped out of all the little difficulties that befall a young and inexperienced teacher.

IN BALLROOM DANCING.

Here again,
in this branch of dancing, a system and method has been developed, by which you are first taught how to LEAD or follow your partner, before being taught steps. In modern ballroom dancing, it is very essential that you can lead (or follow) your partner, and this is one of the important points that so many teachers leave out.

Classes of 12 pupils, in which a gentleman partner for every lady is guaranteed, and each pupil is taught to dance their own part, are always starting.

LADIES ARE NOT ALLOWED TO DANCE AS GENTLEMEN.

Private lessons are given at any time by appointment.

SATISFACTION GUARANTEED

OR YOUR FEES REFUNDED.

MAX RIVERS
STUDIO OF DANCING

ABSOLUTELY the last word in modern stage dancing is taught at these studios. It is the most central studio in London with every modern convenience. Every member of the staff is an expert with a thorough knowledge of all branches of theatrical dancing. The Studios are under the personal supervision of Mr. Max Rivers, whose recent productions include :—

"White Horse Inn," Grosses Schauspielhaus, Berlin.
    Do.   do.   do.   Coliseum, London.
       (the theatrical sensation of the Season).
"Land of Smiles," Drury Lane Theatre.
"My Sister and I," Shaftesbury Theatre.
Francis Laidler's " Reply to the Talkies."
And the new " Splinters " Revue.

Call, Write or 'Phone.

LONDON:
WEST END HOUSE,
(Over Rialto Theatre).   3, 4, 5 & 6 Rupert Street, W.1.
Telephone: GERRARD 4413

BERLIN:
DEUTSCHES KUNTSLER THEATRE,
70-71, Nurnburger Strasse.
Telephone: BABAROSSA 9711 · B5.

VALERIE COOPER
SCHOOL OF MOVEMENT

BASED ON THE

LOHELAND METHOD OF GYMNASTICS

Gymnastic Classes and Remedial Treatment under the supervision of **Fraulein Elisabeth Hausrath**, Official Representative of **The Loheland School, Germany.**

THE CURRICULUM INCLUDES
STATIC, DYNAMIC, METRICAL
AND RHYTHMIC GYMNASTICS

RECOMMENDED AND APPROVED BY EMINENT PHYSICIANS AND PSYCHOLOGISTS.

The Directors of the Valerie Cooper School have associated themselves, after many years of individual and widely varying teaching experience, for the purpose of providing a centre in London, where a training in rhythmic movement may be obtained which, being anatomically and physiologically correct, will prevent and cure postural defects and the many diseases arising from them, and give the ability to carry the body with ease and grace, whether for the purposes of ordinary life or for those of sport, dance or drama.

Every incorrect movement wastes nervous energy and deforms the psychic constitution. By acquiring the habit of "rhythmic movement" the student stops this waste and deformation, preserves youthful vigour and flexibility and intensifies his individuality.

Directors :— **VALERIE COOPER**
Rhythmic Movement Certificate, Dalcroze Schools, London and Geneva. Associate of the Royal College of Music, London.
London, Oxford, Bristol, Reading, &c.

BARBARA DUMMETT
Member of Association of Operatic Dancing. Late of Carlton Hotel, St. Moritz.

WRITE FOR BROCHURE

Secretary, **VALERIE COOPER SCHOOL OF MOVEMENT**

Telephone : Fitzroy 1464. **6 Fitzroy Square, LONDON, W.1.**

Professional Training for the Profession ..

The LILIAN LEOFFELER SCHOOL OF STAGE DANCING

91 Great Portland Street, W.1.

The late Mme. Anna Pavlova and M. Serge Diaghileff repeatedly recruited their companies from the pupils of Lilian Leoffeler, many of whom became leading artistes; and that Producers and Managers to-day recognise the value of the training afforded by this School is evidenced by the fact that its pupils are to be found in every production of which dancing forms an important part.

> "The excellently conducted Lilian Leoffeler School..." THE STAGE.
>
> "An instructress who is a genius at her job..." THE REFEREE.

Telephone: Langham 1725.

BERT GRAHAM
School of Stage Dancing

Telephone: TEMPLE BAR 1152.

TAP	ACTS ARRANGED, PRODUCTIONS, TROUPES SUPPLIED (Boys or Girls)
RHYTHM	
ECCENTRIC	*Classes held Every Evening at 7 for Business People.*
ACROBATIC	
WALTZ	Singing, Voice Production by Miss LORNA KERSWELL, Medallist (R.A.M.).
CLOG	
MILITARY TAP	Elocution, Dramatic Interpretation, Amateurs, coached etc. by Miss SYBIL WISE, the well-known West-End Actress.
THE LATEST AMERICAN RHYTHM	LICENSED BY THE L.C.C.
MUSICAL COMEDY	114-116 Charing Cross Road,
BALLET, Etc.	(4th and 5th floors) London, W.C.2.

C. W. BEAUMONT,
75 CHARING CROSS ROAD, LONDON, W.C.2.
Publisher of Books on Dancing.

SOME BOOKS IN DEMAND.

ORCHESOGRAPHY. By Thoinot Arbeau. *Illus. The standard work on Elizabethan dances.* — **25s.**

THE DANCING-MASTER. By P. Rameau. *With 50 plates. The standard work on 18th century dance technique.* — **25s.**

LETTERS ON DANCING AND BALLETS. By J. G. Noverre. *With 12 illus.* — **25s.**

A MANUAL OF THE THEORY AND PRACTICE OF CLASSICAL THEATRICAL DANCING (CECCHETTI METHOD). By Cyril W. Beaumont and S. Idzikowski. *With 100 illus.* — **25s.**

THE THEORY AND PRACTICE OF ALLEGRO IN CLASSICAL BALLET (CECCHETTI METHOD). By Margaret Craske and Cyril W. Beaumont. *Illus.* — **12s. 6d.**

A FRENCH-ENGLISH DICTIONARY OF TECHNICAL TERMS USED IN CLASSICAL BALLET. Compiled by Cyril W. Beaumont. — **3s. 6d.**

MARIE TAGLIONI. By André Levinson. *With 16 illus.* — **16s.**

A HISTORY OF BALLET IN RUSSIA. By Cyril W. Beaumont. *With Intro. by A. Levinson. 30 illus.* — **21s.**

¶ Complete Catalogue of Publications sent post free on application.

POLAND REHEARSAL ROOMS.

Phones: Gerr. 5176-7-8.   **49 POLAND STREET, W.I.**

Telegrams: "STAREVUE, RATH, LONDON."

THE **FINEST** REHEARSAL ROOMS IN THE **WORLD**

Café. Private Call Offices. Dressing Rooms. Central Heating.
Rehearsal Theatre with Stage.   Footlights and Front Lime.
Ballroom with Stage.

Proprietors: DOROTHY AND NEWMAN MAURICE.

NEW MANAGEMENT. NEW IDEAS. NEW DECORATIONS.

Same Manageress—DOROTHY MAURICE.

LEARN HOW TO MOVE WITH

Easy Grace and Rhythmic Beauty

Apply:

Marcelle Valerie

Subjects Taught:
(a) Greek and Expressive Dancing.
(b) Dalcroze Eurhythmics & Ear Training
(c) Relaxation. Scientific Breathing.
(d) Physical Culture (Swedish System).
(e) Ballet Technique (Cecchetti Method).

KENSINGTON GARDEN STUDIOS, Studio D.:
29 HIGH STREET, NOTTING HILL GATE, Tel. Park 6186.

EVERY DANCER should read—

"MIME"

By

Mark E. Perugini.

POST **2/6** FREE

from

"The Dancing Times" Office,
25 Wellington Street, Strand, W.C.2.

ANELLO and DAVIDE

Continental Toe Ballet Shoe Makers,

MILAN.

No connection with any firm of similar name.

Shoes as supplied to :—
Late Diaghileff's Russian Ballet, Mmes. Pavlova, Lopokova, Nemchinova, Astafieva, Anton Dolin, etc.

Speciality :—
Ballet Shoes approved by and made for Association of Operatic Dancing of Great Britain.

Special reductions in price of Tap Dancing Shoes.

Write for Price List.

71 NEW COMPTON ST., W.C.2.
Near Palace Theatre.

TEMPLE BAR 5019.

PRINCESS YVONNE

Photographic Studios

102 Charing Cross Road,
LONDON, W.C.2.

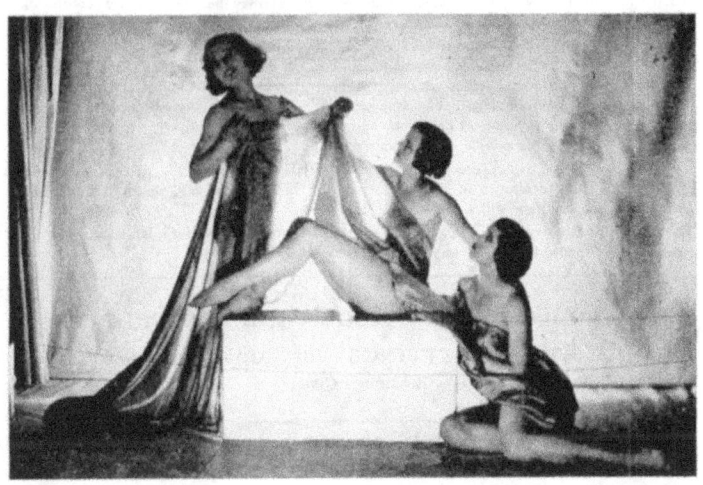

Phone: TEMPLE BAR 4874.

Special Prices to all Professionals and Pupils.

Recommended by:—
MISS JOSEPHINE BRADLEY.
CONE SCHOOL OF DANCING.
MADAM LEA ESPINOSA.
MADAM JUDITH ESPINOSA.

BURNET'S
FANCY DRESS FABRICS

TRIMMINGS, ACCESSORIES & HOSIERY
suitable for
National, Historical, & Fancy Dress Costumes,
School Plays and Dancing Displays.

> Much time can be saved, any chance of disappointment may be avoided, by consulting Burnet's in matters connected with Fancy Dress—whether for Costume Balls or for Theatrical Performances.
>
> Few, indeed, are the probable requirements—either for fabrics or accessories—which are not included in the actual stocks always maintained by Burnet's. Many of the materials are of exclusive design, unobtainable elsewhere. The large and varied character of the stock greatly aids in the task of selection, and in this Burnet's staff of experts are ever ready to afford valuable advice and assistance.
>
> Catalogues are issued which comprise many of the fabrics in frequent use: Tights and Hosiery, and the Accessories in constant demand—spangles, crowns, wands, wings, hats, wire shapes, etc. These will be forwarded on request.
>
> No catalogue can, however, do justice to the resources of Burnet's, and inquiries for special requirements, in case of any difficulty, are always welcomed.

SPECIAL OPERA HOSE, TIGHTS AND ELASTIC BELTS.

FABRIC STAGE SETTINGS for Amateur Theatricals.
Estimates Given.

Patterns and Illustrated Price List on application.
When writing, kindly indicate the special use for which patterns and lists are desired.

B. BURNET & CO., LTD.,
22 Garrick Street, Covent Garden,
LONDON, W.C.2.

TUBE—LEICESTER SQUARE.

Telephone: Telegrams:
Temple Bar 3972 & 4893. " Covent, Westrand, London."

CASANI SCHOOL OF DANCING.

SOME PRESS OPINIONS.

Dancing Times: Santos Casani has capped all by taking by far the largest and most handsome ballroom premises in the Metropolis towards Piccadilly Circus in Regent Street. They are three very large rooms.

Daily Graphic: The Daily Graphic representative visited the dancing school of Santos Casani, the well-known teacher, yesterday and saw forty or fifty men and women from all over the country learning to become teachers themselves.

Natal Advertiser: Casani is the only ballroom dancer to have topped the bill at the Coliseum. In addition he is the holder of many other records, for instance the only man in England to broadcast dancing by wireless, the only man to teach by phonofilms, and the only dancer to exchange steps by telephone between London and New York at the cost of £5 per minute.

Daily Sketch: Santos Casani is, I suppose, the champion director of dance. Casani's place is a real dance factory with all three floors going at once.

Dancing Times: There is no gainsaying the fact that amongst ballroom teachers and demonstrators there is no one in the country who has such an immense popular following as Santos Casani. I know from information given to me by managers in big Palais, especially in the provinces, that Santos Casani and his partner favourably affect the box office receipts in a way that is truly remarkable, and that as a consequence he can demand prices which read as a fairy tale to others. Casani also scores in so much as he possesses a gift of showmanship. How few of our demonstrators possess this.

Daily Despatch: Casani is another of those restless artistic people who sparkle in the arts profession, for not only is he to be found in every part of the country demonstrating the latest dances, but incidentally finds time for film demonstrations.

Dancing Times: For half an hour I watched Mr. Casani give a lesson to a provincial teacher. I must say I was very much impressed by the extremely clear way he demonstrated the why and wherefore of everything. Casani is essentially modern in his teaching.

Dancing Times: Familiarity with Casani's method of teaching certainly does not breed contempt, rather it increases one's admiration. Mr. Casani danced with some half-dozen of his articled pupils separately, in order to show the improvements which each had made with one month's tuition. It was an evidence of efficiency of teaching.

Radio Times: By George Grossmith. Santos Casani is not only a brilliant teacher but a teacher of teachers. Listeners will have appreciated from his first lesson the simplicity of his method.

Vogue: In any case, training is the first essential test at the Casani School of Dancing. So absolutely precise is his method of instruction and his carefully planned four and six months course that produces impeccably efficient and undoubtedly successful teachers.

Evening News: The most popular performance at the Coliseum this week appears to be the demonstration of the new French Tango by Santos Casani and his partner. The graceful movements were followed with absorbed attention last night.

Southend Times: Europe's greatest Tango experts, Santos Casani and partner, proved a remarkable attraction.

Special facilities for Foreign and Provincial Teachers.

Originals of the above press cuttings may be inspected at the Casani School, 90 Regent Street, London.

See Pages i and xvi. Telephone: REGENT **4438-9.**

The "AUTOMATIC" Revolving Spotlight.
WITHOUT A DOUBT—THE MOST WONDERFUL LIGHTING EFFECT EVER PRODUCED.

The Outfit consists of a Special Lantern, fitted with Four Powerful Lenses, which is revolved by means of a clockwork Motor. The Lantern is surrounded by a Handsome Framework, finished in an Oriental Copper Colour, and fitted with Eight Beautiful Colours. The Apparatus is complete with a 500 Watt Lamp and Flex ready for use. When the effect is required simply switch on and Four Powerful Beams appear and sweep round the Hall in a blaze of constantly changing Colour and in penetrating every corner make a most Wonderful and Spectacular Effect.

NO OPERATOR— ONLY ONE LAMP, THE EFFECT OF FOUR SPOTLIGHTS. May be fitted with Electric Motor for **£7** Extra if required.

PRICE, ABSOLUTELY COMPLETE WITH 5 HOUR MOTOR
£5 15s. 6d. CARRIAGE PAID. Delivery from Stock.

Actual Manufacturers of Every Description of Lighting Apparatus.

Full Size Revolving Mirror Bowls, **£5.** Spotlights, **30/-** Floodlights, Gelatines, etc., etc. Send for Illustrated Catalogue. Large Stocks, Lowest Prices in the World.

D. WALTER AND CO.
107 NEWINGTON CAUSEWAY, LONDON, S.E.1
'Phone : HOP 6049

DANCE, CARNIVAL & ADVERTISING
NOVELTIES
DECORATIONS and PRESENTS.

Phone: CHANCERY 7654.

LARGEST SELECTION IN LONDON

Phone or Write for List **X**

COME AND VISIT OUR SHOWROOMS.

Victor G. Ginn & Co.
16 RED LION SQUARE, HIGH HOLBORN, (Close to Holborn Tube) LONDON, W.C.1.

TEA ROOM TABLES
AND CHAIRS OF EVERY DESCRIPTION. Suitable for Hotels, Cafes, Dancing Rooms Lounges, Bar Rooms.

Glass Top Octagonal.   *Send for Catalogues and Price List to :*   Tiled Top.

THE KAFA TABLE Co.,
5-7 Church St., Shoreditch, London, E.2.
Tel. No.: Bishopsgate 1739.

Tables made in
GLASS
 TILES
  RUBBER
   LINO
    BAILE
     COPPER
      BRASS
PLAIN WOOD

Inlaid Glass Top.

Manchester Agents and Showrooms,
7 Cathedral Yd.,
Gt. Ducie St.,
MANCHESTER

Regent 4438-9.   Principal: SANTOS CASANI.

The Casani School of Dancing
90 REGENT STREET, PICCADILLY CIRCUS.

Three Large Studios.

THIS SCHOOL WILL BE OPEN THROUGHOUT THE YEAR FOR TRAINING STUDENTS AND FOR PRIVATE LESSONS.

Guarantee to teach you fundamental steps of any dance in

3 Private Lessons—£1-1-0.

PRIVATE LESSONS daily by a qualified staff in the Waltz (new and old), Fox-trot (slow and quick), New Tango, etc., from **10 a.m. to 10 p.m.**, under the personal supervision of

SANTOS CASANI
Britain's Leading Authority on Ballroom Dancing.

"Casani's Guaranteed Training."

DANCING AS A CAREER.

It is a positive fact that there is an excellent opportunity for young people to take up Ballroom Dancing as a career, and earn between £5 and £10 per week, to teach for themselves, or act as Hostesses, etc.

The training takes roughly between four to six months and, compared with any other profession, is very short, and the cost is most reasonable.

SANTOS CASANI is offering a special sound course of training for students, which is of unrivalled value.

This course will include 150 private lessons.

To be a successful Teacher, it is imperative that you should be trained by the best-known school to the general public. There is no doubt that **CASANI** is the most talked-of name. Anything to do with dancing on the film, radio or newspaper articles throughout the world, is nine out of ten times **CASANI**, which speaks for itself.

Anyone intending to take up dancing as a profession and wish to avail themselves of this wonderful offer are invited to visit the **CASANI SCHOOL** and see for themselves the method of training and style of dancing. Intending students will be given a test free. There is no charge for the interview, and you are under no obligation. Write for particulars and appointment.

Don't you think that there are too many dance societies; too many World's Champions; and far too many worthless titles and abbreviated qualifications which only mislead the general public, but really mean nothing. But there is only one successful **CASANI METHOD**.

SPECIAL CASANI METHOD CORRESPONDENCE COURSES.

UNITY IS STRENGTH.

Learn the **CASANI METHOD**, work together and be successful.

For full particulars apply :—THE SECRETARY, 90 Regent Street, W.1.

Buy SANTOS CASANI Dance Shoes from Messrs. W. Abbott and Sons, Ltd., 82 Regent W.1, and all branches.

Practice Classes—Tuesdays, 8.30 to 10.30, 3/-

See pages i and xiii.   Telephone: REGENT 4438-9.

WHO'S WHO IN DANCING
1 9 3 2

BEING A LIST OF ALPHABETICALLY ARRANGED
BIOGRAPHIES OF THE LEADING MEN AND
WOMEN IN THE WORLD OF DANCING

COMPILED BY THE PUBLISHERS AND EDITED BY
ARNOLD HASKELL
AND
P. J. S. RICHARDSON

LONDON
THE DANCING TIMES, LTD.,
25 WELLINGTON STREET, STRAND, W.C.2

The Association of
OPERATIC DANCING
of Great Britain

Patroness:
HER MAJESTY THE QUEEN

President:
MADAME ADELINE GENÉE

Council:

MADAME KARSAVINA   MISS PHYLLIS BEDELLS
MR. D. G. MACLENNAN   MR. FELIX DEMERY
MADAME JUDITH ESPINOSA   MISS K. DANETREE
MR. P. J. S. RICHARDSON

Entrance Examinations (Elementary Certificate) are held four times a year.

Examinations for the 'Intermediate' 'Advanced' and 'Solo Seal' Certificates, also the 'Intermediate Teachers Certificate' are only open to Members and are held at frequent intervals.

CHILDREN'S EXAMINATIONS
which are not limited to Members or pupils of Members are held twice a year and are divided into five grades.

For full particulars write to

The Secretary,
Association of Operatic Dancing,
154 Holland Park Avenue, London, W.11.

CONTENTS

	PAGE
PREFACE	5
ASSOCIATIONS AND SOCIETIES—	
Great Britain	7
Belgium	13
Denmark	13
France	13
Germany	14
Switzerland	15
United States	15
South Africa	16
STAGE DANCING COMPETITIONS	17
"DANCING TIMES" CUP WINNERS	18
BALLROOM COMPETITION WINNERS	19
BIOGRAPHIES	21

THE IMPERIAL SOCIETY OF TEACHERS OF DANCING

(With which the Cecchetti Society is Incorporated)

(Founded in London, 1904, membership over 2,000).

Headquarters: 113/117 Charing Cross Rd., London, W.C.2

President - Major CECIL H. TAYLOR

BRANCHES

OPERATIC ASSOCIATION. For Teachers of the Operatic Association's System of Training.
CLASSICAL BALLET. For Teachers of Maestro Cav. Enrico Cecchetti's System of Training.
GENERAL TEACHERS'. For National, Character, Step and other dancing.
GREEK. R.G. Section. For Revived Greek Dancing.
  N.M. Section. For Miss Madge Atkinson's Method.
BALLROOM. For Specialists in Modern Ballroom Dancing.

OBJECTS

The elevation and advancement of the Art of Dancing.
The fraternal co-operation of properly qualified Teachers of Dancing for the safeguarding of their mutual interests.
The adoption of a comparatively uniform system of instruction.
The establishment of an Annual Technical School to afford Members special opportunities for the cultivation of a higher standard of proficiency and skill.
The holding of an Annual Congress.
The founding of an Emergency Fund for the temporary relief of Members in distress.
The holding of Lectures and the reading and discussion of Papers upon Dancing and allied subjects.
The publication and distribution to Members of the Society's Journal.

MEMBERSHIP

The degrees of Membership open to qualified teachers are:
MEMBERSHIP. For teachers, over 21 years of age, who have occupied responsible positions in the actual teaching of dancing for a period of years.
REGISTRATION FEE AND SUBSCRIPTION. The Registration Fee is One Guinea. The Annual Subscription to any one Branch is One Guinea and to each additional Branch Half-a-Guinea.

PART MEMBERSHIP

ASSOCIATESHIP. For teachers who have not had three years' experience as responsible teachers of dancing or who have not attained the age of 21 years.

INFORMATION

APPLICATION FORMS and further particulars may be obtained from the General Secretary, Mr. F. W. CRUTCHETT LESLIE, 113/117 Charing Cross Road, London, W.C.2.

PREFACE.

WHEN, considerably over a year ago, having come to the conclusion that the compilation of a " Who's Who in Dancing " was very desirable in the interests of the dancing profession, we consented to act as Editors, we did not realise the magnitude of the task we had undertaken.

Possibly we placed too much faith in the co-operation we hoped to receive from those whose biographies would have to be included in the volume. We did not contemplate that hundreds would have to be written to three, four and even five times in order to obtain the necessary particulars. We certainly never thought that even after five communications there would be, in many instances, no reply forthcoming.

Had we not known the Profession very well, we might have taken this as a sign that the book was not wanted, but we were well aware of the fact that, as a rule, the dancer is decidedly backward in the matter of publicity, and we feel sure that the very first to object to the omission of their names will be those who did not reply to our requests or make any demand for inclusion.

Under these circumstances it is obvious that the book must show many omissions, and that owing to the delay in publication important events in the lives of many dancers may have occurred since they forwarded their biographies, which are not recorded.

We feel, however, that even with these faults, " Who's Who in Dancing " will prove of considerable value as a book of reference.

We have dealt with Great Britain as fully as possible ; but in the case of the rest of the world we have only referred to a very few of the more important personalities, choosing those about whom we are from time to time hearing in this country.

It is our present intention to publish a second edition in 1934. In that, with the help of readers who, we hope, will notify us of omissions and inaccuracies, something nearer our ideal of a book of reference will be attained.

ARNOLD L. HASKELL.
PHILIP J. S. RICHARDSON.

May, 1932.

The Midland Association of Teachers of Dancing

(Estd. 1920.)   (Affiliated to the National Association of Teachers of Dancing.)

Headquarters :—32 PARKHURST ROAD, HOLLOWAY, LONDON, N.7.   (*Branches in the Midlands and West of England*).

President :—H. VIVIAN DAVIES, London.

Membership open to Teachers passing the Association's Examination in—Ballroom, Operatic, National and Tap Dancing, etc.

Advantages :—Social, Legal, Benevolent, Technical, Monthly Meetings in all Councils with expert technical instruction in every branch. Juvenile section with special technical classes. Annual Dinner and Dance. Conference and Competitions.

This year's Conference and Competitions will be held in London, on May 14th, 15th, 16th and 17th, 1932. Twelve handsome Trophies, Medals and Diplomas are offered, covering all branches.

Entrance Fee £1-1-0.   Annual Subscription £1-1-0.

For particulars of Membership, etc., apply—**General Secretary,**
'*Phone: Sydenham* 5425   **Mr. H. D. Brittain, 76 High Street, Penge, S.E.20.**

THE BRITISH ASSOCIATION OF TEACHERS OF DANCING

Registered under the Friendly Societies' Act, 1896.

Annual Subscription One & Half Guineas.—Entrance Fee One Guinea.

Open to all Teachers of Ballroom, Operatic and Display Dancing.

Technical School of Instruction at Quarterly General Meetings and during five days at Annual Conference. No additional Fees.

Registered Office :
Ladbroke Hall, Ladbroke Grove, KENSINGTON, W.10.

All communications to the Gen. Sec.:
W. H. CADMAN, King's Hall, Stretford, MANCHESTER.
Tels.: Longford 1293 and Sale 3847.

ASSOCIATIONS AND SOCIETIES

A list of the Dancing Associations and Societies in England and of the more important ones in the United States and on the Continent.

GREAT BRITAIN.

Allied Dancing Association.

Founded in Liverpool in 1922. An amalgamation of local teachers, who may be members of other Associations, for the purpose of raising the standard of ballroom dancing in the district. Arranges frequent Technical Classes by prominent demonstrators, and organises the annual "Allied North of England Dancing Championship," with finals at the Grafton Rooms, the Association's headquarters. Membership is secured by Examination, the Syllabus of which is laid down by the "Official Board," on which this Association is represented.

President: (1931-2) Mr. J. Killen.

Secretary: Mr. Walter Fletcher, 6 Blucher Street, Waterloo, Liverpool.

Association of Ballrooms and Dance Halls.

A recently formed Association, not of Dance Hall managers, as might be thought, but of the Halls themselves. It is the outcome of the Annual Meetings between the "Official Board" and the managers of Dance Halls. Is under the Chairmanship of Capt. J. Russell Pickering, of the Royal Opera House Dances, and is very representative of the principal popular ballrooms in this country. Was formed to promote, improve and protect the business interests of its members. Has already done a considerable amount towards effecting co-operation between Dance Hall managers and teachers of Dancing.

Membership is open to Companies, Firms, Corporations or Persons controlling rooms or halls for the purpose of ballroom dancing.

Secretary: Mr. A. R. Foggo, 23 Bedford Row, London, W.C.1.

Association of Operatic Dancing of Great Britain.

Founded in London on December 31st, 1920, for the purpose of improving the standard of Operatic Dancing and the elevation and advancement of the Art of Dancing generally in the British Empire. Candidates for Membership must satisfy the Council of the Association that they have a knowledge of the correct Elementary technique of Operatic Dancing. Members are subsequently expected to take in turn the "Intermediate," "Advanced" and "Solo Seal" Examinations. There are now upwards of 1500 members.

A new Examination, open to Members only, and known as the "Intermediate Teachers' Certificate," was instituted in January, 1932, to test the teaching ability of the candidates.

In addition to the above Examinations, which are held at regular intervals, the activities of the Association include "Scholarship Classes," which are special weekly free lessons given to selected pupils of members, special "free classes" given by Members of the Council to all Members, numerous "Lectures" on dancing and the sister arts, a "Technical School" lasting one week in the summer and occasional displays. On three occasions Examiners have been sent to South Africa, where there are many Members. The "Operatic Association Gazette" is published four times a year and issued free to members.

The Association stresses the educational and physical value of dancing for young children by holding twice a year "Children's Examinations" in simple Operatic and Greek Dancing to encourage poise, line and physical development. These Examinations, which are not confined to Members or Members' pupils, are in five grades, and attract about four thousand candidates each year. The "Greek" section is arranged in conjunction with the "Association of Teachers of the Revived Greek Dance."

Her Majesty the Queen graciously gave her patronage to the Association in 1928.

President: Madame Adeline Genée, I. et A.

Council: Madame Karsavina, Miss Phyllis Bedells, Madame Judith Espinosa, Miss Kathleen Danetree, Mr. D. G. MacLennan, Mr. Felix Demery and Mr. P. J. S. Richardson.

Secretary: Mr. P. J. S. Richardson, 154 Holland Park Avenue, London, W.11.

Association of Teachers of the Revived Greek Dance.

Inaugurated by Miss Ruby Ginner at Stratford-on-Avon in 1923 to standardise the teaching of the Revived Greek Dance, and to promote mental and physical development by means of the Revived Greek Dance. Admission is by examination, held twice yearly, both for teachers and students. Candidates who are successful in the teachers' examination may become members on payment of an entrance fee and annual subscription.

In conjunction with the "Operatic Association," "Children's Examinations are held twice a year. "The Link," the Association's journal, is edited by Mr. Mark E. Perugini, and is published four times a year.

President: Miss Ruby Ginner.

Secretary: Miss F. Willoughby Brown, Philbeach Hall, Philbeach Gardens, S.W.5.

Ballet Club.

Founded in October, 1930, to present seasons of ballet in its own small theatre in Ladbroke Road before members and their guests. The Directors are Madame Marie Rambert, Mr. Ashley Dukes, Mr. Frederick Ashton and Mr. Arnold Haskell. The company consists of the "Marie Rambert Dancers," but "guest artists" are frequently invited to dance at the performances. In addition to giving revivals of many famous ballets, the Club has done a great deal to encourage the young British choreographer, and has produced numerous original ballets by Frederick Ashton, Susan Salaman and Anthony Tudor.

Secretary: Mr. Anthony Tudor, 2a Ladbroke Road, W.11.

British Association of Teachers of Dancing.

Founded in 1892. An Association formed to assist professional teachers of dancing to acquire knowledge of the latest developments in all branches of dancing. Membership is gained by Examination. Examinations are held in all the principal cities and towns in the country. This was the first Dance Association to be formed in this country.

President: (1931-2) Mrs. W. H. Cadman.

Secretary: Mr. W. H. Cadman, King's Hall, Stretford, Manchester.

British Ballet Organisation.

Founder and Organiser: Miss Louise Kay, Woolborough House, Lonsdale Road, Barnes, London, S.W.13.

Camargo Society.

Had its origin in a suggestion made by Mr. P. J. S. Richardson and Mr. Arnold Haskell in October, 1929, to a few prominent dancers, artists and musicians that it might be possible to produce original and classic ballets before a subscription audience four times a year at a West End theatre. The proposal assumed definite shape at an "Inaugural Dinner," which was held under the Chairmanship of Madame Adeline Genée at the Hotel Metropole on 16th February, 1930.

During its first season (1930-1) the "Society" fully justified its existence, and by its production of works of such artistic significance as Lambert's *Pomona*, Gretry's *Cephalus and Procris*, Walton's *Facade*, Milhaud's *La Creation du Mond*, and Vaughan William's *Job*, established itself so firmly in public esteem as to receive an invitation to participate in the Ninth Festival of the International Society for Contemporary Music at Oxford, when *Pomona* and *Job* were given with conspicuous success.

The Society's principal choreographers have been Ninette de Valois and Frederick Ashton, but ballets have also been arranged by Phyllis Bedells, Nicolas Legat and Trudl Dubsky.

Annual subscriptions are four, three, two or one guinea according to the seat desired. Donations are needed that the work of the " Society " may fulfil its mission of maintaining a high standard of production.

Madame Karsavina is the Vice-President of the " Society," and the Committee consists of Madame Lopokova, Miss Bedells, Madame Rambert, Miss de Valois, Miss Cone, Miss Penelope Spencer, Mr. Edwin Evans, Mr. Haskell, Mr. Tysser, Mr. P. J. S. Richardson, Mr. Anton Dolin, Mr. Stephen Thomas and Mr. Constant Lambert. Mr. J. M. Keynes is Honorary Treasurer.

Secretary: Mr. M. Montagu-Nathan, 5/24 Campden House Court, London, W.8.

Dancers' Circle Dinners.

A series of " Dinners " inaugurated by *The Dancing Times* in 1920 for the purpose of enabling members of the profession to meet one another and discuss matters of interest. Twenty-six have been held at irregular intervals, and much valuable work—notably the founding of the " Association of Operatic Dancing " and the institution of the " Children's Examinations "—has resulted.

English Folk Dance and Song Society (The).

Formed in 1911 with the object—(*a*) to preserve English Folk Dances, Folk Music and Singing Games, to make them known and to encourage the practice of them in their traditional forms ; (*b*) to encourage research into and promote knowledge and practice of English Folk Song and Dances by means of schools, classes, examinations, lectures, demonstrations, festivals and other like methods ; (*c*) to prepare and publish, for sale or otherwise, journals, records, reports and other literature as may seem desirable for the said knowledge and practice.

The Society has 50 branches in the Counties and larger towns of England, and two in America. The only forms of dancing dealt with by the Society is Folk Dancing, *i.e.*, Country Dancing, Morris Dancing and Sword Dancing.

President and Chairman of Committee: The Lady Ampthill, C.I., G.B.E.

Director: Douglas Kennedy.
Secretary: Mrs. F. C. Jenkins.
Offices: Cecil Sharp House, 2 Regent's Park Road, London, N.W.1

Faculty of Dancing.

One of the branches of the " Faculty of Arts." Lecture-demonstrations on matters of technical interest to dancers are given at frequent intervals, to which members are admitted free and may purchase tickets for their friends. Displays by well-known dancers and also by debutantes (selected at an audition) are given, and members have the right to attend all functions organised by other branches of the " Faculty of Arts." The " Faculty " has a small but excellent theatre and a suite of handsome Club Rooms, fully licensed, at which meals may be obtained at a most reasonable price. The entrance fee is two guineas and the annual subscription a similar sum.

Chairman: Mr. P. J. S. Richardson.
Vice-Chairman: Mr. G. P. Catchpole.
Honorary Secretary: Miss Thora Darsie, Princes Arcade, 190-195 Piccadilly, London, W.

Imperial Society of Teachers of Dancing (with which the Cecchetti Society is incorporated).

The Society was founded in 1904 and now consists of over two thousand members.

The Society is divided into five Branches, viz. : Operatic Association, Classical Ballet, General Teachers, Greek and Ballroom.

The Operatic Association Branch is

founded on French traditional methods of training; the Classical Ballet follows the system of training devised by Maestro Cav. Enrico Cecchetti.

The General Teachers' Branch includes in its membership teachers whose knowledge is general rather than special. The General Branch also deals with National and Character Dancing, Mime and Deportment.

The Greek Branch is divided into two sections: the Revived Greek which follows the Ruby Ginner method, and the Natural Movement Section which follows the method of Madge Atkinson.

The Ballroom Branch is for specialists in modern Ballroom Dancing. The Branch has a combined membership and associateship of about 1000. The Branch Committee consists of leading West End teachers and exponents of modern ballroom dancing.

It was the original members of this Committee which carried out so successfully the novel and intricate work of codifying the modern ballroom technique, and to them is therefore due the present pre-eminence of British ballroom dancing.

The Society organises an Annual Technical School to assist members to attain a higher standard of proficiency and to keep in touch with the latest developments. Each member receives a copy of the Society's Journal which is published bi-monthly.

The Degrees of Membership are: Members, Licentiates, and Fellows. There is also a grade of Associate, but this grade does not entitle the holders to the privileges of full membership.

Members must not be less than twenty-one years of age and, in addition to the years of training, must have occupied responsible positions in the *actual teaching of dancing* for a period of three years. They must also pass an Elementary examination approved by the particular Branch or Section to which they seek admission.

Candidates for Licentiateships must pass an Intermediate examination approved by the particular Branch or Section they wish to enter.

Fellowships are confined to those members who have passed an Advanced examination, and have occupied a responsible position in the actual teaching of dancing for a period of five years.

Candidates of any age over sixteen years, and Professional Dancers over fourteen years of age, may enter for the above examinations.

Examinations for each Branch are held in London four times a year, at roughly equal periods. In the case of the Ballroom Branch there are six Examinations annually, instead of the usual four. Examinations are also held in the provinces as occasion demands.

There are three grades of examinations, Elementary, Intermediate and Advanced, except in the General Teachers' and Ballroom Branches, the former having Elementary and Intermediate only, while the latter makes a distinction between the examinations for Associateships and Memberships.

Examinations for children are also held by the Classical Ballet, Revived Greek and Ballroom Branches.

Syllabi for each examination are available for the guidance of prospective candidates.

President: Major Cecil H. Taylor.
Past-President: Mrs. Dora Bedford.
General Secretary: Mr. F. W. Crutchett Leslie, 113-117 Charing Cross Road, London, W.C.2.

Incorporated London Academy of Music.

Founded in 1861 and Incorporated in 1915. Examinations in Ballroom and Ballet Dancing were instituted in 1928. In addition to London, centres are in Manchester, Cardiff and Leicester. Teachers, Performers, and Grade Certificates are awarded.

Secretary: Mr. G. Gordon Harvey, Incorporated London Academy of Music, Queens Gate Hall, Harrington Road, South Kensington, London, S.W.7.

International Dancing Masters' Association.

Founded in July, 1930, by the incorporation of the English, Premier, Universal and Yorkshire Associations, with the object of raising the standard of dancing. Membership is obtained by Examination, the syllabus for which is that laid down by the Official Board of Ballroom Dancing, on which this Association is represented.

President: (1931-2) Mr. H. Gilliver.
Secretary: Mr. Robert Gledhill, Carlton Chambers, Bradford.

Lancashire Dancing Association.

Founded in 1927 by Miss Alicia Cottrell, who is President. Embraces all branches of dancing. Instituted to help improve the standard of dancing.
Secretary: Mdme. Clara Cottrell, 4a West Crescent, St. Annes-on-Sea, Lancashire.

Liverpool Association of Teachers of Dancing.

Founded in 1919, but was reconstructed and renamed in 1921. Membership is open to all teachers of ballroom, stage and classical dancing, and is obtained by examination, the syllabus of which is that laid down by the Official Board, although the Association is not represented on that Board.
President: (1931-2) Mr. Arthur Hughes.
Secretary: Mr. A. Torpey, 14 Walton Road, Kirkdale, Liverpool.

Manchester Association of Teachers of Dancing.

Founded in 1903. Covers all forms of dancing. Membership is obtained through examination, the Ballroom section of which is that approved by the Official Board, on which this Association is represented. Examinations are held monthly, or as occasions require. Meetings are held on the second Sunday of each month. Registered Office, 210 Plymouth Grove, Manchester. In 1927 the Association organised and officiated for the *Evening Chronicle* All For Dancing Exhibition, one of the most successful exhibitions held in Manchester.
President: (1931) Miss Ethel Finnigan.
Hon. Secretary: Mr. A. Smith, 202 St. Mary's Road, Moston, Manchester.

Midland Association of Teachers of Dancing.

Founded in 1920. Covers all branches of dancing. Membership obtained through examination. Is represented on the Official Board, and adopts its syllabus for ballroom examinations. Has a Juvenile Section. Is affiliated to the National Association. Holds monthly meetings. Headquarters, Morgan's Academy of Dancing, 32 Parkhurst Road, Holloway, London, N.
President (1931-2): Mr. H. Vivian Davies.
Secretary: Mr. H. D. Brittain, Estcourt Hall, 76 High Street, Penge, London, S.E.20.

National Association of Teachers of Dancing.

Founded in 1907, its objects being to afford facilities for social intercourse and technical improvement in dancing. All forms of dancing covered. Membership obtained by examination. Examinations are held monthly in London, Manchester, Liverpool, Newcastle, York and Glasgow. The Headquarters of the Association are at the Criterion Restaurant, Piccadilly Circus, London. Graded Children's Examinations are held in Operatic and Greek Dancing. Ten Silver Trophies are awarded for Operatic Competitions at the Annual Festivals.
President (1931-2): Mr. W. A. Greenwell.
Secretary: Mr. F. C. Barlow, 55 Wellington Street, Woolwich, London, S.E.18.

Northern Counties Dance Teachers' Association.

Founded in 1925 to further the interests of teachers of Ballroom Dancing, and to provide facilities for technical improvement in that dancing. Membership is obtained through examination, the syllabus for which is that approved by the Official Board, on which the Association is represented.
President (1931-2): Mr. W. A. Greenwell.
Secretary: Mr. J. S. Marston, 80

High West Street, Gateshead, Co. Durham.

Northern Dance Teachers' Association.
An Association formed to give members the benefit of Technical Instruction in all forms of dancing, and also legal and other advice. Membership is open to all who can prove two years' actual experience in teaching dancing. When elected, members must take the examinations within six months of date of election. The Association is represented on the Official Board, and adopts its syllabus for ballroom examinations. Examinations are held quarterly. Children's Examinations are held. Postal Tuition is available for members.
President (1931-2) : Mr. Winn Morelle.
General Secretary : Mr. Ted E. Levey, 11 Blackett Street, Newcastle-on-Tyne.

Northern Ireland Society of Dance Teachers.
A newly-formed Society of Teachers of Dancing which has already done quite a considerable amount for the furtherance of the art of dancing in Ireland.
President : Miss Rosalie Haines.
Secretary : Mr. W. Home, 4th Fifth Avenue, Bangor, Co. Down, Ireland.

Official Board of Ballroom Dancing.
This is a Committee of well-known ballroom teachers who, collectively, are representative of all branches of the ballroom teaching profession in this country.
Without in any way interfering with the internal arrangements of any particular Association, its object is to lead the Profession along those lines which will increase the popularity of dancing with the general public.
It is the outcome of an " Informal Conference " in April, 1929, when a Committee was appointed for this purpose by the two hundred prominent teachers who were present. This Committee then reported to a further " Informal Conference " in July of the same year, and received a mandate to remain in existence conditionally upon it making itself more representative of the ballroom profession as a whole than it was at that moment.

It had, before this second " Conference " was held, already named and described the simplest Basic Steps of the Fox-trot, Quick-step, Valse and Tango, and recommended that these should be taught by all teachers to all pupils, and it had strongly urged the use of the slogan " Dancing for Health."

It deprecated the launching of " freak " dances by individual members of the profession, as these helped to confuse the public.

It had also brought about a meeting between the teachers and a representative body of Managers with a view to more harmonious working between the two branches of the dancing profession.

After the second " Conference," acting on the principle that it should not be easier to enter the dancing profession through one door than another, it drew up a suggested syllabus for a ballroom examination, and agreed that all those Associations which adopted the principle of that syllabus should be entitled to representation on the " Board." As a result the " Board " became considerably augmented and thoroughly representative of ballroom dancing in this country.

The " Board " has again met the Managers, both in 1930 and 1931, and the way is being cleared for a combined publicity campaign to be held in the near future.

The " Board " has drawn up a set of " Rules " governing Competitions which have been accepted by the Managers, and are already in force in a great number of dance halls throughout the country, and it also considers the case of any amateur who, having committed an act of professionalism, is desirous of returning to the amateur ranks.

The Chairman of the Board since its inception has been Mr. P. J. S. Richardson.

The original members of the Board were : Miss Josephine Bradley, Miss Grace Cone, Mrs. Ruby Peeler, Miss Adela Roscoe, Miss Muriel Simmons,

*Miss Molly Spain, Miss Eve Tynegate-Smith, Mr. F. C. Barlow, Mr. H. Bloodworth, Mr. Santos Casani, Mr. A. Cowan, Mr. H. Vivian Davies, Mr. W. A. Greenwell, Mr. F. W. C. Leslie, Mr. Alex Moore, Monsieur Pierre, Mr. H. St. John Rumsey, Mr. Victor Silvester, Mr. W. Maxwell Stewart, Major Cecil H. Taylor.

The above members co-opted: Mr. Frank Ford, Mr. Sydney Stern.

Subsequently the Associations agreeing to the "Examination Syllabus," named the following as their representatives to sit on the Board:

"Allied Dancing": Mr. J. Mercer and Mr. Walter Fletcher.
"British Association": Mr. W. H. Cadman and Mr. D. T. Foster.
"International D.M.A.": Mr. W. Collinson, Mr. Harry Clarke ("Yorkshire A."), Mr. N. Markland ("Premier"), Mr. Frank Bullars ("Universal").
"Lancashire A.": Mr. B. S. Hayward.
"Manchester A.": Mr. A. Wantling.
"Midland A.": Mr. H. E. Keston.
"National A.": Mr. F. C. Barlow and Mr. H. Bloodworth.
"Northern Counties": Mr. C. J. Daniels.
"Northern D.T.A.": Mr. T. E. Levey.

Address: C/o *The Dancing Times*, 25 Wellington Street, London, W.C.2.

Scottish Country Dance Club.

Founded in 1928, this Club was instituted for the practice of Scottish Country Dancing as distinct from Solo and Ballroom Dancing. Membership is gained by election.

Treasurer: Mrs. Elizabeth MacLachlan.
Secretary: Mr. Reg. Grant, Scottish Country Dance Club, 98 St. Martin's Lane, London, W.C.2.

United Kingdom Alliance of Professional Teachers of Dancing.

An Association of Teachers of Dancing which is affiliate with the United Professional Teachers of Dancing of America.

---

* *Co-opted in place of Mr. Alec Millar, who resigned on leaving the profession.*

Secretary: Mr. A. Hanson, 5 Salem Street, Bradford.

BELGIUM.

Union Professionelle des Professeurs de Danse et de Maintien de Belgique.

An Association for Teachers only.
President: Monsieur N. Bonnecompagnie, 51 Rue St. Bernard, Bruxelles.
Secretary: Monsieur M. Mottie, 49 Rue Breughel, Anvers.

DENMARK.

Terpsichore (Society for Teachers of Dancing).

Denmark's leading society for teachers of all branches of dancing. Founded in 1923, the President being Georg Berthetsen, former ballet dancer at the Royal Theatre, Copenhagen.

Address: Vibenstrusgrade 4, Copenhagen.

FRANCE.

Academie des Maitres de Danse de Paris.

An Association of Teachers of Dancing.
President: Mme. Lefort.
Address: 2 Boulevard St. Denis, Paris, France.

Federation Internationale de Danse.

Founded in Paris in 1923. Membership open to all Unions, Associations, Syndicates, and International Federations of Teachers of Dancing and Professional Dancers.

Official Organisation of the World's Dancing Championships, which are held under the patronage of the Ministers de l'Instruction Publique et des Beaux-Arts.

Is affiliated to the Syndicat Nationale des Professeurs de Danse et Danseurs Professionels.

President: M. Camille de Rhynal.
Address: 5, Rue de l'Abbe-Gregoire, Paris, France.

Syndicat National des Professeurs de Danse et Danseurs Professionels.

Founded in 1925. Is affiliated to

the Federation Internationale de Danse. Membership open to teachers of dancing, professional dancers, *maitres de ballet*, choregraphic artists.
President: M. Camille de Rhynal.
Secretary: M. Poigt, 5 Rue de l'Abbe-Gregoire, Paris, France.

Union des Professeurs de Danse de France.
An Association of Teachers of Dancing.
Address: 98 Rue Demours, Paris, France.

Union Internationale des Choregraphes.
An Association of *Maitres* and Teachers of Dancing. Has members in countries throughout Europe.
President: M. Valentin de Summera.
Secretary: M. Raoul Gunther.
Address: 115 Avenue Parmentier, Paris, France.

GERMANY.

Allgemeiner Deutscher Tanzlehrerverband.
The largest association of ballroom teachers in Germany.
Address: 2, Berliner Tor, Hamburg 5, Germany.

Anna Pavlova Society.
A Society formed in Berlin after the death of Anna Pavlova to preserve the memory and traditions of that dancer, and for the furtherance of dancing in general.
Secretary: Anna Pavlova Society, Charlottenstrasse 50/51, Berlin, W.8, Germany.

Deutsche Tanzgemeinschaft.
An Association of dancers from the " modern " schools only. The majority of members are independent and are not connected at all with the theatre. Membership gained by passing the entrance examination of one of the schools which belong to the Association.
President: Dr. Felix Emmel.
Address: Kurfurstendamm 119/120, Halensee, Berlin, Germany.

Deutscher Gymnastikbund.
An Association formed for the development of hygienic, rhythmic and dance-gymnastics from a pedagogical point of view. Has no interest in dancing as an art, or in the theatre. Works in co-operation with the Boards of Education. Is chiefly an organisation for gymnastic clubs.
Address: Innsbruckerstrasse 14/15, Schoneberg, Berlin, Germany.

Deutscher Tanzerbund.
This Association is open for membership to all dancers connected with the theatre—ballet and " modern " dancers. Has done a great deal to improve the position, both financial and social, of the theatrical dancer. Is also an employment agency.
Address: Rupprechstr 10, Mannheim, Germany.

Reichsverband zur Pflege des Gesellschaftstanzes E.V.
Established November 4th, 1931, for the cultivation of ballroom dancing. Membership is not for individuals, but is open to clubs, hotels and holiday resort administrations. Amateur ballroom dancing only is covered. Has organised a number of dance tournaments, and controls all the important Amateur Competitions in Germany.
President: County Judge Von Spoenla.
Secretary: Dr. Neuman, Kant Strasse 8, Charlottenburg, Berlin, Germany.

Reichsverband Deutscher Tanzlehrer.
An Association for Teachers only. Covers all branches of dancing.
Address: 46 Hallische Strasse, Leipzig, N.22, Germany.

Sezession Moderner Tanzlehrer E.V.
An Association of Teachers of Ballroom Dancing, and Professional Ballroom Dancers. Examination syllabus based on Victor Silvester's books.
Address: Kurfurstendamm 23, Berlin, W.15, Germany.

SWITZERLAND.

Ligue Internationale des Championnats de Danse.
An Organisation of Competition Dancers, amateur and professional.
General Secretary: A. Traber, Sonnenquai 1, Zurich.

Union Choregraphique Suisse.
President: A. Traber, Sonnenquai 1, Zurich.

Syndicat National Suisse.
President: A. Traber, Sonnenquai, 1, Zurich.

UNITED STATES.

NATIONAL TEACHERS' ORGANISATIONS.

American Society of Teachers of Dancing.
Organised 1879, and incorporated October 31st, 1883. Formed with the object of securing advancement in the art of dancing, an identical method of instruction, to correct and remedy existing abuses, modify, compose and arrange dances with suitable music, and promote social intercourse among its members. All forms of dancing are covered. Membership open to teachers of three years experience, who are balloted for by committee. Life Members limited to teachers who have been members of the Society for 30 years and have retired from business. Honorary members are limited to teachers of the Art who have distinguished themselves in foreign countries, and to eminent teachers of dancing in America.
President: R. W. Vizay, 2029 Wisconsin Avenue, Milwaukee, Wis.
Secretary: Philip S. Nutt, 26 Columbia Avenue, Vineland, N.J.

Concert Dancers' League.
The Committee numbers amongst its members Miriam Marmein, Agnes Boome, Sara Mildred Strauss and Doris Humphrey.
Secretary: Mr. Louis Rever Morris, 66 Fifth Avenue, New York.

Dancing Masters of America, Inc.
Founded in 1926 by the consolidation of the "American National Association" and the "International Association," which date from 1884 and 1894 respectively. Covers all forms of dancing. Holds a four-week Technical School each year.
Secretary: Mr. Walter U. Soby, 553 Farmington Avenue, Hartford, Conn.

LOCAL ASSOCIATIONS.

Associated Dancing Teachers of Southern California.
Secretary: Miss Elisa Ryan, 1500 So. Figueroa Street, Los Angeles, Calif.

California Association Teachers of Dancing.
Secretary: Miss Rose Moore, 1334 McAllister Street, San Francisco.

Chicago Association of Dancing Masters.
The Chicago Association is the largest dancing masters' organization in the United States with the exception of the big national, "Dancing Masters of America." It started as an organization for teachers of social dancing and managers of ballrooms, but as years went on teachers of ballet joined in great numbers, and now the teachers of social dancing are far outnumbered in the membership. The Association holds an Annual Conference and Normal School. Mr. Wm. J. Ashton has been Secretary of the Association since its inception, except for one year when he was President. Mr. Thomas Birchler, who is Editor and Publisher of "The Dancing Master," has held office as Vice-President of the Association for several years, and for the last three years has been President.
Secretary: Wm. J. Ashton, 6711 Stony Island Avenue, Chicago, Ill., U.S.A.

Cleveland (Ohio) Dancing Teachers' Association.
Incorporated September 1st, 1919.
President: Mr. Robert Burns, 1316 Giddings Road, Cleveland, Ohio.

Dancing Teachers' Club of Connecticut, Inc.
Secretary : Miss Florence Umstatter, Bridgeport, Conn.

Florida Society of Teachers of Dancing.
Secretary : Miss Nora Brown Kennedy, 1712 Market Street, Jacksonville, Florida.

Georgia Association of Dancing Masters.
Secretary : Mr. S. Louis Domb, 95 Edgewood Avenue, Atlanta, Georgia.

Louisiana Association of Dancing Masters.
Secretary : Miss Olga Peters, 838 Lowerline Street, New Orleans, La.

Michigan Dancing Teachers' Association (The).
Secretary : Miss Madge Fraser, 1507 Woodward Avenue, Detroit, Mich.

New York Dancers' Club.
Recently founded by Miss Margaret Severn, who is well known in the United States as a dancer and teacher, this Club is a business, social and residential headquarters for professional dancers, teachers and students. It has the support of a great number of prominent members of the dancing profession. Has an Employment Register.
Address : 24 West 54th Street, New York, U.S.A.

New York Society Teachers of Dancing, Inc. (The).
Secretary : Mr. William E. Heck, 154 South 8th Street, Newark, N.J.

North Carolina Dancing Teachers' Association (The).
Incorporated May 16th, 1930.
President : Mr. Leo Byrum, 218½ So. Green Street, Greensboro, N.C.

North Carolina Society Teachers of Dancing (The), Inc.
Incorporated May 16, 1930.
Secretary : Miss Florence Burkhimer, 212 Providence Road, Charlotte, N.C.

North-Eastern New York State Council of Dancing Teachers.
Secretary : Mr. Fred. Herbert, 214 Clinton Street, Schenectady, N.Y.

Ohio Association Teachers of Dancing, Inc.
Secretary : Mr. La Rue C. Hope, 3244 Meadowbrook Boulevard, Cleveland, Ohio.

Philadelphia Dancing Association, Inc. (The).
Secretary : Miss Rudy K. Hoeflech, 336 Westmont Avenue, Westmont, N.J.

Pittsburgh Society for the Improvement of Dancing.
Secretary : Miss Camille G. Carey, 511 N. Euclid Avenue, Pittsburgh, Pa.

St. Louis Dancing Teachers' Association.
Secretary : Mr. George A. Goerger, St. Louis, Mo.

Texas Association Teachers of Dancing (The).
Secretary : Miss Dorothy Bonner, 314 West Woodlawn Avenue, San Antonio, Texas.

Utah Association of Dancing Teachers.
Secretary : Mrs. L. P. Christensen, Salt Lake City, Utah.

Western New York State of Dancing Masters.
Secretary : Mr. Thomas A. Riley, 1840 Bellevue Avenue, Syracuse, N.Y.

Wisconsin Society Teachers of Dancing.
Secretary : Miss Cleo Smith, 65 South Main Street, Fond du Lac, Wis.

SOUTH AFRICA.

South African Dancing Teachers Association.
Secretary : Mrs. Smith, Box 768, Johannesburg.
Works in close association with the " Operatic Association " and the " Imperial Society " of England.

STAGE DANCING COMPETITIONS

The following is a list of the principal Stage Dancing Competitions, giving the month in which they are usually held and the address of the Secretary from whom full details of the events are obtainable. Entries, as a rule, close about one month before the date of the Competition.

All England.
In aid of the "Sunshine Homes for Blind Babies." The principal competition of the year. Heats, which are held in various provincial towns, commence in January; the Semifinals take place in London in March; and the Grand Finals, generally at the Scala Theatre, just before Easter.
Organiser: Mrs. Claremont, M.B.E., National Institute for the Blind, Great Portland Street, London, W.1.

Balham and Streatham.
June.
Hon. Secretary: Mrs. Elsie Weller, 73 Klea Avenue, Clapham Common, London, S.W.4.

Beckenham.
March. (Not held in 1932).
Hon. Secretary: Mr. G. Crease, 23 Kelsey Park Road, Beckenham, Kent.

Beddington, Carshalton, Wallington and District Festival.
March.
Hon. Secretary: Mrs. A. J. Hudson.

Bedfordshire.
March.
Joint Hon. Secretaries: Mr. G. H. Thomas and Mr. A. C. Wildman, 40/42 St. Peters, Bedford.

Blackpool.
May.
Forms portion of the "Blackpool Dance Festival," and is the most important event of its kind in the North of England.
Secretary: Mr. J. H. Clegg, Winter Gardens, Blackpool.

Brighton.
May.
Hon. Secretary: Mr. Lewis Mennich, 44 Montpelier Road, Brighton.

Bristol.
March.
Hon. Secretary: Mrs. W. E. Fowler, 5 Priory Road, Tyndalls Park, Bristol.

Carshalton.
(*See* BEDDINGTON.)

Cork.
April.
Secretary: Cork Eisteddfod, Queen Street, Cork, Ireland.

Croydon.
April.
Secretary: Mr. Thomas Cook, 7 Katharine Street, Croydon.

Epsom.
March.
Hon. Secretary: Major J. Milne Davidson, "Woodgate," Ashtead, Surrey.

Guernsey.
November.
Secretary: Miss Madelaine Vaughan, Fontcouvert, Queens Road, Guernsey, C.I.

Hampstead and Hendon.
February—March.
Hon. Secretary: Mr. Peter Eliot, 173 Adelaide Road, London, N.W.3.

Hastings.
March.
Hon. Secretaries: Musical Festival Offices, 9 Verulam Place, St. Leonards-on-Sea.

Jersey.
April. (Not held 1932.)
Secretary: Mrs. Reg. Grandin, 14 Royal Crescent, Don Road, Jersey, C.I.

Lewisham.
May.
Secretary: Mr. G. H. Loman, 71 Hazelbank Road, Catford, London, S.E.6.

Liverpool and Southport.
January.
Details from Dancing Times, Ltd., 25 Wellington Street, Strand, London, W.C.2.

London (City of).
April.

Medway Towns.
November.
Joint Hon. Secretaries: Mr. J. P. Farmer, 5 Melville Barracks, R.M., Chatham; and Mr. J. W. Alexander, 86 High Street, Chatham, Kent.

Mill Hill.
February.
Hon. Secretary: Mr. Aubrey L. Titford, 7 Hale Grove Gardens, Mill Hill, London, N.W.7.

Norbury.
November.
Secretary: Mr. Thomas Cook, 7 Katharine Street, Croydon, Surrey.

North Hackney and Stoke Newington.
May.
Hon. Secretary: Musical Festival, 36 Oldhill Street, London, N.16.

North of England.
May.
Hon. Secretary: Mr. A. Charlton Curry, 8 Ellison Place, Newcastle-on-Tyne. *Held at* Newcastle-on-Tyne.

Pedlars Fair.
July.
Secretary: Mrs. Claremont, M.B.E., National Institute for the Blind, 224 Gt. Portland Street, London, W.1.

South-east London.
March.
Details from The Dancing Editor, Lewisham Newspaper Co., Ltd., Loampit Vale, London, S.E.13.

Stratford and East London.
April-May.
Secretary: Mr. E. L. Holford, 41 Nightingale Lane, London, E.11.

Sutton and Cheam.
October.
Hon. Secretary: Mr. Leonard Bennett, Sutton's Music Centre, Grove Road, Sutton, Surrey.

Wallington.
(*See* BEDDINGTON.)

Wimbledon.
February.
Hon. Secretary: Mrs. Bennett, 79 Worple Road, Wimbledon, London, S.W.19.

" DANCING TIMES " CUP WINNERS.

The *Dancing Times* Cup is presented each year to the School whose pupils do best in the "All England (' Sunshine ') Solo Competition." The winners and runners-up have been as follows:—

1925—Winners: Cone School.
        Second: MacLaren School.
1926—Winners: Cone School.
        Second: MacLaren School.
1927—Winners: Cone School.
        Second: MacLaren School.
1928—Winners: Judith Espinosa School.
        Second: Mrs. Freda Grant's School.
1929—Winners: Cone School.
        Second: Atkinson-Suffield School.
1930—Winners: Ripman School and Kathleen Danetree School.
1931—Winners: Atkinson-Suffield School.
        Second: Bromova School and Phyllis James School.
1932—Winners: Maude Wells School.
        Second: Irene Hammond School.

BALLROOM COMPETITIONS
Winners of the most important Ballroom Competitions held in England since the War.

Ivory Cross (Open—Fox-trot).
   1921 and 1922—Mr. G. K. Anderson and Miss Josephine Bradley.

"Daily Sketch" (Amateurs only).
   1922—Fox-trot: Mr. G. K. Anderson and Mrs. Rey.
        Valse: Captain G. Foster and Miss Flora le Breton, and Mr. V. M. Brooks and Miss Lipman (divided).

World's Championships (held in England for three years).
   1923—Champions: Mr. Victor Silvester and Miss Phyllis Clark.
        Amateur: Mr. Cecil Reuben and Miss Flora le Breton.
        Mixed: Mr. Cecil Reuben and Miss Beryl Evetts.
   1924—Champions: Mr. Maxwell Stewart and Miss Barbara Miles.
        Amateur: Mr. Cecil Reuben and Miss Jackson.
        Mixed: Mr. G. K. Anderson and Miss Josephine Bradley.
   1925—Champions: Mr. Maxwell Stewart and Miss Barbara Miles.
        Amateur: Mr. Collard and Miss Vera James.
        Mixed: Mr. C. Raphael and Miss Phyllis Haylor.

"Star" Championships.
   1925—Mr. Leonard Ritte and Miss Beryl Evetts.
   1926—Professional: Mr. Alec Millar and Miss Phyllis Haylor.
        Amateur: Mr. Basil Ward and Mrs. Peggy Allen.
   1927—Professional: Mr. Frank Ford and Miss Molly Spain.
        Amateur: Mr. M. E. Moehly and Miss Irene Raines.
   1928—Professional: Mr. Sidney Stern and Miss Mae Walmesley.
        Amateur: Mr. M. E. Moehly and Miss Irene Raines.
   1929—Professional: Mr. Sidney Stern and Miss Mae Walmesley.
        Amateur: Mr. George Morris and Mrs. Peggy Allen.
   1931—Professional: Mr. Graham Godwin and Miss Celia Bristowe.
        Amateur: Mr. and Miss Wells.
   1931—Professional: Mr. R. H. Philp and Miss Ella Scutts.
        Amateur: Mr. and Miss Wells.

"Columbia" Amateur Championship.
   1928—Mr. R. H. Talmage and Miss Marise Cordery.
   1929—Mr. George Morris and Mrs. Peggy Allen.

Professional Championship of Great Britain.
   1928—Mr. Maxwell Stewart and Miss Pat Sykes.

British Championships (Blackpool).
   1931—Professional: Mr. Maxwell Stewart and Miss Pat Sykes.
        Amateur: Mr. J. Pike and Miss V. Ford.
   1932—Professional: Mr. Timothy Palmer and Miss Kathleen Price.
        Amateur: Mr. John Wells and Miss Rene Sissons.

Scottish National Championships.
   1928—Professional: Mr. Alex Warren and Miss Celia Bristowe.
   1929—Professional: Mr. Alex Warren and Miss B. M'Gregor.
        Amateur: Mr. A. Sclanders and Miss J. Fraser.
   1930—Professional: Mr. R. H. Philp and Miss Ella Scutts.
        Amateur: Mr. A. Sclanders and Miss J. Fraser.
   1931—Professional: Mr. R. H. Philp and Miss Ella Scutts.
        Amateur: Mr. A. Sclanders and Miss J. Fraser.
   1932—Professional: Mr. J. Telford and Miss Betty McGregor.
        Amateur: Mr. A. Steel and Miss B. Ramsey.

The Association of Teachers of the Revived Greek Dance
Founder and President - - - **RUBY GINNER.**

RULES OF MEMBERSHIP. Teachers of Dance may become Members by passing an examination on the Syllabus set by the Committee, provided they have had 2 years' training and 3 years' teaching experience, or 3 years' training and 2 years' teaching.
Membership Fee, £1 1s. 0d. Yearly Subscription, £1 1s. 0d.
Advanced Membership is obtained by passing an examination on an Advanced Syllabus not later than 2 years after becoming a member; this examination is compulsory.
PRIVILEGES OF MEMBERSHIP. The free use of the library of the Association; four copies a year of the Association Journal, entitled "The Link"; special classes, lectures and demonstrations; participation in stage productions; a Certificate of Membership entitling the holder to teach the Revived Greek Dance.
Students passing either grade of the Students' Examinations may join the Student Associate's Branch. Yearly Subscription, 10s. 6d.
Further particulars from :—
The Secretary, A.T.R.G.D., Philbeach Hall, Philbeach Gardens, S.W.5. Frobisher 2767.

Allied Dancing Association.

YOUR SUCCESS will be ACHIEVED in taking a short cut to the PROFESSION by becoming a member of the **A.D.A.** *The Association which is Different.*

We have it! Either in Modern or "Old Time." So can you! Join now! *Entrance Fee* **10/6**, *Annual Subscription* **10/6**

Hon. Secretary, WALTER FLETCHER,
6 Blucher Street, Waterloo, LIVERPOOL.

LIVE Teachers of Dancing should join the LIVE Association!

The Manchester Association of Teachers of Dancing
(Registered under the Friendly Societies' Act, 1896).

BALLROOM AND OPERATIC MEMBERS. Meetings Monthly.

Enquiries to—Alf. Smith, *Hon. Sec.*, 202 St. Mary's Road, Moston, Manchester.
'Phone: **Failsworth 1536.**

INTERNATIONAL DANCING MASTERS' ASSOCIATION

Headquarters: **Empress Ballroom, BLACKPOOL.**

ENTRANCE FEE, £1-1-0. ANNUAL SUBSCRIPTION, £1-1-0.
Rule Books sent on receipt of P.O. for 1/-.

Branch Areas: **Lancashire, Yorkshire, Midlands, South of England, South Wales, Scotland.**

Membership open to all who pass the Association Examination.

Gen. Secretary—**Mr. Robert Gledhill, Carlton Chambers, BRADFORD.**
'Phone 3606.

BIOGRAPHIES

A

ABRAHAMS (Madame), A.; general teacher. Member Imperial Society. Has been a teacher for over 20 years.
Address: Avalon Private Academy, 22 Rosehill Road, Wandsworth, London, S.W.18.

ADDISON, Errol; operatic and tap dancer. Holder of Cecchetti's personal certificate. At the age of 15 was *premier danseur* at Covent Garden. Toured with the Diaghileff Ballet for over three years, and danced with Gertrude Mitrenga for six years, touring the world. Now dancing with Iris Kirkwhite. Technically is one of the most brilliant male ballet dancers of to-day.
Address: 90 Selwyn Avenue, Richmond, Surrey.
Best Photos: Lenare, London.

ADKINS, Thomas Charles, B.A.; teacher of English Folk Dancing. Holder of the Advanced Certificate of the English Folk Dance Society since 1925. Was President of the Cambridge University Morris Men in 1926. Now a Member of the E.F.D.S. Headquarters' Teaching and Demonstrating Staff; also Assistant Examiner. Has taught at E.F.D.S. Vacation Schools since 1927. Leeds and Wharfedale Branch Teacher. Secretary of the E.F.D.S. Federation of Yorkshire Branches. Member of Demonstration Team which visited France, Germany, Czecho-Slovakia, Austria, Belgium, etc., for the Folk Arts Congress in 1928 and 1930.
Address: " St. Oswald's," Guiseley, Yorkshire.

AJELLO (Madame), Elvira Giulietta (Mrs. Roberts); general teacher, specialising in traditional Irish dancing. Member of the Imperial Society of Teachers of Dancing (Cecchetti branch) and Member of the National Society of Teachers of Dancing. Has lectured before the Operatic Association on Irish Dancing, and has instructed many of the well-known teachers of to-day in the Dances of Ireland. Has been a general dance teacher since 1916. Studied Irish Dancing in Ireland. Has studied the Ballet in various London Schools, but principally under Miss Margaret Craske. Has written articles on Irish Dancing in *The Dancing Times*, and is the author of an instructional book shortly to be published on " Solo Dances of Ireland." Member of the Scottish Clans' Association. Has a school at 22 Castle Chambers, Torquay.
Address: 37 Third Avenue, Daison, Torquay, Devon.
Best photos: Swaine, London.

AKHURST (Miss), Dorothy; teacher of all branches of dancing. A Member of the Association of Operatic Dancing of Great Britain, and of the Imperial Society of Teachers of Dancing—Operatic and General Branches. Principal of one of the oldest established schools in south-west London. Originally trained by Frederic Browning, and later by Mdme. Judith Espinosa.
Address: The Studio, 68 Manville Road, London, S.W.17.

ALANOVA (Miss); concert dancer of Scottish parentage but born in Russia and trained at the Imperial School. Was a member of the Diaghileff Company, and after appearing in small parts in " Wake Up and Dream " took some of Tilly Losch's more important numbers after that lady had left. Has appeared in cabaret in the West End, and given highly successful recitals in New York, Paris, Vienna and London.

ALBERTO AND SYLVIA (Albert Edmonds and Sylvia Taperell); juvenile ballroom exhibition dancers.

First became known to the general public through Santos Casani, who presented them in exhibitions and demonstrations at dance halls throughout the country. They were the winners of the "World's Professional Juvenile Ballroom Championship," and second in the Adult Step Dancing Competition in Paris in 1930. Have received training from Miss Josephine Bradley and the Max Rivers School, in addition to Santos Casani. Have won a number of minor competitions.

Address: 238 Westminster Bridge Road, London, S.W.1.

ALEXANDER, Jack; tap dancer. Began dancing in concert work in India. Since his return to London has appeared in cabaret, specializing in tap dancing.

Address: C/o Madame Horrocks, 438 Camden Road, London, N.7.

Best Photos: Jaye and King, Brighton.

ALGERANOFF, Harcourt; character dancer. Studied under Laurent Novikoff, Anna Pruzina, Koshiro Matsumoto Fujima (Japanese dancing) and Uday Shankar (Hindu dancing). Became a member of Mme. Pavlova's company in 1921, subsequently dancing with her in all parts of the world. Partnered her in the *Russian Dance* and *Oriental Impressions*. Is brilliant in the *Gopak*. The first Englishman to study and perform Japanese dances. Introduced the Central European School of Dancing to the English public during a "Pavlova" season at Covent Garden in September, 1927, with a first performance of *The Bogeyman*, a solo arranged by Max Terpis. Acted as choreographer and danced with Menaka in Bombay at a recital of Hindu Dancing in December, 1928.

Address: The Studio, 103 Gower Street, W.C.1.

Best photos: Furley Lewis, of Northolt Junction, Pollard Crowther, of London, and E. I. Hori, New York.

ALLAN (Miss), Maud; dancer. Born in Toronto. Studied music in Berlin, where she took a diploma. Made her *debut* as a dancer at Vienna in 1903, where she made an immediate appeal, and during the following years appeared in most of the important cities of Germany, Switzerland, Austria and Hungary, dancing before King Edward at Marienbad in 1907. Made her first London appearance in the spring of 1908 at the Palace Theatre, where she remained until the November of that year. Her dance entitled "The Vision of Salome" made a great sensation, and amongst other popular numbers of her repertoire were those to Mendelssohn's "Spring Song" and Chopin's "Marche Funebre." Was dancing in Russia in 1909, and returned to the Palace Theatre in 1911. In 1917 she appeared at the Ambassadors Theatre, when she particularly featured the "Blue Danube" and the "Valse Triste" of Sibellius. In 1932 played the Abbess with great distinction in the revival of "The Miracle" at the Lyceum.

Address: West Wing, Regents Park, London, N.W.1.

ALLEN (Miss), Violet; general teacher. Co-Principal with Miss Lydia Banks of the Violet Allen School of Dancing, which has been established since 1912.

Address: 55 Darlington Street, Wolverhampton, Staffs.

Best photos: Whitlock & Son, Wolverhampton.

AMIES (Miss), G. E. M. (Mrs. Anthony Hemming); teacher of ballroom dancing specialising in children's work. Member of the Midland Association of Teachers of Dancing. Daughter of Mdme. H. Amies, of Birmingham.

Address: 3 Fentham Road, Birchfield, Birmingham.

AMIES, Henry; ballroom teacher. Past President Midland Association Teachers of Dancing; Member International Dancing Masters' Association. With his wife is Co-Principal of the Amies Dancing Academy, which makes a big feature of old-time dancing. (*See* Mrs. AMIES.)

Address: Amies Dancing Academy, Chain Walk, Birchfield, Birmingham.

AMIES (Mdme.), Minnie; teacher of ballroom dancing. Founder of the Midland Association of Teachers of Dancing (now affiliated to the National Association), and has held the position of Technical Instructress and Examiner to that Association; also to the Universal Association. Diplomée and Member of the U.K.A. Opened Academy in 1900. Has done a great deal to foster modern ballroom dancing in Birmingham, but also supports the old-style dancing to a great extent.
Address: Amies Dancing Academy, Chain Walk, Birchfield, Birmingham.
Best photos: Mason, Birmingham.

ANDERSON, George Kenneth; amateur ballroom dancer. Hon. Member Imperial Society of Teachers of Dancing. Took part in various amateur dancing contests in U.S.A. and England. Danced at one time in competitions with Josephine Bradley, and with her helped in the development of the Slow Fox-trot.
Address: Tavistock Mansions, Tavistock Place, London, W.C.1.

ANDERSON, Ted; ballroom dancer and teacher. Has acted as Manager of ballrooms in Newcastle for some considerable time, and gives frequent demonstrations of exhibition, fancy and ballroom dancing. Was on the Executive Committee of the North of England Children's Dancing Tournament, 1930-31.
Address: Heaton Assembly Rooms, Newcastle-on-Tyne.
Best photos: Princess Yvonne, Newcastle and London.

ANDERTON (Miss), Jean; teacher of all branches of dancing. Member of the Imperial Society of Teachers of Dancing. Trained under Paul Valentine (late Ballet Master to Covent Garden Opera), and with Miss Olive Deets. Has been Principal Dancer at a number of leading theatres. Opened school in 1916. Author of "History by Dramatic Method"—in collaboration with Miss Viola Compton (James Nisbet).
Address: 5-6 Sherwood Street, Piccadilly, London, W.1.
Best photos: Basil; Hana, London.

ANDERTON (Miss), Lily G.; general stage teacher. Member of National Association of Teachers of Dancing (Ballroom and Operatic Branches). Winner of National Trophy (Operatic section) in London, 1927.
Address: "Daisy Mount," Walton Lane, Walton, Liverpool.
Best photos: Morath's Pictorial Press, Liverpool.

ANDREAE (Miss), Felicity; operatic dancer, who has appeared in several "Camargo Society" productions and in recitals at the "Faculty of Dancing." At the latter has produced her own small ballets, and shows promise both as a dancer and a choreographer. Trained by Miss Bedells, is an "Intermediate Member" of the "Operatic Association."
Address: 22 Acol Road, London, N.W.6.

ANDREE, Jules (Miss Julia Helena Andrew); operatic and character dancer. Member and Holder of the Elementary Certificate of the Operatic Association. Danced in Carl Rosa Opera Company at Covent Garden for two seasons as principal "male" dancer. Has appeared in her own act in cabaret in London and the provinces. Trained "The Daily Mirror Eight" which toured the country in 1931.
Address: 20 Vancouver Road, Forest Hill, London, S.E.23.
Best photos: Hana, London.

ANDREWS, Joseph; teacher of ballroom dancing. Member of the Imperial Society of Teachers of Dancing. Well known as a professional dancer, he has judged a number of competitions, and has given demonstrations, first in association with Miss Audrey Phillips, later with Miss Amy Greenwood, and is now again with Miss Phillips at her school.
Address: Knightsbridge Hotel, London, S.W.1.
Best photos: Angus Faith, London.

ANDREWS, Leonard; teacher of ballroom dancing. On leaving the army commenced to dance as an amateur and won over thirty com-

23

petitions. Started as a professional at Miss Belle Harding's School, and in 1925 went to the Mostyn Hotel with Mr. Maxwell Stewart and Miss Barbara Miles. Was also at the Piccadilly Hotel for two years. Entered the "Star" Dancing Championships and reached the Finals in the years 1925, 1926, 1927, 1928 and 1929. Joined Miss Barbara Miles as her partner in 1927 and won the Yale Blues Championship in 1928. Judged the Columbia Championship. For some time afterwards was teaching with Miss Eleanor Candler.

Co-Author, with Miss Candler, of "Modern Ballroom Dance Instructor" (Geographia, Ltd.).

Address: 38 Dartmouth Park Hill, London, N.W.5.

Best photos: Janet Jevons, London.

ANITA (Miss); ballroom teacher. Opened her school in London eight years ago. Features tap-dancing and limbering in addition to ballroom work. Received training from Mrs. Vernon Castle. Has judged and demonstrated a great deal at dances, and also organised dances and competitions.

Address: Victory House, 99 Regent Street, London, W.1.

Best Photos: Claude Harris, London.

ANSTEE (Miss), Vera (Mrs. W. Claremont Martin); general teacher. Also features health culture and fencing. Intermediate Member of Association of Operatic Dancing. Was first trained by Miss Damie Beach; afterwards by Mr. Espinosa and Mr. T. C. Askew. Founded the Tulse Hill School of Dancing in 1922. Gives exhibitions and cabaret numbers with her partner at London hotels.

Address: The Studio, 173 Tulse Hill, London, S.W.2.

Best photos: Marian Lewis, London.

ARCULUS (Miss), Marjorie; ballroom teacher. Has received training in all branches of dancing.

Address: 58 Lower Hastings Street, Leicester.

ARGENTINA; Spanish dancer. Born in Buenos Aires of an Andalusian mother, and a Castillian father who was *premier danseur* of the Opera, Madrid, where she made her *debut* at the age of 9. Was *première danseuse* at 11. She left the opera to appear on her own and was first "discovered" in Paris. She has since toured the world as a soloist in dances of her own creation, the best known being *Danse Rituelle du Feu* (da Falla). Appeared with immense success at three matinées in London in June, 1931.

André Levinson says of her:

"She has developed an incredible fullness and variety. In her the spirit of the Occident triumphs over the lure of the Orient. She has once more reconquered Andalusia from the Arabs."

Best photos by d'Ora, Paris.

ARGENTINA, Cesar; ballroom teacher, specializing in the Tango. Has a well-known School in London.

Address: 9 Great Newport Street, London, W.C.2.

ARGYLE (Miss), Pearl; classical ballet dancer. Pupil of Mdme. Marie Rambert. Member of the Ballet Club Company. Created the role of "Venus" in *Mars and Venus*. Has appeared in *Les Sylphides*, *Aurora's Wedding*, *L'Apres Midi d'un Faune*, *Carnaval* (Chiarina), and with Leon Woizikowsky in the *Pas de deux* from *The Gods Go a-begging*, etc. Created leading role in *The Lady of Shalott*. Danced in Cochran's "Helen."

There is a section on Pearl Argyle in the book entitled "The Marie Rambert Ballet" by Arnold L. Haskell (British-Continental Press, Ltd.).

Address: 13 Palace Court, London, W.2.

ARGYLL (Miss), Jill; teacher of dance and mime. Trained under French, Italian and Russian teachers, and also at Royal Opera House, Berlin. Has twenty-five years' teaching experience in well-known girls' schools and colleges, including Bergman Osterberg Physical Training College. Principal of own Training School in London for stage, film and amateur work, with

continental branches. Original Member of Chez-Soi Company.
Address: 30 Dorset Street, Baker Street, London, W.1.
Best Photos: Bertram Park; Angus Faith, London.

ASHCROFT (Miss), Gwendolyn (Mrs Gwendolyn Hodgson); general teacher. Member of the Imperial Society (Ballroom Branch); Member Operatic Association; Member A.T.R.G.D. Opened her School at the Queen's Hydro, Blackpool, in 1921.
Address: "Norwood," Squire's Gate, Blackpool.

ASHTON, Frederick; dancer and choregraphist. Born in Ecuador. Pupil of Massine, but principally trained by Marie Rambert. First appearance in "Riverside Nights" in 1926. Toured Europe with Rubinstein and Nijinska, and later appeared as *premier danseur* at Karsavina-Rambert seasons at Lyric Theatre, Hammersmith, at Arts Theatre Club with Lydia Lopokova, and in "Marriage à la Mode" at the Lyric Theatre. *Premier danseur* of Ballet Club. Partnered Karsavina in her ballet *Valse Fantaisie* at the third Camargo performance. Created the choregraphy of many ballets, including *Leda, Pomona, Façade, Mars and Venus, Capriol Suite, Passionate Pavane, Lady of Shalott, The Lord of Burleigh* and *Rio Grande*. Recently appointed a Director of the Ballet Club.
Address: 9 Earl's Court Square, London, S.W.5.
Best Photos: Lenare, Cecil Beaton, London.

ASPLEY (Miss), Grace; teacher of all branches of dancing, specialising in acrobatic and cabaret work. Has a successful School of Dancing in Derby.
Address: 10 Breedon Hill Road, Derby.

ASTAFIEVA, Seraphine; Russian dancer and teacher. Holds the diploma from the Imperial Russian Academy, St. Petersburg. Finished education in Russian Imperial Theatrical Academy, and danced in the Maryinsky Theatre. Left the stage after three years for marriage, and went as volunteer nurse in the First Aid Flying Column during the Russian-Japanese War, and was decorated after being wounded at the front. Returned to the stage and joined the Diaghileff Co. in 1911 during the first English season as principal artiste in *Cleopatra, Scheherazade* and *Prince Igor*. Travelled with Diaghileff through all principal European capitals and left the Company in 1914 for engagement at Imperial Theatre, Budapest, where she created the ballets of *Judith, Hashish,* and Trilogy of *Dream of Love*. Signed contracts for Berlin and the Metropolitan Opera House, New York. Refused German contract owing to War, and lost the one for U.S.A. through the disappearance of her German Impressario. Established school in London in 1915. Organised and appeared in 201 charities during the War, mostly with Lady Paget, for which she received Royal thanks. Was responsible for the whole production of the Russian opera, *Coq d'Or*, for Sir Thomas Beecham at Drury Lane, and several other productions, including the Swinburne Ballet at the Coliseum. Has since trained several celebrated dancers, including Dolin, Markova, Divina and Charles.
Address: 152 King's Road, Chelsea, London, S.W.3.
Best photos: Raphael, London.

ATKINSON (Miss), Madge; teacher of natural movement. Miss Atkinson has been teaching in Manchester for over twelve years, and is in partnership with Miss Mollie Suffield. She studied originally with Annea Spong, pupil of Isadora Duncan. Is a Fellow and Vice-President of the Imperial Society of Teachers of Dancing and has founded the Natural Movement branch of that Society. She has done a great deal of work in organising classes and lecture lessons on Natural Movement for the Educational Authorities in the North. Is a professor at the Royal Manchester College of Music for Natural Movement, Mime and Gesture. The Bergman Osterberg Physical Training College, Dartford, along with many other well-known institutions, has chosen to specialize in her method of Natural Movement. She was Ballet Mistress for Miss Horniman during the last years of the Gaiety Theatre, Manchester, and ran several seasons of her own productions there. Although she takes a keen interest in all forms of dancing she has worked upon, and specialized in, Natural Movement, visiting Greece and Italy in furtherance of her studies. She is interested in Historical Dancing, and has done important research work, especially among the old charts in the British Museum. She has produced many well-known ballets for the Grand Opera Festivals held in Manchester, two of the best known being the Venusberg Ballet in " Tannhauser" and the Brocken Ballet in " Faust." She has also arranged ballets for " Aida " and " Samson and Delilah " and many other operas. With her partner she has given matinées during the opera seasons accompanied by the Hallé Orchestra and the Leeds Symphonic Orchestra. At the Mid-day concerts, which were one of the musical ventures of the City, she has given many recitals. For five consecutive years has won with her partner the *Dancing Times* Cup at the North of England Dance Festivals (Blackpool and Scarborough), and with her has several times been runner-up at the finals of the Sunshine All England Competitions in London. During the last two years she has worked in co-operation with the hospitals with Remedial Exercises based on her method of Natural Movement.

Books: Reference to Miss Atkinson's work may be found in " Physical Training for Girls " by Mary Johnstone B.Sc. (Sedgwick & Jackson, Ltd.).

Address: 259 Deansgate, Manchester.

Best photos: Ingham, Bowdon, Cheshire ; and T. Longworth Cooper, Sale, Cheshire.

B

BALANCHINE, George; dancer and choregraphist. Born in Petrograd 1907, studying at Imperial Theatrical Ballet School and at Imperial Conservatoire of Music. Worked in Imperial Theatres as dancer and producer, leaving Russia in 1927. Joined Diaghileff's Company and produced *The Nightingale, Barabau, Pastorale, Jack-in-a-Box, Neptune, The Cat, Apollo, Gods go a-begging, The Ball* and *Prodigal Son*. After Diaghileff's death produced a ballet *Aubade* (Poulenc) at Champs-Elysée Theatre, Paris, and other ballets for the Theatre Royal Copenhagen. Created and produced ballets for C. B. Cochran's productions in London, and later for Sir Oswald Stoll's Theatres.

Address: 5 Passage Doisy, Paris.

BALLIOL, Carl (R. W. Willey); adagio dancer. Carl Balliol, previously known as R. W. Willey, was well-known for his tap dancing. His father, who won the championship of the world in 1904, was " Will Lannon," and he gave his son his first lessons in Lancashire clog dancing at the age of 3. Willey, or Balliol, first appeared as an Adagio Dancer in 1923, when, at the suggestion of Tom Arnold, he produced a ballet with Dorothy Neville, which was one of the successes of " The Melody Box." He met and first worked with his present partner, Merton, in 1927. For the first six months the dancers found their British nationality and names a handicap, but they eventually secured engagements abroad, and were featured on the Riviera, from whence they were engaged to appear at the most exclusive London clubs. They were renowned for the " Swallow Dive " and " Frog Leap," which became the sensation of London.

Address: 17 Carleton Road, London, N.7.

Best photos by Lenare, London ; and Schneider & Robertson, Berlin.

BAMFORD (Miss), Freda; operatic and character dancer. Intermediate Member of Operatic Association. Is a prominent member of the Vic-Wells' Ballet Company, and danced the Witch in *The Jew and the Bush* with them ; also took the lead in *Danse Profane*. Appeared with Anton Dolin's Company at the London

Coliseum, dancing in *Rhapsody in Blue, Revolution*, etc.
Address: "Beverley," Battle, Sussex.
Best Photos: Pearl Freeman, London.

BANISTER, Frederick Charles; dance hall manager. Was at Cricklewood Dance Hall as Assistant Manager and Host from 1925 to 1926, and afterwards Manager at the Locarno, Glasgow, for a year. Is now General Manager of the Plaza, Glasgow. Acted as M.C. for "World's Championships" and "Star" Finals prior to leaving for Scotland. Judged in "Star" Heats for three seasons. Judge in Scottish Championships.
Address: 246 Bath Street, Glasgow, Scotland.

BANKHEAD (Mrs.), Jenny T.; ballroom teacher. A pioneer of first-class ballroom dancing in Scotland. Dancing with an amateur partner, was the first couple from Scotland to do well in London competitions, gaining fourth place in the Open Championship of the World in 1924 at the Queen's Hall, London, and in 1925 was placed second in the Mixed World's Championship, also winning the Open Championship of Scotland in the same year. Is prominent on Board of Judges in all large Scottish competitions.
Address: 25 Bank Street, Glasgow.

BANKS (Miss), Lydia; general teacher. Co-Principal with Miss Violet Allen of the Violet Allen School of Dancing, Wolverhampton, which has been established since 1912.
Address: 55 Darlington Street, Wolverhampton, Staffs.
Best photos: Whitlock & Son, Wolverhampton.

BARBOUR (Miss), Joyce; tap dancer. Has appeared in a number of leading West End shows, including Mr. C. B. Cochran's "Evergreen" at the Adelphi Theatre.
Best photos: Sasha, London.

BARLOW, Frederick C.; general teacher. Past President and Examiner of the National Association of Teachers of Dancing. Now General Secretary to the Association, which position he has held for some years.
Address: 55 Wellington Street, Woolwich, London, S.E.18.

BARNETT, Stanley G. General Secretary of the Dartford Dancers Association, which he founded towards the end of 1931.
Address: 36 Home Gardens, Dartford, Kent.

BARRIE (Miss), Barbara; operatic teacher. Intermediate Member Operatic Association. Pupil of Miss Phyllis Bedells, and has appeared at several West End theatres. Is a clever designer of costumes and décor for dancing.
Address: 115 Maida Vale, London, W.9.

BARTLEY (Miss), Ena; general teacher. Advanced Member Operatic Association. Fellow Imperial Society (Ballroom, Operatic and General Branches). Trained in Birmingham. Was assistant to Miss Grace Cone at Brighton 1919-20. Started own connection in 1920. In 1928 opened new studio with the largest private ballroom in Birmingham. Was the sponsor of "Rhythm Dancing."
Address: 187 Broad Street, Birmingham.
Best photos: A. E. Lane, Birmingham.

BARTON (Miss), Marjorie; general teacher. Advanced Member Operatic Association. Associate of Imperial Society's Classical Ballet and Greek Sections (Intermediate) and Advanced Member Operatic Association.
Address: 6 Glenluce Road, Blackheath, London, S.E.3.

BASTABLE (Miss), Ivy Ruthven; general teacher and dance journalist; specialist in Scottish Dancing. Began to teach in 1927. Has written articles on dancing for *The Dancing Times, The Gateway*, etc.
Address: 91 Kenilworth Avenue, Wimbledon Park, London, S.W.19.

Best Photos: Le Dernier Cri, London.

BATEMAN (Miss), Madge; teacher of natural movement dancing. Fellow of the Imperial Society of Teachers of Dancing, and Member of their Natural Movement Branch Committee. Trained by Miss Madge Atkinson, and has danced in all Miss Atkinson's productions in both solo and group work for many years. During the Opera Festival seasons in Manchester danced in the Venusberg Ballet from "Tannhauser," "Aida," "Samson and Delilah" and "Faust." Appeared twice at "Sunshine Matinees." For the past six years has been a teacher with the Atkinson-Suffield School. Specialises in social work, and holds large classes each week in the poorer districts of Manchester, including one at the Manchester University Settlement, Ancoats, and another at the Collyhurst Guild of Social Service.

Address: Fernyhurst, Palatine Road, West Didsbury, Manchester.

Best Photos: Longworth Cooper, Sale, Cheshire.

BATTINE-WILLIAMS (Miss), Gwen (Mrs. G. S. Hughes); ballroom and operatic teacher. Member Imperial Society (Ballroom). Trained under Mdme. Bizet Michau, of London. Gained a very large teaching connection, which she sold in 1917 when she married. Resumed teaching in 1923, and now has an important school in Liverpool.

Address: 4a Colquitt Street, Liverpool.

Best photos: Dobson, Liverpool.

BEACH (Miss), Damie; general teacher, specializing in operatic and tap dancing. Member Operatic Association. Her School, the Norwood Academy of Dancing, is well known.

Address: 331 Norwood Road, London, S.E.24.

Best Photos: Mannell, London.

BEAUMONT, Cyril W.; critic, historian, and writer on dancing. Hon. Fellow of the Imperial Society of Teachers of Dancing, and Vice-President and Member of the Examining Board of the Classical Ballet Branch (Cecchetti Method). Editor of *The Dance Journal*. Has taken an active interest in dancing since 1912, particularly in the history and technique of classical ballet. Served for three years (1922-24) as critic of theatrical dancing to *The Dancing World*. In 1922 organised the foundation of "The Cecchetti Society" for the preservation and propagation of the Cecchetti Method of training for classical ballet. When Maestro Cecchetti went to Italy in 1923, Mr. Beaumont was made President at the former's request. The following year the Society amalgamated with "The Imperial Society of Teachers of Dancing," and Mr. Beaumont became a Vice-President of their Classical Ballet Branch, which position he has continued to occupy, and in the same year was elected an Hon. Fellow of the Imperial Society, and also appointed Editor of *The Dance Journal*.

Mr. Beaumont has written a number of themes for ballets and dances, several of which, such as *Bal Mabille*, *Circus*, *Touch*, *Promenade*, etc., have been publicly performed. He furnished the historical article, "Costume for Ballet," for the collective volume on theatrical costume entitled "Robes of Thespis" (1928), and has written a number of books relating to dancing, besides making available in English translations three of the most important classics of French dance literature: "Orchésographie," by Thoinot Arbeau; "Lettres sur la Danse et les Ballets," by J. G. Noverre; and "Le Maitre à Danser," by P. Rameau. He has also contributed numerous critical and historical articles on dancing to *Artwork*, *The Dance Journal*, *The Dancing Times*, *The Dancing World*, *Fanfare*, *The Mask*, *Observer*, *Theatre Arts Monthly*, etc.

Author of many books and pamphlets, including the following: "A Manual of the Theory and Practice of Classical Theatrical Dancing (Cecchetti Method)," in collaboration with S. Idzikowski; "The History of Harlequin," "Enrico Cecchetti: A Memoir," "The Theory and Practice of Allegro in Classical Ballet (Cecchetti

Method)" in collaboration with M. Craske; "A History of Ballet in Russia (1613-1881)," "A French-English Dictionary of Technical Terms used in Classical Ballet"; "Fanny Elssler" (all published by C. W. Beaumont); "A Bibliography of Dancing (The Dancing Times, Ltd.).
Address: 75 Charing Cross Road, London, W.C.2.
Best Photos: Swaine, London.

BEDELLS (Miss), Phyllis (Mrs. Ian MacLean); danseuse and teacher of Operatic Dancing. Original Member of Committee of Operatic Association; Fellow Imperial Society of Teachers of Dancing; Member of Committee of Faculty of Dancing and of Camargo Society. Born in Bristol, 1893, and studied under Madame Cavalazzi, Cecchetti, Pavlova, Alexander Genée and Nicholas Legat. First appearance in *Alice in Wonderland* at Prince of Wales Theatre, 1906. Engaged 1907-1915 at Empire, Leicester Square, appearing in *The Belle of the Ball, The Debutante, Ship Ahoy*, etc.; succeeded Genée and Kyasht as *première danseuse*, 1914, appearing in *The Dancing Master, The Vine*, etc., and at the Palace Theatre in "The Passing Show." Joined Albert de Courville, 1916, appearing in "Razzle Dazzle," "Zigzag," 1917, at the Hippodrome; "Smile," Garrick Theatre; "Hotch-Potch," Duke of York's Theatre, etc., 1918; "Box o' Tricks" and "Joy Bells," Hippodrome, 1919. Opened with Novikoff a season on tour of Russian ballets produced by Komissarjevsky, 1920, and appeared at Alhambra in "Johnny Jones." In 1922 re-appeared at Empire as The Spirit of the Past in "The Smith Family." Opened large School of Dancing in Bristol, and danced in "By the Way," Apollo Theatre, 1925, later dancing for several seasons with Anton Dolin. With own company appeared in *The Three Bears* at Palladium and on tour. Has given series of Dance and Piano Recitals with Prince George Chavchavadze; danced in Madame Genée's revival of *Robert the Devil*, first Camargo performance, and in Legat's *Straussiana*, second Camargo performance, 1930-1931. Produced and danced in *Chopin Ballade* (Camargo, November, 1931).
Address: 115 Maida Vale, London, W.9.
Best Photos: Sasha; Peter North; Lenare; Yvonne, London.

BELCHER, Ernest; teacher of operatic, character and exhibition ballroom dancing. Began professional career as *premiere danseur* at the Alhambra Theatre at the age of 19. Following this danced principally in vaudeville throughout the Empire, Moss and Stoll, Gibbons, and syndicate theatres. His partners were Dorothy Graham and Dorothy Edwards. With the latter became known as "The Celestes," and were recognized ballroom experts. He left London for New York in 1913, and played the Keith Circuit in New York and adjacent territory. In 1916 went to Los Angeles, and there opened his own school, which has become one of the principal schools in the country. Mr. Belcher has done a very considerable amount of work for the films, having trained or directed innumerable "stars" in Hollywood in dance sequences.
Address: 607 South Western Avenue, Los Angeles, California, U.S.A.
Best photos: Keystone, Los Angeles.

BELLAMY (Miss), Eileen ; operatic, stage and ballroom teacher. Holder of the Intermediate Certificate of the Operatic Association. Acted as *Maîtresse de Ballet* at the Aldwych Theatre at Christmas, 1924, at the Apollo Theatre at Christmas, 1926, and to Mr. H. V. Nielson's production, *Bluebell in Fairyland*, for five years. Has introduced and conducts a "Postal Dance Service."
Address: "Halcyon," Riversdale Road, Thames Ditton, Surrey.

BELLENDEN - CLARKE (Miss), Diana; general teacher. Is teaching in Southsea and district, and her pupils won the Silver Medal for Senior Group dancing in the All England Sunshine Competition, 1931.
Address: Charlton House, South Hayling Island, Hants.

BENNETT (Miss), Marjorie; general teacher and principal of Blue-Bird School of Dancing, specializing in children's work. Was trained at Ansty College of Dancing, Birmingham.
Address : 113 Torquay Road, Paignton, S. Devon.
Best Photos : Robsons, Paignton.

BERNEY (Miss), Ruth; operatic dancer and teacher. Was Children's Examiner to the Operatic Association 1924-30, and a teacher of the Association's "Scholars" 1926-30. Miss Berney is herself a pupil of Espinosa, and holds his Advanced Diploma and Honours Certificate. She obtained the Advanced Certificate of the Operatic Association in 1924. Is now a teacher of the British Ballet Organisation's Children's Classes, and has the full teaching Diploma (Advanced and Solo Standards) of that organisation.
Address : 47 Victoria Street, Mansfield, Notts.
Best photos : Ellis, Mansfield.

BERRY (Miss), Joyce; classical and character dancer. Studied with Astafieva and Nijinska. In 1924 danced in Nigel Playfair's production of "The Duenna" at the Lyric, Hammersmith. Has since toured with Anton Dolin's Company as soloist. Danced at the London Palladium in The Chaperon Ballet for Phyllis Bedells. Has studied Japanese dancing with Toshi Komori. Has worked continuously with Nijinska in all her recent production for the Russian Opera Company at the Champs Elysées Theatre, Paris, and in Madame Ida Rubinstein's productions.
Address : 41 Tite Street, Chelsea, London, S.W.3.
Best photos : Yevonde, London.

BEST (Miss), Mary; operatic and ballroom teacher. Member of the Ballroom Branch of the Imperial Society. Has taught in Margate and district for the past twenty-two years. From 1919 to 1924 was Dance Hostess at the Queen's Highcliffe Hotel, Margate. Works chiefly amongst the Boarding Schools in the Isle of Thanet.
Address : The Grosvenor School of Dancing, Harold Road, Margate.

BESTE (Miss), Joan (Mrs. Hugh Symonds) ; general teacher. Intermediate Member of the Operatic Association ; Member of the Ballroom Branch Imperial Society. Received training from Miss Florence Purcell and Miss Elsa Brunelleschi. Was finalist for the Senior Cup in "All England Solo Dancing Competition" in 1928, and in the same competitions gained silver medals in 1926, 1927 and 1929. Also won three silver medals in the first dancing competitions held at the Croydon Festival. Opened School seven years ago at 8 Wellesley Road, Croydon, and now has a good connection with a branch at Cheam, Surrey.
Address : "Lavenders," Church Hill, Merstham, Surrey.
Best photos : Hana ; Stiby, London.

BEWICKE, Hilda (Mrs. D'Arfa) ; operatic dancer. Was *première danseuse* with Pavlova. Danced important roles in Diaghileff's Russian Ballet, such as Papillon in *Carnaval*, Chinese in *Aurora's Wedding*, etc.
Address : Teheran, Persia.

BIRCHLER, THOMAS; general teacher. Editor of *The Dancing Master*. Vice-President Chicago Association for several years, President for three years ; Member Dancing Masters of America, Inc. Was a newspaper reporter and editor, and in 1916 studied dancing under R. G. Huntinghouse, Chicago, Vestoff and Serova, later under Louis Kretlow. Then began to teach social and ballet dancing, and managed club balls and class schools. In 1924 edited *The Terpsichorean*, the accepted trade journal of the dancing profession in America.
Address : 6243 Champlain Avenue, Chicago, Ill.

BISHOP (Miss), Edith (Mrs. J. H. Randell) ; ballroom, operatic and national teacher. Examiner and Member of Executive Council of British Association of Teachers of

Dancing. Belonging to a family whose dance-teaching dates back one hundred years, Miss Bishop assisted her father until 1914 at Kilburn Athenæum and has since specialized in modern ballroom dancing at her own studio.
Address: Buckland House, 28 Quex Road, West Hampstead, London, N.W.6.

BISHOP, Will; eccentric and "tap" dancer, associated with many successful pre-War ballets at the Empire Theatre, notably *Faust* (1895), *The Press* (1898), *Round the Town Again* (1899) and *Old China* (1901). Danced at one of the earliest "Sunshine Matinees.
Address: 2 Park Lane, London, W.1.

BIZZELL (Miss), Lilian; ballroom teacher and demonstrator. Member of the Imperial Society; b. 1907.
Address: 38 Ebury Street, Belgravia, London, S.W.1.
Best photos: Janet Jevons, London.

BLACKEBY, Harry; teacher of ballroom, national, folk and Morris dancing. Late Hon. Secretary to Midland Branch of the British Association of Teachers of Dancing. Elected Hon. Member in 1930. Fellow of the British Association of Physical Training. Acted as Physical Education Instructor since 1897, but adopted dancing as a profession in 1913.
Address: 41 Eastbourne Street, Walsall, Staffs.
Best photos: N. Bullock, Walsall.

BLAIKLEY (Miss), Nancy; Greek and classical ballet dancer and teacher. Advanced Member A.T.R.G.D. Licentiate of the Imperial Society (Classical Ballet Section). Children's Examiner of the A.T.R.G.D. Holder of the Diploma of the Ginner-Mawer School. Is Visiting Teacher at the West of England Academy, Bristol, and has own private connection in Hampstead and Finchley in North London.
Address: Northbrook, 133 Holden Road, Woodside Park, London, N.12.

BLAKE, Francis P.; ballroom and eccentric dancer. Has been a professional dance partner at Dunedin Palais de Danse, Edinburgh, the Plaza, Dublin, and is now at the Rialto, Liverpool. Has appeared in cabaret.
Address: 2 Montpelier Terrace, Upper Parliament Street, Liverpool.

BLOODWORTH, Harry; ballroom teacher. Examiner for National Association. President 1922-1923; has served on Informal Committees during last ten years, and is now on Official Board.
Address: Mascot House, 43 Stamford Hill, London, N.16.

BLUNT, Edward W. J.; ballroom dancer and teacher. Member Syndicat Nationale des Professeurs de Danse et Danseurs Professionnels (France). Commenced professional dancing in 1921, and was employed by the Wimbledon Palais de Danse until 1927. Has won a number of competitions, the chief amongst them being the "World's Championship (Paris), 1927-8, Championship of the Côte d'Azur, 1928-9 (Nice), and came third in the World's Championship in Paris (1926-7). Winner of the World's Mixed Ballroom Championship, 1931, and of the International Ballroom Championship at Vichy in 1931. Winner Ballroom Championship of Switzerland, held at Zurich, January, 1932. Inventor of the "Skating Charleston," introduced in 1927. Opened his school in 1928.
Address: "Balmoral," 52 Queen's Road, Wimbledon, London, S.W.
Best photos: Russell & Sons, Wimbledon.

BOALTH (Miss), Anny; dancer and teacher of Central European dancing. Member of the German Dancers' Association, and the Laban Association; Examiner in Münster Town Academie, 1927, and also in Breslau in 1928. Holds the Laban Certificate and Diploma. Trained at the School of Rudolf von Laban. Member of the Laban group, and has appeared in Laban productions of *Agamemnon's Death, Don Juan, Ritterballet* (by

Beethoven), *Tannhauser* at Bayreuth, and Chamber Dance Recitals. Toured with Chamber Dance Group of Hamburg in Shakespeare productions; "Faust" by Goethe, etc.; at the Deutsches Schauspielhaus, Hamburg; Stadtheater, Altona. In 1925-26 was teacher at the East German Gymnasium and Dance Institute at Breslau, and in 1926-27 was teacher at the Town Academie of Dancing, Music and Elocution in Münster. Danced at the Handel's Festivals. In 1928 was again in Breslau. In 1929 became a partner of the Laban School at Prague, and gave recitals in the town theatre. In 1930 visited London, and in October of that year appeared at the Camargo Society's first production. Has a Central European School of Dancing in London.

Address: 13 Blomfield Road, London, W.9, and Bismarckallee, 43 Ahrensburg, Hamburg, Germany.

Best photos: Wilcke, Hamburg; Carola and Balzar, Prague; and Anthony, London.

BODENWIESER (Frau), Gertrud; teacher of dancing. Professor at the Staate Akademie Für Musik und Darst Kunst, Vienna; President des cremiums der Behördlich genehmieten Schulen für Künstlerischen Tanz, Vienna; Member of the Prufungskommission für das Lehrant in Rhythm, Gymastik und Künste Tanz, Vienna. First appeared in public in 1919, later giving dance recital with first pupils. Became Professor of Dancing in two famous girls' colleges in Vienna and of the State Academy in Vienna, dancing being included for the first time in the curriculum of a government art school. Principal of own School of Dancing in Konzerthaus, Vienna, where own method of Central European Dancing is taught. Formed with best pupils the Gertrud Bodenwieser Tanzgruppe, which appeared at the London Coliseum in 1929 for a month.

Address: Universitatsstrasse, 10, Vienna, IX.

Best Photos: Zimbler, Vienna.

BOEHME, Frint ; dance author and dance critic with big influence in Berlin. *Author* of numerous books and articles. Some of the best known are: "Der Tanz der Zukunft," "Tanzkunst."

BOGGAN (Miss), Jean; teacher of operatic, Greek and ballroom dancing. Trained by Espinosa and Miss Ethne Skinner.

Address: 38 Vivian Avenue, Hendon, London, N.W.

BOÏELLE (Miss), Jeannette; general teacher and dancer, and teacher of fencing. Member of Committee and Judge of Dancing Sections of the Jersey and Guernsey Eisteddfod. Judge at Jersey Dancing Championships, 1927-1930; teacher at Jersey Green Room Club; Recitalist at the Musical Classics in Dance, Jersey and Guernsey, 1930-1931. Producer of pageants, etc., since 1925.

Address: The Studio, 56 David Place, St. Helier, Jersey.

Best Photos: Albert Smith, Jersey.

BOLM, Adolph; balletmaster and dancer. Formerly with the Imperial Ballet in Petrograd; Diaghileff's Russian Ballet; Metropolitan Opera Company, New York; Chicago Opera Company; Colon Opera, Buenos Aires; Chicago Allied Arts, and the Adolph Bolm Ballet. Born in Petrograd and educated in the Imperial Ballet School in Petrograd, from which he graduated with first prize. Became soloist of the Imperial Ballet at the Marinsky Theatre. As a young artist organised a small ballet company, with Anna Pavlova as *ballerina*, which he took to Europe, appearing in Riga, Stockholm (where he was decorated by the King of Sweden with the medal Litras Artibus), Copenhagen, Prague and Berlin. In 1909 joined the Diaghileff Ballet as *premier danseur*, scoring tremendous success in *Prince Igor, Petrouchka, Fire Bird, Carnaval, Cleopatra* and *Tamar*, appearing in Paris, London, Monte Carlo, Berlin, Vienna and South America. He was also Ballet-Master and staged several ballets. In 1915 he helped Diaghileff to re-organize the company, and prepared all the ballets for the first North American tour as Ballet

Master and first dancer. After two seasons of trans-continental tours of the United States, and a season in Spain, he decided to stay in New York. He was engaged by the Metropolitan Opera Company to produce Rimsky-Korsakoff's *Coq-d'Or*, which caused a great sensation. In 1927 he arranged a spectacular ballet on a revolving stage at the Century Theatre in New York; founded his *Ballet Intime*, touring the country for the benefit of the American Ambulance in Russia, and produced the first dance prologues for moving picture houses in New York at the Rivoli and Rialto Theatres. In 1919 he produced *Igor* and Stravinsky's *Petrouchka* for the Metropolitan Opera Company, and during the same season the ballet by John Alden Carpenter, *The Birthday of the Infanta*, for the Chicago Grand Opera Company. In 1920 he appeared with his dancers in London, returning to continue with the Metropolitan Opera Company until 1923, during which year he left the Metropolitan to become ballet-master of the newly-organized Chicago Civic Opera, when he founded the Adolph Bolm School of the Dance, now having several branches. In 1924, together with John Alden Carpenter, the composer, and other notable persons, he founded the Chicago Allied Arts, Inc., an organization consisting of a small Symphony Orchestra and the Adolph Bolm Ballet, for the production of modern music and ballet. For the opening performance in November, 1924, Tamara Karsavina was invited as guest dancer, appearing for the first time in Chicago. For four seasons this organization produced many ballets by modern composers. In 1925 he was re-engaged by the Metropolitan to make an entirely new production of Stravinsky's *Petrouchka*. The same year he was engaged to give *Coq-d'Or*, *Petrouchka* and other ballets at the Colon Theatre in Buenos Aires. In 1928 he was invited to participate in the Elizabeth Sprague Coolidge Music Festival at the Library of Congress Auditorium in Washington, D.C., where he produced the World's *première* of Stravinsky's *Apollo Musagetes*, which was specially composed for the occasion. His activities now consist of touring, performing with his ballet, teaching, lecturing and writing on the Dance. He is also working on a project for the Chicago 1933 World's Fair, which it is hoped will be the meeting-place of the dancers of the world. Adolph Bolm is Chairman of the Dance Committee for the Chicago World's Fair, for which he will also prepare several new ballets by modern composers. Is the author of a book entitled "The Dance," which is now in course of preparation.

Address: The Adolph Bolm School of the Dance, 162 E. Ohio Street, Chicago, Ill.

Best photos: Hoppé, London, and Goldberg, New York.

BOSUSTOW (Miss), Grace; general teacher. Has a well-established School of dancing at Watford and Ealing.

Address: 24 Mortimer Road, Ealing, London, W.

BOURNE, Edward Wentworth; Dance Hall Manager. Entered into Dance Hall management in 1920, and has been manager at Sherry's and the Regent Dance Hall at Brighton; the Southport Palais de Danse; the Rialto Ballroom, Liverpool, and, for the past four years, the Astoria Dance Salon, London.

Address: 25 Lancaster Court, Newman Street, W.1.

BOYD (Miss), Clarice; ballroom teacher. Trained under Alfred Baker in 1928. Took over the Baker School of Dancing, Plymouth, in 1930.

Address: Links Hotel, Thurlestone, S. Devon.

BRADBURN (Miss), Madge ; operatic and ballroom teacher; *b*. 1907. Intermediate Member Operatic Association. Fellow of the Imperial Society (Ballroom), and Licentiate Member (Operatic). Holder of the I.L.A.M. Bronze Medal for Elocution. Received operatic training from the Bush School, acrobatic and step from the Askew School, and Ballroom from

Miss Eve Tynegate-Smith. Opened own school in 1926. Is Ballet Mistress to the Derby Opera Company, and Dancing Mistress to several leading schools in Derby. Holds classes in various parts of the county. Makes a speciality of exhibition ballroom dancing, and gives many cabaret shows. In 1932 gained the "Intermediate Teachers' Certificate" of the Operatic Association.
Address: The Studio, 129 Osmaston Road, Derby.
Best photos: Winter, Derby.

BRADLEY Miss, Josephine (Mrs. Wellesley-Smith); ballroom dancer and teacher; Vice-President of the Ballroom branch of the "Imperial Society." First came into prominence when she won an "Open Fox-trot" Competition at the "Embassy Club" in November, 1920, dancing with an amateur, Mr. G. K. Anderson. The following year with the same partner she won both the "All-England Fox-trot" Competitions organized by the "Ivory Cross." These competitions definitely settled the form of the fox-trot. In 1924, with Mr. Anderson, she won the "Mixed" section of the "World's Championship" at the Queens Hall, London. Upon the reorganization of the "Imperial Society" and the founding of its Ballroom Branch, Miss Bradley took an active part in the proceedings, and ultimately became Vice-President of the Branch, an office which she still holds. She has played a very big rôle in the evolution of the technique of modern ballroom dancing, and with her late husband, Mr. Wellesley-Smith, was one of the most popular "demonstrators" appearing before the public. For the past five years she has been Chairman of the Judges of the "Star" Ballroom Championships, and is in considerable demand as a judge at competitions throughout the country.
Address: 6 Basil Street, Knightsbridge, S.W.1.
Best photos: Peter North, London.

BRAHAM, Philip; ballroom teacher. Member of the National Association of Teachers of Dancing. World travelled. Has taught dancing in almost every British colony, and also other countries, including North and South America, and Japan.
Address: 92 Holland Park Avenue, London, W.11.

BRAITHWAITE (Miss), Margaret; operatic dancer, trained by Miss Kathleen de Vos. Was runner-up for the "Senior Cup" at the "All England Solo Competition" in 1928, and has appeared in a Cochran revue when she understudied Tilly Losch. Is now a prominent member of the *corps de ballet* in "Waltzes from Vienna" at the Alhambra.
Address: 97 York Mansions, London, S.W.10.

BRANDENBURG, Hans; well-known German author and pioneer, with big influence for the ideas of modern dancing and specially dance-drama. Collaborator with Rudolf von Laban in Munich and Ascona.
Author of the following books: "Der Moderne Tanz," "Das Theatre und das neue Deutschland."

BRAYBROOKS (Miss) D. A. Member of the Association of Teachers of the Revived Greek Dance, and Holder of Advanced Certificate of the Imperial Society. Local Organiser for Children's examinations. Is Principal of the Dorothy Braybrooks School of Dancing at Bradford.
Address: Park Royd, 32 Keighley Road, Bradford.

BRETHERTON (Miss), Monica H.; general teacher, but specializes in ballroom dancing. Member Imperial Society (Ballroom, Operatic and Greek Branches; Advanced Member Association of Teachers of the Revived Greek Dance, and holds their Honours Certificate. Member British Ballet Organization. Has taught in Liverpool and district since 1918. Introduced first tea dances in Liverpool, and also first cabaret at the Adelphi Hotel. Came first and second in the first "Ivory Cross" Competitions held in Liverpool. School won the "All

England Dancing Competition" Cup in 1929 and 1930.
Address: 6 Lord Street, Liverpool.
Best photos: Chidleys, Liverpool.

BRIDGEWATER (Miss), Ailsa Madeline; operatic and ballroom dancer and teacher. Member of the Imperial Society of Teachers of Dancing (Classical Ballet and Ballroom Branches). Member of the P.D.A., and holder of the Advanced Certificate of the Incorporated London Academy of Music. Received training from Leon Leonidoff of Toronto and Montreal, Mr. H. St. John Rumsey, and Miss Margaret Craske. Was the first person to broadcast dancing by means of the Baird process of Television in connection with the B.B.C.
Address: Thanet House, Egmont Road, Sutton, Surrey.

BRIGGS, Hedley; ballet and character dancer; actor; designer of masks and costumes. Started stage career as actor at Birmingham Repertory Theatre in 1923; went to Festival Theatre, Cambridge, in 1926. Met Ninette de Valois who was choregraphic director there, and was persuaded to dance. Partnered Penelope Spencer in 1928-30 at the Arts Theatre Club, etc. Danced with Ninette de Valois at the Old Vic, Lyric, etc. Went to Abbey Theatre, Dublin, for first production of Yeats' *Fighting the Waves*. Danced with Lopokova in Stravinsky's *L'Histoire du Soldat* in 1928. Designed costumes, masks, décor for Ninette de Valois, Anton Dolin, Anna Ludmila, etc., and *Danse Sacrée et Profane* for Camargo Society. Danced in the first Camargo performance, October, 1930.
Author of an article entitled "The Mask," printed in *The Dance Journal*, April and June, 1930.
Address: 19 Taviton Street, London, W.C.1.
Best Photos: Beck & MacGregor; Anthony, London.

BRITTAIN, H. D.; ballroom teacher. Has been established since 1904. Member of the National Association of Teachers of Dancing. Was President in 1920-21, and a Member of the Executive Council and Examiner for six years. Member of the Midland Association, and was President in 1927-28; Member of Supreme Council, and Examiner since 1920. Was elected General Secretary in 1930. Is a strong supporter of sequence dancing, and has won a number of diplomas and medals for this type of dancing. Won the "Handley Shield" of the National Association in 1927.
Address: 76 High Street, Penge, London, S.E.20.
Best Photos: Bates and Son, Penge, London.

BROMOVA (Mdme.), Anna; teacher of all branches of stage dancing. Trained by Cecchetti, Mordkin, Kosloff, Volinine and Morosoff. Toured Canada and U.S.A. with Michael Mordkin's Company before the war. Became a member of the Imperial Russian Ballet under Diaghileff. Principal Dancer to Theodore Kosloff's Company, partnered by Alexis Kosloff and later by Serge Morosoff. Principal dancer in and producer of "Valentine" at St. James's Theatre, London. Opened School of Dancing at Gunnersbury, 1916.
Address: 13 Grange Road, Gunnersbury, London, W.4.
Best Photos: Miriam Lewis, London.

BROOKS (Miss), Iris; general teacher. Member Imperial Society of Teachers of Dancing (Classical Ballet, Revived Greek, and Ballroom Branches). Member of the Association of Teachers of the Revived Greek Dance. Trained at the Ripman School of Dancing.
Address: Southwood Lodge, Newbury, Berkshire.
Best photos: Margaret Neste, Paris.

BROWN, Alfred E.; ballroom teacher. Member British Association of Teachers of Dancing, 1899-1908; Vice-President, 1904; Member Executive Council; Founder and Secretary Universal Association of Teachers of Dancing, 1907-1930; Hon. Member Union des Professeurs de Danse, Paris; Secretary International Danc-

ing Masters' Association, 1930-1931; Born in Leicester, 1872, and began teaching 1894. Has held many positions as Lessee and M.C. of important ballrooms and dance halls in Blackpool and Halifax, and is now teaching in Halifax. Inventor of 26 Novelty dances, including the King's Waltz, which was accepted by H.M. the King in 1913 in commemoration of his visit to Blackpool.
Address: 37 Lister Lane, Halifax, Yorkshire.
Best Photos: Bamber, Blackpool.

BROWN (Miss), Beatrice A.; teacher of operatic and ballroom dancing. Intermediate Member Operatic Association. Licentiate of the Imperial Society (Operatic). Licentiate of the British College of Physical Education. Author of " Group and Solo Dances" (Saville & Co., Ltd.).
Address: 24 Westmoreland Road, Barnes, London, S.W.13.
Best photos: Stabey, London.

BROWN (Miss), Constance; ballroom teacher. Member of the Imperial Society. One of the Principals of the Nottingham Academy of Dancing.
Address: Brerby House, Burns Street, Nottingham.

BROWN (Miss), Hylda; general teacher. Member of the Operatic Association, and Fellow and Life Member of Imperial Society (Operatic and General Branches).
Address: 20 Penkett Road, Wallasey, Cheshire.

BRUCE (Miss), Audrey; general teacher. Member of the Association of Operatic Dancing; Member of Operatic, Ballroom, Cecchetti (Elem.) and General Branches of Imperial Society, and is an Examiner for the General Branch and on that Committee. Trained with Florence Purcell, and latterly opened School of Dancing at Wimbledon.
Address: Bruce-Collins School of Dancing, 61 Worple Road, Wimbledon, London, S.W.19.

BRUNELLESCHI (Miss), Elsa; operatic and Spanish dancer and general teacher. Member of the Arts Theatre Club, Camargo Society and the Society of Guitarists. Holder of Maestro Cecchetti's original Certificate. Studied under the following masters: Alonso Sanchez at Madrid; Pauleta in Barcelona; Realito and Rodriguez, Seville; Mme. Mariquita and Simarra at Paris; and with Maestro Cecchetti in London and Paris. Has successfully appeared in London, the Continent and South America. *Première danseuse* at Covent Garden Opera House, London, and Liceo de Barcelona, etc. Is the principal teacher of Spanish Dancing in this country.
Hobby: Guitar playing and Swimming.
Address: Westbourne Hall, 26 Westbourne Grove, London, W.2.
Best photos: Basil, London; and Mandel, Paris.

BUCK (Miss), Nancy; ballroom teacher. Associate of the Imperial Society's Ballroom Branch. Trained by Mrs. Jack Buckley, and was teaching with her for two years. Now has own teaching connection in Hove.
Address: Flat 1, 106 Lansdowne Place, Hove, Sussex.

BUCKLEY (Mrs.), Jack; ballroom dancer and teacher. Member of the Ballroom Branch of the Imperial Society. Dance Hostess at the Hotel Metropole, Brighton. Is partnered by Mr. Allen Cavanagh.
Address: Studio, 21 Lansdowne Road, Hove, Sussex; Private address, 24 Salisbury Road, Hove, Sussex.

BUCKLEY (Miss), Mona; solo dancer and general teacher. Trained at the Vandyck School. Has also studied under Miss Belle Harding, Espinosa and others. Had a teaching connection at Cricklewood for two years, one at Clacton-on-Sea for five (this is now carried on by an assistant), and for the past five years has had a studio at the Portman Rooms, Baker Street, London, at which remedial work is a big feature. Has judged a number of ballroom competitions.
Address: The Portman Rooms, Baker Street, London, W.1.

BULLARS, Frank; ballroom teacher. Member International Dancing Masters' Association, and Vice-President of that Association for 1931; also examiner and adjudicator. Member and examiner of the British Association of Teachers of Dancing. Member of the Official Board of Ballroom Dancing. Adjudicator at the British Amateur and Professional Championships, 1931.
Address: Victoria Academy of Dancing, St. Sepulchre Gate, Doncaster.

BULT (Miss), Mildred; general teacher. Life Member of and was for two years Vice-President of the Operatic Branch of the Imperial Society. Member of Council and Fellow of the Imperial Society (Certificated Operatic (Cecchetti) and Ballroom Sections). Principal of first real Training College (Residential) for Teachers of Dancing. Opened at the Grafton Rooms, Bedford, in 1910, and moved to present address in 1922.
Author of " Devonshire Dances " (Curwen).
Address: Bedford College of Dancing, 5 Kingswood Road, London, S.E.19.

BURNS, Robert; ballroom teacher. President Cleveland Dancing Teachers' Association, Inc.; Vice-President, The Dancing Masters of America, Inc.; Member, The Ohio Association of Teachers of Dancing, and Member, The Pittsburgh Society for the Improvement of Dancing, and holds certificates of these associations. Has been teaching modern and American Folk Dancing for twelve years, and has originated a number of new dances.
Address: 1318 Giddings Road, Cleveland, Ohio, U.S.A.
Best Photos: Bern, Cleveland.

BURROWES (Miss), Leslie; was the first English girl to take the Diploma of the Mary Wigman School at Dresden. She has given Recitals in Germany, France and England, and has done distinguished work for the " London Theatre Company."

BURY (Miss), Joy; general teacher Member Operatic Association (Advanced Certificate); Member Imperial Society of Teachers of Dancing (Ballroom and Cecchetti branches). Danced in ballet produced by Novikoff for *The Betrothal*, Gaiety Theatre, London, in 1922. Head assistant at the Cone School 1922-1926, and at the James Meyer School of Dancing, Amsterdam, 1926-1928; is now principal of the Raybury School of Dancing, Folkestone.
Address: 133a Sandgate Road, Folkestone.

BUSH (Miss), Noreen (Mrs. Victor Leopold); general teacher, specializing in operatic work. Holder of the " Solo Seal " of the Operatic Association. Member of the Cecchetti Branch of the Imperial Society. Teacher of Ballet and Mime to the Royal Academy of Music and the London scholars of the Association of Operatic Dancing of Great Britain. Her school was founded in 1915 by her mother, the late Mdme. Pauline Bush, and is one of the best known in the country, having particularly brilliant successes in operatic dancing. Was assistant to Espinosa, and danced at Daly's Theatre, London. Also appeared at the Operatic Association's Special Matinee at the Gaiety Theatre, London.
Address: 48 Forest Road West, Nottingham, and 36 Fellows Road, Hampstead, London, N.W.3.
Best Photos: Freckleton's Studios, Nottingham.

BUTTERWORTH (Miss), Audrey; teacher of operatic, ballroom and Greek work. Member of the Imperial Society — Ballroom and Cecchetti branches; Intermediate Member of the Operatic Association. One of the principal teachers in Liverpool. In 1932 passed with Honours the " Intermediate Teachers' Examination " of the Operatic Association.
Address: Crane's Buildings, Hanover Street, Liverpool.

BYRNE, Talbot Leggett; general teacher. Mr. Leggett Byrne inherited his ability for teaching from his mother, the late Madame Leggett Byrne, formerly Miss Leggett, of London, who was for many years Head Assistant to Mr. and Mrs. Nicholas Henderson, of Newman St., London, and a pupil of Monsieur Coulon, of Paris. Mr. Leggett Byrne is ably assisted by his wife, who also cames from a dancing family, being a daughter of Mrs. Haines, who taught in Belfast for over twenty years. They have a large teaching connection in Dublin, and for thirty years have had charge of social functions at Dublin Castle, and on the occasion of a Royal garden party at the Vice Regal Lodge produced an outdoor ballet by their small pupils before H.M. The King and Queen, who afterwards congratulated Mr. and Mrs. Leggett Byrne on the children's performance. During the visit of the late Queen Victoria to Dublin, their class at the Chief Secretary's Lodge was attended by Princess Ena of Battenberg, afterwards Queen of Spain. Have given numerous performances both in Dublin and London, for Charities, by which over £1,200 has been raised. Mr. Leggett Byrne was the first to start Ballroom Championships in Dublin, and the first to introduce evening dress "Cinderellas" at popular prices in Dublin.

Author of "Terpsichore: her Votaries and Fashions" (Illustrated Advertising Association, Ltd., London).

Address: 27 Adelaide Road, Dublin, Ireland.

Best Photos: Lafayette, Dublin.

C

CABRERA (Mrs.), W. J.; ballroom teacher. Member of the Imperial Society of Teachers of Dancing. Co-principal with her husband of the "Cabrera School of Dancing." Winner with Mr. W. J. Cabrera of the Eastern Counties Championship, 1924. Semi-Finalist in the World's Dancing Championships, 1924. Judge of a number of important competitions, including the London and Southern Counties Championships, the "Star" Championships, and the "Columbia" Amateur Ballroom Dancing Championship of Great Britain.

Address: 8 Ventnor Villas, Hove, Brighton, Sussex.

CADMAN (Mrs.), Margaret; Vice-President, 1930, and Member of Executive Committee Operatic Section of the British Association of Teachers of Dancing. Member of Society of Teachers of Dancing, Belgium. Co-Principal with her husband and daughter of the Cadman School of Dancing at King's Hall, Stretford, Manchester. (*See also* W. H. CADMAN.)

Address: West Bank, 39 Washway Road, Sale, Manchester.

CADMAN (Miss), Margaret Sancta; ballroom and operatic teacher. Trained at the Royal Academy of Dramatic Art in London 1921-7, and was a pupil of the late Louis d'Egville. With her partner, Miss Allan, and under the professional names of "Margaret Sancta and Apryl," has toured the foremost towns of England, Scotland, Holland, Belgium and Germany during the last few years as exhibition dancers. Is co-principal of the Cadman School of Dancing at Kings Hall, Stretford, Manchester.

Address: West Bank, 39 Washway Road, Sale, Manchester.

CADMAN, W. H.; ballroom and operatic teacher. President British Association of Teachers of Dancing, 1923-4, 1924-5. President Manchester Association of Teachers of Dancing in 1925. Member of the Manchester "Dancers' Circle." Member Nederlandsche Vereeniging van Danslareeren. Opened the King's Hall, Stretford, as a Dancing Academy in 1903, and it has continued up to the present time without a break, during the war being carried on by Mrs. Cadman. During the summer of 1914 Mr. Cadman acted as M.C. at the Empress Ballroom, Blackpool, and with his wife introduced a successful "round dance" called the "Mary Gavotte." The following year saw him in "active service" in France. In 1919 he leased the White City

Ballroom, Manchester, and for a number of years held some very popular dances there.
Address: West Bank, 39 Washway Road, Sale, Manchester.

CALLADINE (Miss), Florence; general teacher (*see Miss Hettie Calladine*). In partnership with her sister has school of dancing in Sheffield, and is responsible for the secretarial and general management of the School; also for most of the music.
Address: 4 Hanover Square, Sheffield.
Best photos: Ethel Eadon, Sheffield.

CALLADINE (Miss), Hettie S.; general teacher. In partnership with her sister, Miss Florence Calladine, has taught in Sheffield and district for the past 26 years. Was trained with Mr. Archie Webster, of Manchester and Newcastle, and was for some years with the Haines School. Studied Operatic work with Mr. Espinosa, Greek with Miss Ruby Ginner, and Ballroom with Miss Eve Tynegate-Smith. Has taught and lectured on Folk Dancing in various countries. Is also interested in the British Ballet Organisation.
Address: 4 Hanover Square, Sheffield.
Best photos by Ethel Eadon, Sheffield.

CAMBAGE, A. C.; teacher and exponent of Ballroom Dancing. With his wife, has family dancing connections extending over 45 years in the district of North-east Lancashire. Were managers of the Ritz Ballroom, Nelson, and the Empress Ballroom, Burnley. Are now at the Imperial Ballroom, Nelson. Trained and taught by Mr. Morry Blake and Mr. Robert Sielle and Miss Annette Mills. Are popular demonstrators and well-known teachers.
Address: 181 Hibson Road, Nelson, Lancs.
Best photos by Laurence, Blackburn, and Taylor, Burnley.

CAMBAGE (Mrs.), A. C.; is a teacher and exponent of Ballroom Dancing with her husband, as above.
Address: 181 Hibson Road, Nelson, Lancs.
Best photos by Laurence, Blackburn, and Taylor, Burnley.

CANDLER (Miss), Eleanor; ballroom dancer and teacher. Member of the Imperial Society of Teachers of Dancing. Was Principal of the Verity Studio of Dancing, but has now gone into partnership with Miss Muriel Simmons. Has judged and demonstrated at many leading competitions. *Author* of "Modern Ballroom Dance Instructor."
Address: 235 Regent Street, London, W.1.
Best photos by Janet Jevons, London.

CANSINO, Angel; teacher of Spanish dancing. Instructor to the American "Dancing Masters' Association." Son of Antonio Cansino, a well-known teacher of Spanish dancing in Madrid. Made his professional *début* in Madrid at the age of 10. Has appeared in the best theatres of America, England, Spain and South America for sixteen years. Has been teaching in Carnegie Hall, N.Y., for the past four years, during which time he has arranged dances for many well-known stars, such as Ada May, Fred Stone, Dorothy Stone, Paul Haakon, Rosita Moreno, Dario and Irene, Clifford and Higgins, Robert Woolsey, Walter Catlett, Nina de Marco and many others.
Books: Author of "The Art of Playing the Spanish Castanets."
Address: Carnegie Hall, Studio 839, New York City, U.S.A.
Best photos: Fabio Ruberti, New York.

CARD (Miss), Helen; operatic and ballroom teacher. Member of Imperial Society; holds Intermediate Certificate Operatic Association; Executive Member, Examiner and Lecturer of the National Association of Teachers of Dancing and the Midland Association of Teachers of Dancing. Was trained by Miss Florence Purcell, Espinosa and Victor Silvester. Has specialized successfully in the training of children, and is now conducting a successful school in partnership with Mr. Vivian Davies.

Author of a treatise on " Elementary Operatic Training for Children."

Address: 18a Crawford Street, Baker Street, London, W.1.

Best Photos: Hana (now Navana), London.

CARLOTTA (of Carré and Carlotta); adagio, acrobatic and interpretive dancer. Received operatic training from Miss Elsie Stevenson, of Sydney, Australia, and later from Miss Eunice Weston. Is of Spanish descent, and is sister to the Australian writer, Edith M. England. Carré and Carlotta were chosen for the *premières* at all leading theatres in the larger cities in Australia, and since coming to this country have made very successful appearances in West End hotels and theatres, etc. They have also been successful on the films. (*See also* CARRÉ.)

Address: 53 Belgrave Road, Victoria, London, S.W.1.

Best photos: Ruskin, Melbourne, Australia.

CARPENTER, Fred; operatic dancer, trained by Mordkin in America, where he appeared in several John Murray Anderson productions, notably " The Young King," which has recently been revived in " Bow Bells." Appeared in England in February, 1930, in exhibition dances with Frances Mann at Ciro's Club, doing a very unusual and clever number in masks entitled " The Prom." Subsequently danced in Jack Hulbert's " Follow a Star " and assisted in the arrangement of the dances. Has now a very prominent part in " Bow Bells " at the Hippodrome.

CARRE (of Carré and Carlotta); adagio and interpretive dancer. Member of the Australasian Society of Physical Education; 1st Class Instructor's Certificate of the Royal Australian Naval Physical Training and Dancing School. Studied Ballet under members of the Pavlova Company during their visits to Australia; also under Miss Elsie Stevenson, of Sydney, and Miss Eunice Weston, now of Melbourne, Australia. Is of Basque descent, and inclines towards the dances of Spain. (*See also* CARLOTTA.)

Address: 53 Belgrave Road, Victoria, London, S.W.1.

Best photos: Ruskin, Melbourne, Australia.

CARSON (Miss), Sylvia; teacher of rhythmic movement and ballroom dancing. Holds Diploma of the Bedford Physical Training College. Member of Conjoint Society of Massage and Medical Gymnasts (First Class Honours). Member of the Ling Association of Gymnastic Teachers. Teacher of Dancing and Gymnastics at Bexhill-on-Sea, Sussex, during which time produced original dance scenes and ballets for public performances; lectured and demonstrated on Rhythmic Dancing; produced open air displays of dancing for various charities. From 1923 to 1929 was Dance Hostess at the Sackville Hotel, Bexhill-on-Sea, and on the Continent. In 1930 opened private School in London.

Author of " Little Rhythmic Dances " (Saville & Co.). Contributor to the *Dancing Times*, *Child Education*, *Teacher's World*, etc., and has other books in course of preparation.

Address: 52 Queen Alexandra Mansions, London, W.C.1.

CARTER (Miss), Allie (Mrs. C. M. Jones); general teacher. Hostess at the Grand Pump Room, Bath. Was trained in operatic dancing by Madame Karina.

Address: 5 Connaught Place, Weston-super-Mare, Somerset.

Best Photos: Goodman, Weston-super-Mare.

CARTER, Misses D. and T.; general teachers. Advanced Members Operatic Association; Members Imperial Society (Ballroom and Operatic Branches) Holders of the Diploma of the Chelsea Physical Training College. Principals of the Chandos School of Dancing.

Address: 108 Chandos House, Palmer Street, London, S.W.1.

CARTIER, Jacques; concert dancer. Spent early years in India and South Africa, followed by seven years at Military School in United States. Ran away from Vanderbilt University to go on stage. Ambition to be actor, and became dancer as matter of necessity. A growing interest in the Dance, and its future—particularly in America—caused him to live with American Indians, learn their language, chants, rituals, ceremonials, and, finally, to be admitted to their tribe (the Hopi, of New Mexico), an honour accorded to only two other white men, both of them Presidents of the U.S.A. Recently made head of the Department of Indian Ritual and Ceremonial (which is the combine of the departments of Music, Costume, Dance and Song of American Indians) of the Rockefeller Foundation Laboratory of Anthropology (which is a branch of the Smithsonian Institute of the U.S. Government). During the past nine years has appeared in New York in John Murray Anderson's "Greenwich Village Follies," Florenz Ziegfeld's "Follies," "Music Box Revue," "Passing Show of 1927," Hammerstein's "Golden Dawn," etc., and has also performed in several successful films. Is now appearing in "Bow Bells" at the London Hippodrome. Last year he took the part of "Christus" in the Hollywood Bowl production of the Passion Play with great distinction. Mr. Cartier created in America the role of the Devil in Stravinsky's "L'Histoire de Soldat," and performed, for the first time in America, the leading roles in *El Amor Brujo* and *The Three-Cornered Hat*. His Chinese ballet, *General Fu*, the book and music by himself, has been produced in New York and Chicago eleven times during the past two years. He is at present working on the score for an Indian dance drama called "Ahul-alanti."
Address: 87 Bedford Street, New York City, U.S.A.

CARVER (Miss), Nora; ballroom dancer and teacher. With Mr. Jack W. Fitton as partner won the Leicestershire Amateur Championship 1929-30. Became a professional dancer in 1931 and, with Mr. Fitton, won the Sheffield and District finals of the British Professional Championships 1931; was runner-up for the Nottingham District Championship 1931. Acted as hostess at the Pier Pavilion Ballroom, Shanklin, Isle of Wight, during the summer, 1931, and inaugurated the Isle of Wight Amateur Dancing Championships, 1931. Is on the staff of the Leicester Palais de Danse.
Address: 4 Tennyson St., Leicester.
Best photos: Ramsden, Leicester.

CARYLL, Jan; operatic and character dancer and choregrapher. Born in New Zealand. Pupil of Estelle Beere, Wellington, N.Z.; Edouard de Kurylo, Warsaw Opera; Seraphine Astafieva, London. Appeared with success in Australia and New Zealand. First London appearance with Marian Wilson Ballet at the Kingsway Theatre as *premier danseur*. Partnered Ninette de Valois at various music halls. Toured with Valeska, Delyse and Colette. Extensive tours in the East and on the Continent as *premier danseur* of own Corps de Ballet. Dance Director of musical shows in principal theatres of various European capitals.
Address: 52 Priory Road, West Hampstead, N.W.6.
Best Photos: Lenare, London; Sasha, London.

CASANI, Santos; teacher and demonstrator of ballroom dancing. Was born in South Africa in 1893. Originally a mining engineer, he served during the Great War in the Royal Flying Corps, when he was very severely wounded and invalided with a life pension. In 1921 he took up dancing as a career and rapidly came to the fore as a teacher and demonstrator. He has appeared at the Empire, Alhambra, Coliseum and countless dance halls in demonstrations of ballroom dancing for many years with Miss Jose Lennard as partner, and has always proved a great attraction. Has broadcast dancing lessons on numerous occasions, appeared in many educational films, and has contributed articles on dancing to over one hundred different periodicals.

He was the sole organiser of the Columbia Graphophone Company's Amateur Dancing Championship of Great Britain, at that time the largest competition of that kind ever held. Is Principal of the School bearing his name, and is a great "showman." Incidentally he is an inventor, a big game hunter, and a boxer and horseman of no mean ability. Since Miss Lennard's marriage has danced with Miss Jean Mence.

Address: 90 Regent Street, Piccadilly Circus, London, W.1.

Best Photos: Güttenberg, Manchester.

CASSEL-GERARD, Leon; ballroom, eccentric and exhibition dancer. Reached the Finals of the World's Championships, Professional and Mixed, in 1924. Won the Lancashire and Cheshire Open and Professional Championship, 1926, and at the age of 18 was Manager of the Assembly Rooms, New Brighton. Joined his teacher, Mr. Malcolm Munro, at the Embassy Rooms, Liverpool, as his Chief Assistant, and assisted him in the creation of the "Twelve O'Clock Follies," a repertory company of dancers who varied their shows weekly. Had a number of successes with an exhibition act, "Leon and Topsy." Was Host at the Palace Hotel, Birkdale, and the County Club, Liverpool, and Manager at the Palais-de-Danse Royal at Leamington Spa. Returned to Liverpool as Host at the Adelphi Hotel. Was responsible for the first stage presentation in the provinces of the "Moochi" at the Shakespeare Theatre, Liverpool. Assisted in the organisation of the World's Championship Heats, and other big events in Liverpool. Adjudicator British Professional Championship, 1928.

Address: Crane's Studios, Hanover Street, Liverpool.

Best Photos: Walden Hammond, Leamington Spa.

CATCHPOLE, Doris; general teacher of dancing. Member of the Imperial Society of Teachers of Dancing; L.I.F.A. Has School with branches at Liverpool, Shrewsbury, Oswestry and Shropshire districts. Visits eight large schools weekly. A special feature is made of classical dancing, original dance composition, dress design and production work.

Address: "Clavis," Christchurch Road, Oxton, Birkenhead.

CATCHPOLE, George P.; Vice-Chairman, The Faculty of Dancing and Director of the Faculty of Arts. Founded the Faculty of Arts in 1921, and designed the Faculty of Arts Theatre. Editor of *The Orbit*. Delegate to International Cinema Congresses at Paris, Berlin and Brussells. Film critic *Daily Dispatch*, 1927-29. Has organised over 100 Art Exhibitions.

Address: 190 Piccadilly, London, W.1.

Best Photos: Yvonne Gregory, London.

CAVE (Miss), Norma; ballroom dancer and teacher. Partnered by Mr. Arthur Milner was the winner of the Championship of Switzerland, 1930; the International Championship, Nice, 1931; the World's Championship, Paris, 1931, and was a finalist in the "Star" Championships in 1929-30-31.

Address: 69 Wigmore Street, London, W.1.

Best photo: Molloy, London.

CECILE (Madame Cécile Hames); ballroom and general teacher. Member Imperial Society of Teachers of Dancing; Certified Teacher of Incorporated London Academy of Music. For the past six years hostess and teacher at the Liberal Club, Leicester; also teaches at private studio, "Melrose," Upper Kent St., Leicester.

Address: 55 St. Peter's Road, Leicester.

CHALIF, Louis H.; Principal of the Chalif Russian Normal School of Dancing, New York, which was established in 1905. Operatic and general teacher. Hon. Member and President for three years, of the American Society of Teachers of Dancing; Hon. Member of Dancing Masters of America; Hon. Member of the Dance Teachers' Club of Connecticut; one of the first organizers and President of the New York Society of Teachers of Dancing; Vice-President of Union International, Paris. Late Balletmaster, Odessa Government Theatre, Russia. Director of a programme of National and Folk Dances at the second convention of the American Playground Association. Director of the Hudson Fulton Celebration, New York. Teacher of Harriet Hoctor (American *Prima Ballerina*) and Marguerita De Laporte (*Prima Ballerina* Metropolitan Opera House, New York), and many others. Member New York Rotary Club and New York Metropolitan Museum of Fine Arts. Organizer of the Dance Art League of America and many foreign Dance Teachers' Societies. Has contributed many dance articles to papers.

Author of "Chalif's Text Books of Dancing," 5 volumes (obtainable in this country from *The Dancing Times*); a Russian Festival Book; Ballets; and individual dances.

Address: 163 West 57th Street, New York, U.S.A.

CHAMIE, Tatiana; ballet dancer. Member of the Diaghileff Ballet. Has danced in various rôles of the classical repertoire, and created the "Street Dancer" in *The Triumph of Neptune*.

CHAMIER (Miss), Alice; teacher, producer and dancer of the revived Greek dance; neo-classic dancing; character dancing and mime. Member of the Association of Teachers of the Revived Greek Dance (advanced honours certificate); also Member of Committee, 1927, 1928 and 1930, and Vice-President, 1928. Is examiner for the Association and for the Children's examinations (Greek branch). First studied with Madame Lancelot in York and Scarborough, 1905. Received professional training at the Ginner-Mawer School, and is holder of the Honours Diploma, Ginner-Mawer School. Also studied under Margaret Craske, Tamara Karsavina, Serge Morosoff, Paul Raymond (Paris Opera Ballet Master), Ecole Jacques Dalcroze (Paris and London). Appeared with Ginner-Mawer Company in London and Stratford-on-Avon, and in own productions with the Association of Teachers of the Revived Greek Dance Company; also in partnership with Helen Wingrave in the Alwin dancers in cabaret in London, Brighton, etc.

Address: 17 York House, Church Street, Kensington, London, W.8.

CHAPLIN (Miss), Dorothy; teacher of operatic, national, folk and character dancing. Advanced Member of the Operatic Association; Advanced Certificate Member of the Espinosa School. Holds full teaching diploma of the Advanced and Solo Standard of the British Ballet Association. Commenced dancing with Miss Susie Boyle and afterwards trained with Mdme. Cormani and Mr. Espinosa. In the autumn of 1924 opened a School of Dancing in Marylebone. In 1927 became deputy assistant teacher at the Espinosa School. In 1928 transferred her school to Hampstead, and later became deputy teacher to the London scholars of the Operatic Association.

Address: 1 Fairfax Road, Swiss Cottage, London, N.W.6.

Best photos: Swaine, London.

CHAPPELL, William; operatic dancer. Trained by Marie Rambert, and member of the Rambert Ballet. Worked with Ida Rubinstein under Nijinska and Massine. Danced with Madame Karsavina in *Mercury*, for which he designed the costumes and decorations. Danced with Lopokova at the Camargo Society, and designed costumes for her season at the Arts Theatre, 1930. Designed costumes and scenery for *Cephalus and Procris, Jackdaw and Pigeons* and *Regatta* at the Old Vic. First English dancer to act the faun in Nijinsky's *L'Apres Midi D'un Faune*. Partnered Alicia Markova and danced with her in *Rio Grande*. Designed costumes for many

productions at the Ballet Club and Rambert seasons at the Lyric and the New Theatres. Danced the part of Mars in the ballet *Mars and Venus* in " Jew Süss."
Address: 7 Redcliffe Gardens, London, S.W.10.
Best Photos: Barbara Key-Seymer, and Paul Tanqueray, London.

CHESTER, Dorice; general teacher. Member of the Imperial Society of Teachers of Dancing (Operatic) ; also Member of the Operatic Association of Dancing of Great Britain.
Address: 35 Norfolk Road, Seven Kings, Essex.

CLARK (Mrs.), I. Grandison; general teacher. Principal of the Grandison Clark School of Dancing, London. Advanced Member of the Operatic Association ; Member of the Ballroom Branch of the Imperial Society ; and a Fellow of the Operatic Branch of that Society. Received early training at the Elaine School of Dancing. After the war took up dancing seriously and studied under Espinosa and Miss Phyllis Bedells, gaining the Advanced Certificate of the Operatic Association. Was coached by Miss Josephine Bradley in ballroom dancing, and in 1924 opened a school in Norbury which grew so rapidly that the present premises were acquired. These premises boast of a particularly fine ballroom which can dance three hundred people. It is known as the Grandison Hall. Every branch of dancing is featured at the school, and the musical comedy section is under the direction of Miss Dorrit MacLaren.
Address: 1262 London Road, Norbury, London, S.W.16.

CLARKE (Miss), Freda; general teacher ; also operatic, ballroom and exhibition dancer. Intermediate Member of the Association of Operatic Dancing of Great Britain. Also Member of the Ballroom Branch of the Imperial Society, and Licentiate Member of the Operatic Branch. Was trained in the Wordsworth system, Skirt-Dancing and Drilling. Has produced a number of successful shows.

Has extended her teaching connection to Bromley and Grove Park. School has been established nearly twelve years.
Address: 20 Northbrook Road, Lee, London, S.E.13.
Best photos: Wayland, Blackheath ; Dalby, Lewisham.

CLARKE, Harry; ballroom teacher. Member of the Imperial Society of Teachers of Dancing. Was judge for the West of Scotland Dancing Championship in 1927, 1928 and 1930, and for the Yorkshire Dancing Championship in 1927 and 1928.
Address: Majestic Ballroom, Pall Mall, Hanley, Stoke-on-Trent.

CLARKE (Miss), Margaret; ballroom and general teacher. Intermediate Member of the Operatic Association. Licentiate of the Imperial Society of Teachers of Dancing. Established School in 1907, and has given a very large number of pupils' displays in aid of local and London charities with exceptionally good results.
Address: 28 St. Kilda Road, West Ealing, London, W.13.

CLARKE (Miss), Nancy; general teacher. Member Imperial Society of Teachers of Dancing (Ballroom and Operatic branches) ; Member Operatic Association ; Member British Ballet Organization (full teaching diploma) ; local organizer for Operatic Association. Has a dancing connection in Nottingham, and teaches all branches of dancing ; is instructress to a dance club in connection with the Nottingham City Business Club.
Address: 9 Western Terrace, The Park, Nottingham.
Best Photos: E. P. Short & Son, Nottingham.

CLEARE (Miss), Doreen; general teacher. Member Operatic Association ; Member Imperial Society of Teachers of Dancing (Ballroom branch). Trained All England " Star " Champion (Musical Comedy) in 1930, and Gold Medallists, Senior and Junior Troupes, at Scala Theatre, judged by Jack Hulbert in 1931. Principal of

the Purcell School of Dancing, the only school using artificial sunshine in its studios.
Address: 95 Wigmore St., London, W.1.
Best Photos: Navana, London.

CLEMSON AND VALERIE (R. Clemson Young and Valerie Leigh); exhibition and ballroom dancers. Certificates held from Monsieur Pierre and Belle Harding for General Ballroom Dancing. Well-known on the continent, having fulfilled engagements at Cannes, Aix-les-Bains, Nice, Biarritz, Le Touquet, Algiers, at famous hotels and casinos; have also appeared at Mayfair, Piccadilly, Ciro's and other London clubs and hotels. Won Premier Prix in International Tournée de Danse in 1928, and were presented with Diplomée des Beaux Arts, Premier Prix d' Elégance, 1929, and Danse d' Elégance de l'Europe, 1930.
Address: 8 Cambridge Street, Hyde Park, London, W.2.
Best Photos: Angelo, Budapest.

CLIFTON - HADDAN, Mary (Mrs. Sanders Walter); teacher of operatic, Greek, ballroom and character dancing. Was articled pupil and assistant to Madame Vincent Glass; also assistant to Miss Belle Harding. Started her own school in 1906, and specializes in children's work.
Address: 7 Waldegrave Road, S.E.19.
Best Photos: Everitt, London, S.E.19.

COLE (Miss), Dorothy; ballroom dancer and teacher. Originally trained by and taught for Miss Josephine Bradley. Winner of World's Tango Championship in 1925, and "Star" Professional Tango, 1925, 1926, 1928, 1930, 1931. Is on the staff at the Empress Rooms.
Address: Empress Rooms, Kensington High Street, London, W.8.
Best Photos: Lenare; Molloy; Claud Harris, London.

COLERIDGE - TAYLOR (Miss), Avril; classical, operatic and musical comedy dancer and teacher. Pupil of B. Soutar, Guildhall School of Music, and of Ernest D'Auban, late of Drury Lane Theatre. Demonstrator in Greek, operatic and musical comedy dancing for the Television.
Address: 188a Finchley Road, London, N.W.3.
Best Photos: Claude Harris; Le Dernier Cri, London.

COLIN (Miss), Jean; musical comedy dancer. Has played lead in many London shows, including "Many Happy Returns," "Five O'clock Girl," "Here Comes the Bride" and "Blue Roses."
Address: 28 Grand Parade, Brighton.

COLLIER, Beatrice (Mrs. Peter Shaw); character dancer, who appeared in several of the old Empire ballets. Was conspicuously successful in "A Day in Paris," where, with Fred Farren, she introduced the Apache Dance to England, and also as the Ayah in "Ship Ahoy."
Address: Sutherland House, Marloes Road, London, W.8.

COLLINS (Mrs.). Since the death of her daughter, Miss Elga Collins, in January, 1931, Mrs. Collins has taken over the direction of the Walthamstow School of Dancing. Every style of dancing is taught. A West End branch of the School, known as the Marylebone School of Dancing, is held in Edgware Road.
Address: Walthamstow School of Dancing, 22 Rectory Road, Walthamstow, London, E.17.

COLLINS (Miss), Nancy; general teacher. Member of the Association of Operatic Dancing of Great Britain. Elementary Member of the Imperial Society of Teachers of Dancing (Ballroom, Operatic, and Revived Greek). Opened a School of Dancing in co-operation with Miss Audrey Bruce in 1927.
Address: 61 Worple Road, Wimbledon, London.

COLLINS, Vere, M.A. (Oxford); amateur ballroom dancer. Educational

Manager of the Oxford University Press, Examiner for the Civil Service Commission, etc. Winner of the Scottish Veterans' Championship (Glasgow, 1929), and of the North of England Veterans' Waltz Championship (Blackpool, 1929) ; Semi-finalist in the " Star " Amateur Championship (1930), and Runner-up in the Dorothy Cole Amateur Tango Championship, November, 1931.
Address : 16 Southway, Hampstead Garden Suburb, London, N.W.11.

CONE (Miss), Gracie; general teacher and specialist in operatic, Greek and ballroom dancing. Advanced and Sub-Committee Member Operatic Association ; Member Revived Greek Association ; Licentiate and Fellow of Imperial Society of Teachers of Dancing (Operatic, Cecchetti, Greek and Ballroom branches) ; Member of all other branches ; Council Member (Ballroom branch). Examiner for Children's Examinations of Operatic Society (Operatic and Greek branches), and for Revived Greek Association. Judge for World's Championships, " Star " and many other Competitions for ballroom dancing, and also at the principal Festivals and Eisteddfods in Great Britain. Winner *Dancing Times* Cup, All England Solo and Duet Competitions in 1925, 1926, 1927 and 1929. Committee " Camargo Society " and Member of the " Official Board."
Address : 20 Stratford Place, Oxford Street, London, W.1.

CONE (Miss), Lillie; general teacher, specializing in babies' work. Member and Sub-Committee Secretary, Operatic Association ; Member Revived Greek Association ; Council Member and Licentiate Imperial Society of Teachers of Dancing (Fellow Operatic and Member of all other branches). Founder of Children's Examinations. Judge of World's Championship Ballroom Dancing, All England Solo and Duet Competitions, Festivals and Eisteddfods. Winner *Dancing Times* Cups, All England Solo and Duet Competitions in 1925, 1926, 1927 and 1929.

Address : 20 Stratford Place, Oxford Street, London, W.1.

CONTI (Miss), Italia. Principal of the well-known Italia Conti School of Stage Dancing, which numbers many of the leading theatrical and dancing stars amongst its pupils. Producer of " Where the Rainbow Ends," which is now in its twenty-first year, and also other successful pantomimes.
Address : 14 Lamb's Conduit Street, London, W.C.1.

COOK (Miss), Iris (Mrs. William Palmer) ; general teacher. Member Imperial Society of Teachers of Dancing (Cecchetti and Ballroom branches). Principal of the Highest Aim School of Dancing, Leicester. Specialist in ballroom and operatic dancing and children's work. Pupil of Margaret Craske and Victor Silvester.
Address : Holly Bank, London Road, Leicester.
Best Photos : Ramsden, Leicester.

COOKE-YARBOROUGH (Miss), Muriel; teacher of rhythmic foundation exercises, Greek, national and ballroom dancing. Member of the Association of Teachers of the Revived Greek Dance. Trained for three years at and holds diploma of the Chelsea College of Physical Education, and has taught under the London County Council and City of Leeds Education Committee as Gymnastic, Games and Dancing Mistress. Started a School of Dancing in Leeds in 1923 for rhythmic and ballroom work only, but now all general branches are taught. By request has arranged two matinées at civic receptions for H.R.H. Princess Mary, Countess of Harewood.
Address : The Hera School of Dancing, 1 Vernon Road, Leeds.

COOKSON (Miss), Grace; Associate of the Imperial Society (Ballroom, Greek and Operatic (Cecchetti) Branches). Is an assistant at the Violet Allen School of Dancing, Wolverhampton.
Address : 55 Darlington Street, Wolverhampton, Staffs.

COOPER, Henry; ballroom teacher. Began dancing 1918; organised Dress Parades with Lady Duff Gordon, 1920; opened Park Lane Dancing School, 1921. Amongst others trained Pat Sykes and Margery Wallis. Arranged dances for Lady Diana Cooper in " The Glorious Adventure," and was filmed for Movietone News and other film companies. Editor-in-Chief of *Dancing Weekly*. Stood as Parliamentary Candidate for Hereford in General Election, 1929. Inventor of the " Chrystal Waltz," 1932.
Address: Park Lane Dancing School, London, W.1.
Best Photos: Foulsham & Banfield; Pearl Freeman, London.

COOPER (Miss), Valerie; teacher of rhythmic movement. Holder of the Dalcroze School Certificate. Associate of the Royal College of Music. Has a School in London. (*See also* Miss BARBARA DUMMETT).
Address: 6 Fitzroy Square, London, W.1.

CORDON (Miss), Renée; general teacher of ballroom, operatic, musical comedy and step-dancing, etc.
Address: Studio, 5 Chapel Ash, Wolverhampton.

COTTRELL (Miss), Alicia; general teacher. President and Examiner of the Lancashire Dancing Association. Member E.F.D.S. Specializes in children's work.
Address: Alicia School of Dancing, 44b The Square, St. Annes-on-Sea, Lancs.
Best photos: Lord, St. Annes-on-Sea.

COULDRIDGE (Miss), Rosa; ballroom and general teacher. Life Member of Imperial Society of Dance Teachers (General and Ballroom branches). Member of Royal Society of Teachers and holds National Froëbel Certificate. For some considerable time has taught dancing in many schools in Devonshire, among them the School for the Blind in Exeter. Is Teacher of Dancing and Health Exercises to the patients of a mental hospital.
Address: 3 Linden Vale, Howell Road, Exeter.

COUSINS, George C.; ballroom teacher of dancing. With Miss Joan Rowe was finalist in Columbia Amateur Ballroom Dancing Championship of Great Britain, 1929. Had teacher's course of training at the Rumsey School of Dancing, London.
Address: The Rhythm School of Ballroom Dancing, 8 Market Place, Rugby, Warwickshire.
Best photos by Speight, Rugby.

COWAN, Andrew; ballroom teacher. Member of the Official Board, also an Examiner of the Manchester Association of Teachers of Dancing, and has been President and Secretary of that Association; Member of the International Dancing Masters' Association. Has been teaching since 1908, and has acted as Adjudicator at the Blackpool Festivals.
Address: 66a Raby Street, Moss Side, Manchester.

COWAN (Mr. and Mrs.), Albert; ballroom teachers. Mr. Cowan is an Examiner of the National Association, and a Vice-President of the Manchester Association of Teachers of Dancing. Together with his wife won the Handley Shield and were Runners-up for the Kempton Trophy of the N.A.T.D. in 1931, and were Gold Medallists of the M.A.T.D. in 1931.
Address: 29 Regent Avenue, Moss Side, Manchester.
Best Photos: Guttenberg, Manchester.

COWLEY (Miss), Joan; specialist in all types of dancing. Advanced Member of the Association of Operatic Dancing of Great Britain. Commenced her career when 13 years of age under the direction of Mr. Ludwig Blattner, of the " Blattnerphone " Company, at the Gaiety Theatre, Manchester. For two years was principal dancer in Mr. Julian Wylie's productions, and was also principal dancer at the Scala Theatre, and the King's Theatre, Hammersmith. Solo dancer at the Empire Theatre, Paris,

47

1931, and now appearing in "Waltzes from Vienna" at the Alhambra Theatre, London.
Address: 42 Powis Square, Bayswater, London, W.11.
Best Photos: Navana, London.

CRANMORE, Janet; teacher of operatic, tap and ballroom dancing. Advanced Member Association of Operatic Dancing; Member Imperial Society of Teachers of Dancing (Ballroom and Operatic branches); Member of Examining Committee of British Ballet Organisation. Became member of the Association of Operatic Dancing in 1922; was principal dancer Wylie Tate Pantomime, 1921-22; toured own act on independent halls, and opened present School in 1924. Was solo dancer in London and provincial cabarets. Photos taken by Walden Hammond were hung in the International Photographers' Salon Exhibition for three years—1928-30.
Address: 75 Hagley Road, Edgbaston, Birmingham.
Best photos by Walden Hammond, Leamington Spa.

CRASKE (Miss), Margaret; teacher of classical ballet. Holder of Enrico Cecchetti's personal Certificate. Fellow of the Imperial Society of Teachers of Dancing, and is an Examiner of their Classical Ballet Branch (Cecchetti Method). Started her dancing with Madame Vandyck, Alexandre Goudin and Madame Astafieva. Studied for four years with Cecchetti, and has also had lessons from Nijinska and Trefilova. Was a soloist in the Royal Italian Ballet, and a member of Diaghileff's Russian Ballet. Has produced ballets for the Carl Rosa Opera Company, and for West End productions. Has a School in London.
Author, with Cyril Beaumont, of "The Theory and Practice of Allegro in Classical Ballet" (C. W. Beaumont).
Address: 7 Dyott Street, London, W.C.1.
Best Photos: Lenare, London.

CRAWFORD (Miss), Mimi; operatic and stage dancer. Pupil of Elise Clerc and Julia Seale. Dancing parts were "Sally" in '. Sally," Winter Garden Theatre, "Alice" in *Alice in Lumberland* Ballet of R.S.V.P. at the Vaudeville Theatre; played lead in *Venetian Wedding* Ballet of "Vaudeville Vanities" with Anton Dolin; also partnered Bobby Howes in tap dance in same revue; appeared in "Co-Optimists of 1930," London Hippodrome. Specially engaged to dance Blue Danube Valse in "Die Fledermaus" at Covent Garden Opera House, 1931, before the King and Queen, being the first English dancer to be given this engagement.
Address: 83 West Hill, London, N.6.
Best photo: Rita Martin, London.

CRESWELL (Miss), Nancy; ballroom teacher. In charge of the ballroom dancing at the Walthamstow School of Dancing.
Address: Walthamstow School of Dancing, 22 Rectory Road, Walthamstow, London, E.17.

CROPPER (Miss), Dorothy Norman; teacher of all branches, also exhibition ballroom dancer. Member of the Faculty of Dancing Masters of America, of the Boston (Mass.) Normal School, and of the Hartford (Conn.) Normal School. President of the New York Society of Teachers of Dancing, 1925-26, 1927-28 and 1930-31.
Address: 141 Carnegie Hall, New York, U.S.A.
Best photos: Aldene, New York; and Robbins & Norris, Boston, U.S.A.

CRUTCHETT-LESLIE, Mrs.; teacher of ballroom dancing. Past President and Life Member of the British Association of Teachers of Dancing; also Life Member of the Imperial Society of Teachers of Dancing.
Address: Disraeli House, 6 Disraeli Road, Putney, London, S.W.15.

CRUTCHETT-LESLIE, F. W.; General Secretary, Imperial Society, 113/117 Charing Cross Road, London, W.C.2.

CUFF (Miss), Betty; operatic dancer. Associate Imperial Society (Classical

Ballet Branch). Member of the Marie Rambert Ballet and Ballet Club. Appeared in all the Seasons of Ballet at the Lyric Theatre, Hammersmith, with Madame Karsavina; in "Waltzes from Vienna" for six weeks, leaving for Season of Ballet at the New Theatre, London, and at Manchester; danced at the "Midnight Ballet" at the Carlton Theatre in *My Lord of Burleigh* and *Façade*.

Address: 57 St. Augustine's Av., South Croydon, London, S.E.

CULL (Mrs.), Blanche; general teacher. First trained at City School, Bristol, later studying under Espinosa and Phyllis Bedells. Appeared as a juvenile at Theatre Royal, Bristol; then toured British Isles and Germany. Danced with Jackson's English Dancers, and produced ballets for pantomimes, revues, etc. Retired from the stage in 1928 and opened School of Dancing at Swindon in connection with the City School of Dancing, Bristol.

Address: 15 Cumberland Road, Swindon, Wilts.

Best Photos: Alfred Wager, Bristol.

CURRY (Miss), Iris; operatic, ballroom and general teacher. Holds classes in Kensington, Barnes, West Hampstead and Woking.

Address: 16 Westmorland Road, Barnes, London, S.W.13.

CUSHING (Miss), Lillian; general teacher, specializing in operatic work. Member of the American Association of Dancing Teachers; Member of the Colorado Association of Dancing Teachers. Was trained by Mr. Luigi Alberteri, with whom she was a favourite pupil. She has one of the largest schools in the Western United States.

Address: 412 Tabor Building, Denver, Colorado, U.S.A.

Best photos: Bramback, New York City.

D

D'AQUILAR, Juan; ballroom dancer and teacher. Aged 28. Born Malaga, Spain. First became prominent in the dancing world in 1922 when he was in the finals of the World's Amateur Championship at the Queen's Hall. In 1924, partnered by his sister, won the "London and Southern Counties" Championship. Turned professional in 1926, after winning several smaller competitions. In 1929, dancing with Edna Deane, tied for first place in the British Professional Tango Championship organised by *The Dancing Times* and the Imperial Society of Teachers of Dancing, and was also runner-up for the World's Tango Championship. Then went to South America, from where he returned last year and opened own school of dancing in Malvern, Worcestershire. Incidentally is a very good all-round sportsman.

Address: Peachfield House Academy, Poolbrook, Malvern, Worcestershire.

DANETREE (Miss), Kathleen; general teacher. Advanced Member of the Operatic Association; also Member of the Council; Intermediate Member of the Cecchetti Society; Fellow of the Imperial Society (Operatic Branch); Special Teacher for "Scholars" of the Operatic Association. Originally trained by Rose Tyrrell of Birmingham, under whose direction she had the honour of appearing before H.R.H. Princess Beatrice. From there she went to the Bush School, Nottingham. Later turned her attention to the Cecchetti method of Operatic Dancing, and is now studying advanced work in this method. In 1926 Miss Danetree won the *Dancing Times* essay competition on "Dancing as an Educational Force," and in the same year was appointed, by the Operatic Association, special teacher for scholars of the Association (Birmingham area). In 1927 was appointed Examiner for Children's Examinations. She has a large residential school at Erdington, and also a branch at Coventry. The school was the first in the provinces to carry off the *Dancing Times* Cup for the "All England Solo Competition."

Address: The Priory School of Dancing, 75 Gravelly Hill North, Birmingham.
Best photos : Walden Hammond, Leamington Spa.

DANIELS, Charles J.; general teacher. Member of the National Association of Teachers of Dancing, and was President in 1920. Past President of the English Association of Teachers of Dancing. Was President of the Northern Counties Dance Teachers' Association in 1930, and Vice-President of the International Union des Choregraphes 1926-1930 (Paris). Has invented many popular sequence dances, and in 1930 won the Handley Shield for the best sequence dance at the Annual Conference of the National Association of Teachers of Dancing. Adjudicated at the Blackpool Festival for two years. Also organized the English heats and judged at the Paris finals of the World's Championships in 1926.
Address: The Bungalow, Westoe, South Shields.
Best photos: Princess Yvonne, Newcastle.

DANILOVA, Alexandra; prima ballerina. One of the most promising pupils of the Petrograd Ballet, Alexandra Danilova received small but important rôles as soon as she made her *début*. After one year in the Imperial Ballet she was engaged by Diaghileff, and remained with the ballet until it was disbanded, being ballerina for some time. She created with great success the leading rôle in *The Triumph of Neptune*. Her best known rôles were in *Le Bal, Pas d'Acier, Les Deux Mendiants, Petrouchka, Carnaval, L'oiseau de Feu, Les Sylphides, Femmes de bonne humeur*, etc. *Première danseuse* in "Waltzes from Vienna," Alhambra Theatre, 1931-2.
A. L. Haskell, in an article on her, says :
" Danilova has the grand manner, the proud carriage of the head, that marks the dancer from the Imperial stage, and she is in the direct classical tradition—alas, the last young dancer to emerge before the revolution."
Address: 5 Passage Doisy, Paris, 17c.
Best photos by M. Dimitriev, Paris ; Joan Craven, London.

DARNBOROUGH (Miss), Hermione; operatic dancer. Associate Member Imperial Society (Classical Ballet Branch). Has taken the part of solo dancer in " Hiawatha " at the Royal Albert Hall ; also solo dancer at the Lyceum pantomimes in 1929-30. Winner of the Senior Cup at the All England Solo Dancing Competition in 1931. A pupil of the MacLaren School.
Address : 33 Chelsea Park Gardens, London, S.W.3.
Best Photos : Janet Jevons, London.

DARSIE (Miss), Thora; classical ballet (Russian) and plastique dancer and teacher ; actress and teacher of acting. Member of Imperial Society of Teachers of Dancing (Inter. Cert. Cecchetti Society), and Licentiate of Guildhall School of Music (Elocution). Hon. Secretary Faculty of Dancing. Has studied under various teachers, including Astafieva, Craske, Massine Volinine and Nicolas Legat. Commenced career as a child dancer. *Première danseuse* Wylie-Tate's " Dick Whittington " in 1914-15. Acted with Ben Greet and at the Old Vic. Appeared with Mme. Karsavina's Company at the Coliseum in 1923. Has given numerous recitals at the Aeolian Hall and at the Faculty of Arts. Danced in Mme. Genée's revival of " Robert the Devil " at first Camargo performance.
Address: C/o Faculty of Dancing, 190-195 Piccadilly, London, W.1.
Best photos: Basil, and Claude Harris, London.

DAVIDSON (Miss), Barbara; teacher of operatic and ballroom dancing. Associate of the Imperial Society.
Address : C/o The Haden School of Dancing 10 King Street, Baker Street, London, W.1.

DAVIES, Byron; specialist in dancing propaganda and cabaret presentation. Is Publicity Manager of Sherry's

Dance Hall, Brighton; the Locarno Dance Hall, London; the Ritz Dance Hall, Manchester; and the Royal Opera House Dances, London. Runs a Cabaret and Band Agency licensed annually by the London County Council. Formerly Publicity Manager to the well-known Hammersmith Palais de Danse (which has ceased to exist as a dance hall); the Birmingham Palais de Danse; Rector's and the Grafton Galleries Club, London; and also Rector's Club in Paris.
Address: 5 Dean Street, London, W.1.
Best photos: Hughes Studios, London.

DAVIES, H. Vivian; general teacher. Past President (1926-7) National Association of Teachers of Dancing; President 1923-4 and 1931 Midland Association of Teachers of Dancing. Examiner and Lecturer to both Associations. Member of the Official Board of Dancing. Trained by Elise Journeaux, Charles d'Albert (Imperial Society) and Crompton (Technique) and has had "refresher" courses with most of the prominent teachers of to-day. First appeared on the Halls in a dancing scena, and later toured in musical comedy. Was a member of Sir Frank Benson's famous Shakespearian Company, and was Assistant Stage Manager under this management at the Court Theatre, London. Represented the N.A.T.D. on the Informal Committee and various Boards; was an official delegate at the affiliation of the M.A.T.D. to the N.A.T.D. Has won the open competition of the Midland Association on four occasions. Is now conducting a successful school in partnership with Miss Helen Card.
Address: The Studio, 18a Crawford Street, Baker Street, London, W.1.
Best Photos: Hana (now Navana), London.

DAVIES (Miss), Margery; teacher of ballroom dancing. Trained by Miss Gem Mouflet. Opened her own school in January, 1931, specializing in children's training.
Address: 16a High Road, Willesden Green, London, N.W.10.

DAVIS (Miss), Joan; teacher of stage dancing, specialising in tap and eccentric work. Has toured extensively with well-known companies. Is Co-Principal with Miss Zelia Raye of the Zelia Raye School of Dancing, London.
Address: 77 Dean Street, London, W.1.

DAWSON (Miss), Hylda; general teacher. Intermediate Member Operatic Association. Member A.T.R.G.D., and Imperial Society (Ballroom, Operatic and Revived Greek Branches). A student of the Cone School, London. Was assistant to the J. B. McEwen School, Glasgow, for the season 1926-27, since which date has been head assistant to Miss Tewson at Tunbridge Wells, Kent.
Address: 8 Guildford Road, Tunbridge Wells, Kent.

DAWSON (Miss), Nena; general and operatic teacher. Associate of Imperial Society of Teachers of Dancing (General and Operatic branches). Has a large dancing connection in Seven Kings, Romford, Brentwood and Upminster.
Address: 14 Elgin Road, Seven Kings, Ilford, Essex.

DEAN (Miss), Norah; general teacher. Advanced Member of the Operatic Association; Fellow of the Imperial Society (Operatic) and Member of their Ballroom Branch. Bronze Medallist I.L.A.M. Trained by Madame J. Espinosa and Mr. Felix Demery. Commenced teaching in Beckenham, Kent, in 1924, and has since worked up a large school in South London. Specializes in children's work. Winner of the Silver Medal for Operatic Dancing in the "All England Solo Dancing Competitions," 1929.
Address: The Studio, 37 Beckenham Road, Beckenham, Kent.
Best photos: Navana, Ltd., London; and Gordon Chase, Beckenham.

DEANE (Miss), Edna; ballroom teacher. Member of the Imperial Society. Trained originally for ballet,

and was with Nicolas Legat for some time. Taught for Miss Josephine Bradley for five years. Tied for first place in Professional Tango Championship, 1928. Won "A.O.F.T. Championship" (Slow Fox-trot) in 1928, and was second in the "Star" Tango Championship, 1930.
Address: 12 Cheniston Gardens, Kensington, London, W.8.

DE BOLTZ, Freda (Miss Winifreda M. L. de Boltz); general teacher. Associate Imperial Society of Teachers of Dancing (Classical Ballet, Operatic and Ballroom branches); Wordsworth Diploma. Trained for three years at Wordsworth College of Dancing, London, and also studied under Margaret Craske, Ruby Peeler and Rachel Macmillan. Principal of Ravenswood School of Dancing, Harrow.
Address: 7 Northwick Avenue, Harrow-on-the-Hill.
Best Photos: Mannell, London.

DE CERJAT, Charles; ballroom teacher. Examiner and holder of Advanced Certificate of Incorporated London Academy of Music; Member of Imperial Society of Teachers of Dancing. Began professional dancing after the war, being trained by Georges Fontana, Marjorie Moss, T. C. Askew and Alec Mackenzie. With Jean McKay had own schools of dancing in West of England, and in 1929 opened branch of Maxwell Stewart School at Bournemouth. Joined Maxwell Stewart at Mostyn Hotel, London, in 1930. Has now left the profession and is studying for the Ministry.
Author of "Dancing Defined" (Bournemouth Guardian, Ltd.).
Address: Mostyn Hotel, Portman Street, London, W.1.
Best Photos: Stuart Black.

DEEMING (Miss), Mavis; ballroom dancer and teacher. Associate of the Imperial Society. Winner of the Lancashire and Cheshire Tango Championship, 1930, and of the Midland Counties Waltz Championship in the same year. In the "Star" Professional Championships for 1931 was fourth in the Waltz and Fox-trot, and third in the Quick-step; also Runner-up in the British Professional Championship of that year. Appointed Hostess at the Café de Paris in 1930.
Address: 20 Adam Street, Portman Square, London, W.1, and 2a Duke Street, London, W.1.
Best Photos: Molloy, London.

DÉ FIGGIS, Alfred; ballroom teacher. Winner of International Solo Charleston Competition in Brooklyn, N.Y., in 1928. Opened School of Dancing in Dublin in 1929, and has been successful in training winners of important competitions in Ireland. Founder of first Dancers' Club in Ireland.
Address: 1 Windsor Villas, Fairview, Dublin.
Best Photos: Ross, Dublin.

DE LA GRANGE (Miss), May; comedienne and tap dancer; teacher of stage dancing. Late Lead in George Edwardes' San Toy Company's production, "Chinese Honeymoon"; principal girl in many pantomimes, and has played own variety turn. Principal of De la Grange Academy.
Address: 80 Ferndale Rd., London, S.W.4.

de LARUN, Edward (E. Arundel Smith); ballroom teacher. Member of the Imperial Society, and on Board of Arbitrators. Member of Faculty of Dancing. Was born in Tasmania in 1868. Competed as an amateur in the World's Championship 1922-23 and reached first twelve with Miss Ivy Gornold at the Queen's Hall. Winner of such minor competitions as entered for. Is now teacher and co-principal with Miss Gornold at the Brighton Branch of the Casani School of Dancing.
Address: C/o Messrs. Grindlay & Co., 54 Parliament Street, Westminster, London, S.W.

de MARE, Rolf. Director of Swedish Ballets. Director of the Opera Music Hall in the Champs Elysees, Paris. Organiser of the Salon du Franc. Organiser of the Official Tournament

of the Comedie-Francaise in Scandinavia. President-Founder of the newly-established Archives Internationales de la Danse in Paris.
Author of " Les Ballets Suedois dans l'Art Contemporian " (Trianon, Paris).
Address : 2 Rue Saint Simon, Paris, France.
Best Photos : Isabey, Paris.

DEMERY, Felix; teacher of operatic, ballroom, musical comedy work, etc. Member of Council and an Examiner of the Association of Operatic Dancing ; Fellow of the Imperial Society ; Member of Committee Faculty of Dancing. Teacher of Dancing at the Guildhall School of Music, London, and Principal of an Academy of Dancing (established 1880) in Bedford. Was *premier danseur* at the Palace Theatre and at the Royal Albert Hall, London. Had notable successes in *The Dawn*, an eighteenth century ballet, and as " Pau-Puk-Keewis " in the dramatised version of "Hiawatha," 1924, 1925-1928 and 1929.
Address : Academy of Dancing, 2 Grafton Road, Bedford.

de MESQUITA (Miss), Bueno; ballroom teacher. Was the first to inaugurate Sunday Tea Dances in London and to organize public Tea and Dinner Dances in Newcastle-on-Tyne. Has taken charge of the dance arrangements at several Dance Halls and Hotels.
Address : " Bueno de Mesquita " School of Dancing, 95 New Bond Street, London, W.

De MORODA (Miss), Derra; classical ballet and character dancer. Teacher. Fellow of the Imperial Society of Teachers of Dancing ; Member of Council and Examiner of the Classical Ballet branch. Hon. Member of the Imperial Society of Hungarian Teachers of Dancing. Pupil of Maestro Cecchetti and holder of his certificate. One of the founders of the Cecchetti Society. *Première danseuse* at the Palladium for many years. Specialises in Hungarian and Greek national dances. Translator of Gregorius Lambranzi's " New and Curious School of Dancing " and author of " Cásrdás és Sor Tánc," both for the Imperial Society of Teachers of Dancing. British representative of " Der Tanz " (Berlin).
Address : 44 Lupus Street, St. George's Square, London, S.W.1.
Best photos : Sasha, London.

DENHAM (Miss), Bunty; ballroom dancer and teacher. Trained by Major Cecil H. Taylor in 1923-4. Was hostess at Southport Palais de Danse 1925-27, and at the Piccadilly Club, Glasgow, 1927-28. Is at present hostess and ballroom demonstrator at the Tricity Restaurant, London, where she has been since 1928. Was the winner of the Ballroom Charleston Championship—Professional and Mixed Sections—in 1925-26 (held in Paris). Came fourth in the World's Professional Championships in 1925-26 (held in Paris). Came fourth in the Flat Charleston Competition held at the Royal Albert Hall in 1926-27, and was the winner of the Northern Section of the " Star " Competitions in 1928-29. Has not entered competitions since.
Address : 27 Lancaster Court, Newman Street, London, W.1.

DERBYSHIRE (Miss), Kathleen; general teacher. Member Operatic Association ; Member British Ballet Organization ; Member Imperial Society of Teachers of Dancing. Opened a School of Dancing in Liverpool, with connections in North Wales, in 1927, where pupils are coached for various examinations and competitions in Operatic and Ballroom Dancing.
Address : 95 Garmoyle Rd., Sefton Park, Liverpool.

de RHYNAL, Camille. President of the Fédération Internationale de Danse. President of the Syndicat National des Professeurs de Danse et Danseurs Professionels de France. Organiser of the " World's Dancing Championships," and a number of other International Competitions.
Address : Villa " Camylena," Avenue du Zuylen, Nice, France.

de VALOIS (Miss), Ninette; operatic dancer, teacher and choreographer. Advanced Member Operatic Association. Holder of original Cecchetti Certificate. Made her first appearance in London as *prèmiere danseuse* in the Lyceum pantomime 1914-15, and appeared there every year until 1918. Partnered Robert Roberty at the Palladium and Oxford Music Halls in 1915. Was *prèmiere danseuse* in Sir Thomas Beecham's Opera Co. at the Palladium in 1918, and at the Italian Opera Season at Covent Garden in the summer of 1919. Danced in E. C. Roll's productions " Laughing Eyes " and " Oh Julie " at the Strand and Shaftesbury Theatres, 1919-20, and with the Lopokova-Massine companies at Covent Garden and the London Coliseum, 1922. Toured the Gulliver circuit with her own company in 1921. Danced in Sir Oswald Stoll's production " You'd be Surprised " at Covent Garden and the Alhambra Theatre, London, in 1923. Joined Diaghileff's Russian ballet for two years in 1923. Partnered Anton Dolin at the London Coliseum in 1926; also in " Whitebirds " at His Majesty's Theatre, 1927. Appeared at the Covent Garden Opera Season in 1928, dancing in " Carmen," " Aida," " Armide," " Samson and Delilah." Was appointed choregraphic director to the Festival Theatre, Cambridge, the " Old Vic " Shakespeare Company, and the Abbey Theatre Dublin School of Ballet the same year. Produced occasional ballets for the first time at the Old Vic Theatre during opera season, 1928-30. Became director and producer to the Vic-Wells Ballet, founded 1931, and produced *Job, Cephalus and Procris* and *Crèation du Monde* among other works for the Camargo Society; also dances and ballets for the production of "Aladdin " at the Lyric Theatre, Hammersmith, and two ballets for " Bow Bells " at the London Hippodrome in the same year.
Address: 21 Taviton Street, Gordon Square, London, W.C.
Best Photos: Vaughan Freeman, Mesdames Morter, and Lenare.

DEVERSON (Miss), Mary; general teacher. Member of Association of Operatic Dancing (Adv. Cert.), and is local organiser for children's examinations in Northamptonshire. Member of Imperial Society of Dance Teachers (Classical Ballet, Greek and Ballroom branches). Trained at the Cone School of Dancing, London. Runner-up for Senior Cup " All England Solo Competition," 1927. Now teaching at the Phyllis James School of Dancing, Northampton.
Address: 81 Abington Street, Northampton.

DEVINE (Miss), Laurie; acrobatic dancer. Was born at Sydney, Australia, and started work there at the age of five in a circus as a contortionist acrobat. Toured the whole of Australasia, U.S.A., Canada, Hawaii, South Africa, England and Western Europe as a variety artist, gradually working out and specializing in acrobatic dancing. First went in for production at the London Pavilion with Mr. Cochran nearly six years ago, and has remained with him practically ever since.
Address: 12 James Street, Covent Garden, London, W.C.2.
Best photos: Frank Davis, Dorothy Wilding and Bertram Park, London.

DE VOS (Miss), Bettina; general teacher. (*See* Miss KATHLEEN DE VOS.)

DE VOS (Miss), Kathleen; general teacher. Is Co-Principal, with her sister, Miss Bettina De Vos, of the De Vos School of Dancing, Manchester Square, London, with branches in Dorset, Devon, Wilts. and Hants.
Address: 11-13 George Street, Manchester Square, London, W.1.

DIAMOND, Joseph A.; ballroom teacher. Member British Association of Teachers of Dancing; Examiner for Scotland and President 1903-1904. Holder of Honours Certificate Society of Arts for Theory and Harmony in Music; Technical Instructor and Musical Director to British Association.
Author of " Rhythm as Applied to Modern Dancing," published in 1926

privately by the British Association for use of its members.
Address: 127 Main Street, Glasgow, C.5.

DILLON (Miss), Gwladys; teacher of stage dancing. Originally trained in both the Italian and Russian Ballet Schools, later specializing in Musical Comedy dancing in all its forms, particularly tap dancing. Late Dancing Mistress at the Gaiety, Winter Garden, Adelphi and Shaftesbury Theatres. Her School has been established in London since 1913, and her pupils have been very successful on the stage.
Address: 17-18 Rupert Street, London, W.1.

DIVINA (Miss), Claire; operatic, adagio and acrobatic dancer. Studied under Lucia Cormani and Seraphine Astafieva. At the age of 14, after two years tuition, made her *début* at the Hippodrome, Golders Green, as a " single " variety act. Spent many years in Variety. Met Lawrence Charles at Astafieva's School, and with him became one of the pioneers of acrobatic dancing. They made their *début* at the Grafton Galleries in 1923, and were engaged by Jack Hylton for the Queen's Hall Roof Garden, where they remained six months. During their seven years partnership, " starred " in almost all the European capitals, and almost every club, restaurant and hotel in London, playing in four West End productions. In Paris created a furore with an Apache dance. In Milan, the " Home of Ballet," " stopped the show " at the Teatro Excelsior and were recalled eight times before the curtain. Invented the Slow-motion Dance and the Swallow Dive swing. Were the first to perform a complete " Adagio " dance on a staircase. Always endeavoured to remain artists as well as sensational. Winners of the " Exhibition " Section of the *Dancing Times* Competition, " Who were the best dancers seen in 1927 ? "
Address: 12 Palace Mansions, Kensington, London, W.14.
Best photos: Lenare, London; Schneider, Berlin; Walery and Sobol, Paris; and Baccharini & Porta, Milan.

DOLIN, Anton (Patrick Healey-Kay); operatic dancer. Member of the Operatic Association. Member Advisory Committee of the Camargo Society, and the Faculty of Arts. Studied dancing with Seraphine Astafieva, Nijinska, Legat, and Enrico Cecchetti. In August, 1923, appeared at the Royal Albert Hall in an Anglo-Russian Ballet. His first rôle with the Diaghileff Ballet was Daphnis in *Daphnis and Chloe*. Remained with the Company until April, 1924. Has since toured Spain, France and Germany. Appeared at the London Coliseum in November, 1924, as Beau Gosse in *Le Train Bleu*; danced in *The Punch Bowl* at His Majesty's Theatre in 1925; was in *Palladium Pleasures* at the Palladium in February, 1926; in *The Charlot Show of 1926* at the Prince of Wales Theatre in October, 1926; in *Vaudeville Vanities* at the Vaudeville Theatre in December, 1926; in *White Birds*, at His Majesty's Theatre, in May, 1927; and in the same year fulfilled numerous engagements with Phyllis Bedells, Karsavina and Nemchinova at the London Coliseum. Made his first appearance in America in January, 1930, in Lew Leslie's *International Revue*. Returned to London, and was engaged by André Charlot for *Charlot's Masquerade*, when he composed the *Manhattan Seranade*, a dance based on the atmosphere that surrounded him whilst in America, which met with a sensational success. Appeared at Covent Garden in Diaghileff's last season, notably in *The Ball*, in which he filled the leading male rôle. He created the rôle of Vertumnus in the Camargo Society's first production of Lambert's *Pomona* (Ashton), and created rôle of Satan in *Job* (De Valois-Vaughan Williams).
Dolin's first notice, after a brilliant display at the Royal Albert Hall, was given by J. T. Grein in the *Sketch*, July 11th, 1923 :—
" A new dancer, Anton Dolin, carried us away in enthusiasm. . . .

Dolin was light as a feather, as graceful as a faun, as wing-footed as Mercury. I for one believe that Dolin, wholly unaffected, immersed in his art, will ere long be proclaimed the rival and successor of Nijinski, and if he remains unspoilt, he may be the greater of the twain, for so far his work is entirely free from poise."

Books on Dolin: "Anton Dolin," by Arnold L. Haskell (British Continental Press).

By Dolin: "Divertissement" (Sampson Law).

Address: 66 Glebe Place, Chelsea, London, S.W.3.

Best photos: Morter, Sasha, Paul Tanqueray, Dorothy Wilding, London.

DOONE, Rupert ; classical ballet dancer and choreographer. First engagement was as understudy to Mr. Espinosa at His Majesty's Theatre. Afterwards appeared with Madame Lopokova's Company at the London Coliseum. Danced in Paris at La Potinière Théâtre. Gave concerts with Cleo de Mérode all over France. Danced at the Champs Elysées as one of the principal dancers in the Swedish Ballet. From there to America. Returned to Paris to dance at the Empire Theatre with Cleo de Mérode. From there to dance at La Cigale Theatre under the direction of Count Etienne de Beaumont, and arranged, under Massine's supervision, his first ballet, *Vogue,* and, under the same supervision, assisted Jean Cocteau with the movements in his production of *Romeo and Juliet.* Returned to England and arranged the ballet and movements for Sir Nigel Playfair's production, *The Duenna.* Returned to Paris and partnered Mdme.Trefilova. Danced with her in *Le Lac des Cygnes (pas de deux)* at the Scala Theatre, Berlin. Returned to London, understudied Massine in C. B. Cochran's production at London Pavilion. Arranged dances and danced at Coliseum with Anton Dolin. Partnered Phyllis Bedells at Palladium, and did his first English tour with her. Danced as soloist to Nijinska under Mdme. Rubinstein's direction at the Paris Opera, partnering Anna Ludmila. Returned to London to join as a soloist the Diaghileff Ballet. Was the last artiste to be engaged by Diaghileff. Since then has undertaken a concert tour with Phyllis Bedells and appeared at the Festival Theatre, Cambridge. Produced *The Enchanted Garden* for the Vic-Wells Ballet in 1932. Studied with Mdme. Astafieva, M. Clustien, Leonide Massine, Mdme. Nijinska, Mdme. Trefilova, Mdme. Egorova, Mdme. Tchernicheva and Miss Craske.

Address: 6 Fitzroy Square, London, N.W.1.

Best Photos: MacNamara, London.

DOUBROVSKA (Madame), Felia; ballet dancer. Left Russia in 1922 and joined Serge Diaghileff's Company, then at the Alhambra Theatre, London, in the "Sleeping Princess." Was with him until his death. Chief rôles: *Sylphides, Fire-Bird, Pastorale, Tamar, Ode,* and the last production under Diaghileff, *The Prodigal Son.* Was with Mme. Anna Pavlova's Company after the death of M. Diaghileff; then in Buenos Aires at the Colon Theatre in *Giselle,* and in June, 1931, appeared at the Lyceum Theatre with the Russian Opera and Ballet Company, taking leading parts.

Books: Mentioned in Propert's "Diaghileff Ballet," with photographs.

Address: 6 Rue d'Auteuil, Paris, 16 C.

Best photo: Yvonde, London.

DUBSKY (Fraulein), Trudi; dancer and teacher of Central European School of Dancing (Bodenwieser method). Certificate of the Vienna State Academy of Music (Dance Faculty). Studied dancing at Vienna State Academy and at private school of Gertrud Bodenwieser. Toured extensively in Europe with the Bodenwieser Ensemble. In October, 1930, opened the Rutherston-Dubsky School of Rhythmic Movement in London, where pupils are trained; recitals given in London and the North. Created and danced in *A Woman's Privilege* (Handel), for Camargo Society, November, 1931.

Address: 33a Cheyne Place, London, S.W.3.
Best Photos: Fimbler, Vienna; D'Ora, Vienna.

DUMMETT (Miss), Barbara; teacher of ballroom and operatic dancing. Member of the Operatic Association. Trained by Mrs. Freda Grant. For three and a half years was Hostess at the Carlton Hotel, St. Moritz, Switzerland (partnered by Mr. Max Carlen). Is now teaching at the Valerie Cooper School, London.
Address: Valerie Cooper School, 6 Fitzroy Square, London, W.1.

DUNCAN, William A. T.; ballroom and acrobatic dancer and teacher. Member National Association Teachers of Dancing. Trained by Mr. T. C. Askew for acrobatic work, and by Mr. Victor Silvester in Ballroom Dancing. Teacher of Acrobatic Dancing at the Hendry School of Dancing, Aberdeen.
Address: 12 Richmond Terrace, Aberdeen, Scotland.

DURYEA, Oscar; general teacher, specializing in ballroom dancing. Past President Dancing Masters of America, Past President and Ex-Secretary New York Society of Teachers of Dancing, Member Imperial Society of Teachers of Dancing. With Dorothea Duryea owns Duryea Studios. Has given large classes, etc., at New York's well-known hotels, theatres and clubs —Biltmore, Ritz-Carlton, etc., etc. Lectured and demonstrated to American Society of Teachers of Dancing, Anderson Club and Dr. Savage Alumni Association, etc. Staged scenes for three days "Pageant of History" under patronage of New York Women's Clubs at Metropolitan Opera House; arranged "Dancing Down the Ages" at a Damrosch Matinée of the New York Symphony Orchestra. Has toured extensively in U.S.A. and Canada.
Author of "How to Dance Well," "Songs and Dances" (John Church Co.).
Address: 135-45 West 70th Street, New York.

Best Photos: Davis & Sandford, New York.

E

EASON (Miss), Marjorie; general teacher. Intermediate Member Operatic Association. Member of the Ballroom Branch of the Imperial Society. Trained by Miss Irene Hammond, of Chester, and later acted as her assistant. After three years teaching in Brighton and London was attached to the Wimbledon Conservatoire of Music, and at the close of 1931 founded with Miss Letty Littlewood the Darlaston School of Dancing, Wimbledon.
Address: Valetta, Cambrian View, Chester, and c/o The Wimbledon Conservatoire of Music, 79 Worple Road, London, S.W.19.
Best Photos: Russells, Wimbledon, and Kent Lacey, Brighton.

EDGE, Mr. and Mrs. L. and G. W.; general teachers. Members and on the Executive Council of the United Kingdom Alliance of Professional Teachers of Dancing. Well known as teachers and exponents of Dancing, and are the winners of several first prize Diplomas, Gold Medals and Trophies. Have invented several Ballroom and Exhibition dances.
Address: School of Dancing, Heathfield Avenue, Crewe, Cheshire.

EDOUARDOWA (Mdme.), Eugenie; teacher of operatic, character, step, tap and acrobatic dancing, etc. Was born in St. Petersburg, and at the age of 9 joined the Imperial Ballet School, and was afterwards for many years at the Imperial Marinsky Theatre, St. Petersburg, as first character dancer, following Maria Petipa. In 1907-8 was first character soloist in the first European tour of Anna Pavlova's company. Since 1920 has been resident in Berlin, where she founded her own Ballet School, through which many well-known artists have passed, including Margaret Wallman, Dorothea Albu, Max Terpis and others. While at Berlin has staged and arranged many ballets—for Max

Reinhardt, the Great Folks Opera, and the Scala and Wintergarten Theatres. Was one of the founders of the Anna Pavlova Society, which, formed in 1931, is hoped will play an important part in the future of Central European dancing.
Address: Kalckreuthstre, 11, Berlin W.62, and Eisenacherstrasse 36-37, Berlin, W.30.

EINERT (Miss), Margaret; general teacher. Member of Faculty of Dancing. Principal of School of Dancing in Liverpool, which opened in 1919. Has lectured for British Association of Science, North of England Educational Conference, Liverpool University, etc. Produced dances for Liverpool Playhouse; organized Liverpool Dancers' Circle; represented *The Dancing Times*. Specializes in production of rhythmic expressionistic dances.
Author of " Rhythmic Dance Book " (Longman's, Green & Co.).
Address: Crane's Studio, Hanover Street, Liverpool.
Best Photos: Burrell & Hardman, Liverpool.

ELLIOTT-CLARKE (Miss), Shelagh; general teacher. Member of the Operatic Association of Great Britain; Member of the Imperial Society; Member of the Association of Teachers of the Revived Greek Dance; Holder of A.L.C.M. Gold Medal for Elocution; Member London Incorporated Academy of Music. The Principal of the Studio School of Dance and Dramatic Art in Liverpool. Was Ballet Mistress with Miss Booth for the L.M.S. Centenary Pageant Ballets, 1930. Her School has recently come very much to the fore in competitions.
Address: Studio School of Dance and Dramatic Art, 6 Colquitt Street, Liverpool.
Best photos: Burrell & Hardman, Liverpool.

ENTERS, Angna; concert dancer. "Choréomime." American soloist, dancer-mime, choregraphist and costume designer. Made her first London appearance at the St. Martin's Theatre in 1928, and her second appearance later in the same year. Her most famous creations are: *Queen of Heaven, Moyen Age, Second Empire, Black Magic, Park Avenoo, Feline, Promenade*, etc. Stanislavsky has proclaimed her as the finest dance talent of America:
"Her actual presentation might be described as 'Woman in many moods, in many lands, in many ages,' and her interpretations were characterized by a rare comprehension of the subtler feminine instincts, and a masterly handling of detail." (*Dancing Times*, March, 1928).

ESCEKAY (Mdme.), Milly; operatic dancer and general teacher. Trained under Lilian Leoffeler at Stedman's Academy. Appeared as Fairy Queen in *Alice in Wonderland*; danced with the British Ballet at Wembley and in *The Immortal Hour* at the Regent Theatre, London; danced with Leighton Lukas, of Diaghileff's ballet, as an independent turn. Principal of large school of dancing at Streatham.
Address: 21 Killiesu Avenue, Streatham Hill, London, S.W.2.
Best Photos: Vaughan & Freeman, London.

ESCUDERO, Vicente; Spanish dancer and teacher. Born at Grenada, Spain, and is of Gipsy origin. Has danced in every country in Europe. For the past five years has devoted his time entirely to Dance Recitals to music by famous Spanish composers. Is a big authority on genuine Spanish dancing, and incidentally was the first to employ the use of metal castanets. Is a designer of costumes and also a painter. Was to have accompanied Anna Pavlova on her tour of the United States in 1931-2, which did not of course take place owing to that famous dancer's death early in 1931.
Address: 12 Rue Victor Masse, Paris.
Best Photos: Steichen, New York.

ESPINOSA, Edward; son and pupil of Leon Espinosa. Was prominent as a dancer for many years and has

arranged many ballets. As a teacher, owing to his remarkable ability to analyse movement, has been very successful. He was one of the original members of the Committee of the "Operatic Association," and for many years was intimately associated with the work of that body. Is now the principal and founder of the "British Ballet Organisation" and has a School of Dancing in London.
Address: Woolborough House, Lonsdale Road, Castelnau, London, S.W.13.

ESPINOSA, Geoffrey; eccentric and tap dancer. Is a son of Madame Lea Espinosa, and a grandson of Leon Espinosa. Partnered by his sister Ray, and George Watson, is one of the "Two Espinosas and Watson" who have appeared at various cabarets and halls with much success.
Address: 26 West Street, Shaftesbury Avenue, London, W.1.

ESPINOSA, Madame; specialist in operatic, tap and all types of stage dancing and production. Wife of the late Leon Espinosa, of the Opera House, Paris, and St. Petersburg. Was principal dancer in every capital in Europe. Is now principal of well-known School of Dancing, London.
Address: 26 West St., Shaftesbury Avenue, London, W.C.2.
Best Photos: Hughes, London.

ESPINOSA (Madame), Judith. Member of the Council of the Operatic Association. Made her *debut* at the age of 5 in Berlin. Was principal dancer at the Opera House, Brussells, for two seasons, and, later, in New York. She danced at the opening of Madison Square Gardens in New York, her father, Leon Espinosa, producing the dancing, and with Edouard Strauss as conductor. She was one of the first to dance on the roof gardens of America. She toured all over America with Sir Henry Irving, and, returning to England, was engaged as principal dancer at the Alhambra. Later she founded her own school, where every branch of dancing is taught.

Address: 17 Great Titchfield St., Oxford Circus, London, W.1.

ESPINOSA (Mdme.), Lea; teacher of stage dancing, specializing in operatic and tap work. Daughter of Leon Espinosa. Made her *debut* at the Queen's Hall at the age of 15, giving a choregraphical matinee, and afterwards was approached by the Manager of the old Empire Theatre to take the place of Adeline Genée in the event of her being absent, but did not accept as her father considered her too young for such a responsibility. Two years later she appeared as Principal Dancer at the Prince of Wales Theatre, and from there danced at practically every theatre in London, at the Opera, Brussells, and in Germany and America. Married in 1904 and retired from the dancing profession until 1913, when she took up teaching with her brother Edward. Then re-appeared on the stage during the War and until 1919, when she started teaching for the Florence Etlinger Academy. In 1921 opened her own School at her present address. Is an expert on what is known as "tap dancing," and has trained many of our leading theatrical people in it.
Address: 26 West Street, Shaftesbury Avenue, London, W.1.

ESPINOSA (Miss), Ray; a daughter of Madame Lea Espinosa. With her brother, Geoffrey Espinosa and George Watson is a member of the act "Two Espinosas and George Watson" which has been so successful.
Address: 26 West Street, Shaftesbury Avenue, London, W.1.

EVANS, John E. ; general teacher. A Past President of the Manchester Association of Teachers of Dancing and Past Vice-President of the United Kingdom Alliance of Professional Teachers of Dancing. Adjudicator at the Blackpool Dance Festival and was M.C. for the first six years it was held. Organising Secretary for the "All for Dancing Exhibition" held at the City Hall, Manchester, in 1919, and has organised Juvenile and Adult Competitions in the Blackpool, Manchester and

Stockport districts. His School has been established in Stockport for 31 years.
Address: The New Hall, Duke Street, Stockport.
Best Photos: Nield, Stockport.

EVE; contortionist and dancer. Has appeared in various C. B. Cochran productions, and when first seen in London created a sensation with her ultra-modern contortionist work. Has studied International Character Dancing. Is at present appearing in "Helen" at the Adelphi Theatre.
Address: 255 Brixton Road, London, S.W.9.
Best Photos: Maycocks, and Dallasons, London.

EVERARD, Jack; ballroom teacher. Member of the Imperial Society of Teachers of Dancing (Ballroom Branch). Commenced teaching at Brighton in 1922; opened a School at Belfast in 1924, and one in London in 1926. Was finalist in the World's Dancing Championship, 1925. Apart from his teaching, which includes Step-Dancing, he runs a Dance Band Agency.
Address: 26 Baker Street, London, W.1.
Best photos: Hana (now Navana), London.

EVETTS (Miss), Beryl; ballroom (Charleston specialist), tap and general teacher. Winner of the first Mixed "World's Championship" with Cecil Reubens, and of the first "Star" Professional Championship with Leonard Ritte. Was the first demonstrator of the "Blues" with Morry Blake and Paul Specht's band at the London Coliseum, and originator of the "Baltimore" with Barry Oliver. Winner of C. B. Cochran's Solo Charleston Championship at the Albert Hall.
Address: 294a Earl's Court Road, London, S.W.5.
Best Photos: Foulsham & Banfield, London.

F

FARLEY (Miss), Netta; ballroom teacher. Trained by Maxwell Stewart. In co-operation with Miss Aileen Dowsett ran the Cadogan School in Sloane Street from October, 1926, to March, 1928. Is at present Principal of the Hyde School of Dancing, 69 Wigmore Street, W.1, where she has been since December, 1928.
Address: 69 Wigmore Street, London, W.1.
Best photos: Molloy, London.

FARREN, Fred; dancer, choreographer and *maitre de ballet*, who was closely associated with many of the successful ballets at the Empire Theatre before the War. Is now producing and teaching.
Address: 3 York Street, Baker Street, London, W.1.

FARRINGTON (Miss), Violet; ballroom dancer and teacher. Trained by Miss Josephine Bradley, and is a Member of the Imperial Society. Is in partnership with Mr. L. Douglas Moseley, and teaches at Hove.
Address: 3 Hove Lodge Mansions, Hove Street, Hove, Sussex.

FAUCHEUX (Miss), Violet; operatic, character and Greek dancer. Started with Miss Ruby Ginner at the age of nine, and remained with her until the age of 18, when she joined Mdme. Pavlova for a London season. Afterwards acted with Miss Sybil Thorndyke in *The Medea*, *The Trojan Women*, and *Advertising April* in 1922. Rejoined Mdme. Pavlova, and with her has visited practically every country in the world. Is still a member of the Pavlova Ballet Company.
Address: 43 Hungerford Road, London, N.7.
Best Photos: Raphael, London.

FAWCETT (Miss), May; general teacher. Trained by Mrs. Douglas Logan, London. In 1918 began to build up connection which extends over Worcestershire, Staffordshire, Shropshire, etc. Specializes in babies' classes.
Address: The Studio, Kingsley Hall, Kidderminster, Worcs.

FAYERS, W. J.; ballroom teacher.

Was teacher in a London school for a year, then opened school in Watford in October, 1930, which has met with a big success. Has an operatic section at his school under the direction of Miss C. M. Page.
Address: "Star" School of Dancing, 41a High Street, Watford, Herts., and at 11 Aynho Street, Watford, Herts.

FEARN (Miss), Nora; general teacher. Member of the Operatic Association, Advanced Certificate, and late Teacher of the Operatic Association Scholars, Notts. District. Was Head Assistant at the Bush School, Nottingham and London, and is now Head Assistant at the Northern School of Dance and Dramatic Expression at Sunderland and Newcastle.
Address: The Studio, 1 Grange Crescent, Sunderland.

FEDOROVA, Sophie; ballet dancer (dramatic mime). One of the original members of the Diaghileff Ballet. Won an instant success at the Company's *debut* in Paris. Specialized in dramatic roles such as "Ta Hor" in *Cleopatra*. Svetloff speaks of her "remarkable fire" and the French critics remark on the fact that she brought a new element into dancing.

FEIST, Hertha; pupil of Rudolf von Laban and member of the "Tanzbuhne Laban." Founder and principal of the Laban School in Berlin, 1923. Has given recitals of solo and group dances in Berlin and other leading towns. Took the leading part in Laban's production of "Don Juan" in Berlin, 1926. Produced the dance-drama "Die Berufung" for the Volksbuhne, Berlin, 1928. Appeared at the Sunshine Matinée in London, 1930 (together with Anny Fligg).
Address: Berlin-Halensee, Georg-Wilhelmstr. 9-11.

FINDLAY (Miss), Elsa; teacher of Dalcroze Eurythmics for actors and dancers. Studied under Dalcroze at Hellerau, Dresden, and began teaching in Manchester in 1914. Taught in School in New York in 1922, and was engaged as first Dalcroze teacher at Denishawn School, American Laboratory Theatre, Columbia University, etc. Has a lecture-demonstration group which appears at Universities and Colleges. Opened studio with Ronny Johansson in 1929, and now appears with her Dance Ensemble in modern dance composition in New York and elsewhere. One of the founders of Concert Dancers' League, inaugurated in 1930.
Address: 264 Fifth Avenue, New York.
Best Photos: Sunami, New York.

FITTON, Jack W.; ballroom teacher. Winner of Leicestershire Amateur Championship 1929-1930. Professional dancer at Leicester Palais de Danse and Pier Pavilion Ballroom, Shanklin. Originator of Isle of Wight Amateur Dance Championship.
Address: 4 Tennyson St., Leicester.
Best Photos: Ramsden, Leicester.

FLATOW (Miss), Ruby; operatic, ballroom and general dancer and teacher. Intermediate Member of the Operatic Association; Fellow of the Imperial Society's Operatic Branch and Member of the General Branch, Had her early training with Madame Karina, amongst others. Has appeared at leading theatres in London and the Provinces and also on the films. Has also originated ballets which have been produced in London and the Provinces.
Address: Leeds Operatic School of Dancing, 47 Mount Preston, Leeds.

FLETCHER, Walter; ballroom teacher. Member of the National Association of Teachers of Dancing; Secretary of the Allied Dancing Association (Liverpool). Has organised the Allied North of England Dancing Championships for the past five years. Represents the Allied Association on the Official Board. Has contributed articles to local press.
Address: 6 Blucher Street, Waterloo, near Liverpool.
Best Photos: Mills' Studios, Liverpool.

FLIGG (Miss), Anny; dancer and teacher of Central European Dancing (Laban Method). Certificate of the Laban School; Member of Associations for Dancing in Germany. Trained at the Laban School and a pupil of Rudolph von Laban and Hertha Feist. In 1925 became a teacher at the same school and a member of the Chamber Dancing Group under Hertha Feist, appearing in Berlin and other towns in Europe. Under Rudolph von Laban danced in *Don Juan*, Berlin and in Tannhaüser Bacchanal, Bayreuth, etc.; danced in London at the Sunshine Matinée in 1929, and the following year opened the Central European School of Dancing in London. Has been engaged by the Royal Academy of Dramatic Art, London, since October, 1931, to take charge of the production of chorus movements in the Greek dance, and suitable plays. Also produces chorus work and gives training in the Laban method.
Address: 72-74 Marylebone High Street, London, N.W.1.
Best Photos: Robertson; Baruch; Becke, Berlin.

FOKINA, Vera (Madame Michel Fokine); ballet dancer. One of the original members of the Diaghileff Ballet, and the original "Chiarina" in *Carnaval*. Has appeared in many rôles of the classical repertoire, and in all her husband's ballets. Has danced with him all over the world—especially in America during the last few years.
Address: 4 Riverside Drive, New York, U.S.A.

FOKINE, Michel; dancer and chorégraphist. Imperial Theatre, St. Petersburg. Educated at the Imperial Schools. Michel Fokine was the first to break away from the old-fashioned five-act ballet, with its complicated scenario, to create the short one-act ballet as we know it in Western Europe, where choregraphy, music and theme are in complete harmony. Fokine was no destroyer, but made full use of all that was best in classicism, dispensing with the many rigid and often illogical formulae. His first attempt in this manner, *Eunice*, caused considerable opposition. The influence of Isadora Duncan was noticeable in this. Fokine was an original member of the Diaghileff company, and its first choregraphist. His most important works are *Prince Igor*, *Pavilion d'Armide*, *Cleopatra* (produced in Russia as *Egyptian Nights*), *Les Sylphides* (1909), *Carnaval*, *Scheherazade*, *The Firebird* (1910), *Narcissus*, *Spectre of the Rose*, *Petrouchka* (1911), *The Blue God*, *Daphnis and Chloe*, *Thamar* (1912), and innumerable divertissements, among them Saint-Saen's *Dying Swan*, which delighted the composer. His last works in England were the ballets for *Hassan* and *Midsummer Night's Dream*.

He has since been teaching, dancing and producing in America with Vera Fokina, his wife.

Studies of Michel Fokine appear in all the leading works on the Russian Ballet.
Address: 4 Riverside Drive, New York, U.S.A.
Best Photos: Goodwin, Stockholm.

FONTANA, Georges; exhibition dancer associated for many years with Marjorie Moss. The dancing of these two, which may be described as a combination of ballroom and ballet work, created a sensation when seen in London, first at the Grafton Galleries and afterwards at the Embassy Club and the "Midnight" Follies. They were soon in great demand at the smart Continental hotels and casinos in France, notably on the Riviera, in Paris and at Deauville, and in the United States they achieved an even greater success and were recognised as the most brilliant exhibition couple of modern times. Fontana commenced his dancing career with Miss Belle Harding.
Address: Manoir de Gaumont, Castelmoran-d'Albret, Gironde, France

FORBES-JONES (Miss), Bessie; operatic and character dancer and teacher. Associate of the Imperial Society (Cecchetti Branch). winner of the Senior Operatic Section of the

All-England Solo Competition in 1931, and of the Senior Cup in 1932. Principal teacher at the Walthamstow School of Dancing.

Address: Walthamstow School of Dancing, 22 Rectory Road, Walthamstow, London, E.17.

FORD, Frank; leading ballroom dancer and teacher. Examiner for Imperial Society of Teachers of Dancing. Winner with Molly Spain of "Star" Professional Championship in 1927 and finalist in 1929; finalist All England Professional Championship in 1928. Judge for "Star" and Columbia Finals; filmed by British Movietone News, Pathé and Gaumont. Since 1925 has been teaching at the Empress Rooms. Gives many demonstrations with Murielle Sturgiess.

Address: 8 Linden Gardens, Notting Hill Gate, London, W.2.

Best Photos: Dorothy Wilding, London.

FOSTER, D. T.; teacher of ballroom, operatic and national dancing; also rhythmic exercises. President of the British Association of Teachers of Dancing in 1920. Is Examiner of the Yorkshire District. Member of the Official Board of Ballroom Dancing; Member Academie des Maîtres de Danse de Paris, 1920; Member Union Professionnelle des Professeurs de Danse et de Maintien de Belgique, 1920; Member Nederlandsche Vereening van Dansleeraren den Hague, 1920; Member Genossenschaft Deutscher Tanzlehrer e.v. sitz Berlin, 1930. Established his School in 1878. Inventor of the "Naval Three Step." Adjudicator in Columbia Semi-Finals and in East Coast Championships.

Address: The Hull School of Dancing, Salisbury Hall, Park Road, Hull, and 274 Beverley Road, Hull.

FOSTER (Miss), Marjorie Helen; general teacher. Associate Imperial Society of Teachers of Dancing (Operatic and Revived Greek Branches); Member Imperial Society (Ballroom Branch); Student's Certificate of Ruby Ginner School of Revived Greek Dancing. Trained at Cone School. Won Senior Group Gold Medal at All England Competition, Scala Theatre, London, 1931. Now has own School in Romford, Essex.

Address: Gay School of Dancing, 95 Eastern Road, Romford, Essex.

FOSTER (Miss), Pam (Miss Pamela Wentworth Foster); operatic dancer. Advanced Member of the Operatic Association of Great Britain, and Holder of their "Solo Seal." Born September 13th, 1914, and started dancing at the age of seven with Miss Kathleen de Vos, of Weymouth. Came to London when twelve and studied with Miss Phyllis Bedells for five years, recently becoming a pupil of Anton Dolin. In 1928 won the "Junior Cup" of the All England Competition with dances arranged by Miss Cone. In 1929 won the "Gold Medal" at the Sutton and Cheam Musical Festival. Has appeared with Miss Phyllis Bedells at the London Palladium; on tour, and has also danced solo at the Commodore Theatre, Hammersmith. Has appeared in two productions of the Camargo Society, and has danced at the Faculty of Arts.

Address: 10 Grosvenor Mansions, 395 Oxford Street, London, W.1.

Best photos: Hana, and Princess Yvonne, London.

FOX (Mr. and Mrs.), J.; ballroom teachers. Members of the British Association of Teachers of Dancing. Principals of Fox's Academy of Dancing in Huddersfield, which has been established 15 years. Mr. Fox is also a Member of the Nederland Ver. v. Dansleeran in Holland.

Address: 85-87 Trinity Street, Huddersfield.

FRANCESCO, Julian; classical and character dancer. Featured dancer of the Chicago Civic Opera, the San Carlo Opera (U.S.A.) and the Berlin Staatsoper. Has fulfilled engagements in several coast to coast American tours, concert engagements in France, Germany, Mexico, Brazil, Uraguay and the Argentine. Was formerly a pupil of Luigi Albertieri, Adolf Bolm,

Leo Staats, Max Terpis and Constantin Kobeloff.
Address: Clearwater Lake, Wisconsin, U.S.A.
Best photos: Robertson, Berlin; Basabe, Chicago.

FRANZEL, Willy; well-known solo dancer of the State Opera in Vienna.
Address: Konzerthuas-Heumarkt, Vienna.

FRASER, "Jimmy," (J. W. Fraser); amusement manager. Has been Manager for nearly ten years of the Marine Gardens Ballroom, Edinburgh, one of the largest ballrooms in Great Britain, where many of the best-known dancing celebrities have made their *debut* to the Scottish public. Does not confine his activities to dancing alone, he being the first to introduce Dirt Track Racing to the Scottish capital, and is also interested in Association Football and Boxing. He introduced Carnera to Scotland.
Address: Marine Gardens, Portobello, Edinburgh.

FREARSON (Miss), Gina; ballroom dancer and teacher. Associate of the Imperial Society. Studied for two years with Alexandre Volinine in Paris, after taking the Imperial Society Examination from the Bush School of Dancing, Nottingham. In 1929 came to England, and continued training with Victor Silvester, after which opened her own school in Wigmore Street.
Address: 131 Wigmore Street, Portman Square, London, W.1.
Best photos: Swaine, London, and Henri Manuel, Paris.

FRENCH, Ruth; operatic dancer and teacher. Advanced member of the Operatic Association. Received training under Nicolas Legat, Michael Fokine, Serge Morosoff and Ivan Clustine. First appeared on the stage in the late Mrs. Percy Dearmer's Children's Plays. Became *première danseuse* of the London Hippodrome, and held the position for four and a half years in five of Julian Wylie's revues, including "Brighter London." In this revue she scored an outstanding success as the "Jackdaw" in the *Jackdaw of Rheims* ballet, playing the part at 603 consecutive performances; also toured the principal towns of England and Scotland with it. She has had the honour of appearing at two Royal Command performances. Later was chosen as *première danseuse* by Mdme. Anna Pavlova for her company's season in South America in 1928, followed by a tour to Egypt, India, Malay States, Java and Australia. Has a School of Dancing in London.
Address: 24 Baker Street, London, W.1.
Best Photos: Lenare; Foulsham and Banfield; Janet Jevons, London.

G

GALL (Miss), Constance; ballroom dancer and teacher.
Address: 30 Brixton Road, London, S.W.9.

GALLOWAY (Miss), Norah; ballroom and tap teacher. Member of the Imperial Society of Teachers of Dancing, and holder of their Certificate. Was trained by Mrs. Cynthia Humphreys and Mr. G. K. Anderson in 1922, and remained with Mrs. Humphreys as head assistant. On Mrs. Humphreys' marriage, became co-Principal with Miss Ruault, of the Humphreys School of Dancing. Was finalist in World's Championship, 1923, dancing with own pupil.
Address: Humphreys School of Dancing, 41 New Bond Street, London, W.1.
Best photos: Hana (now Navana), London.

GARGANICO, F.; ballroom teacher. Member of the Imperial Society and the National Association of Teachers of Dancing. Is at present on the Executive Committee of the latter. Principle of the Knightsbridge Rooms School of Dancing. Has been teaching for ten years. Won the Pearce Shield of the National Association for two consecutive years 1928-9. Was in the

finals of the Charleston Competition held at the Royal Albert Hall in 1926. Has judged a number of ballroom competitions in South-west London. Also acted as judge for the " Amateur Dancer " Competitions.
Address: 58a Brompton Road, London, S.W.3.

GARNISH (Miss), Eileen; ballroom dancer and teacher. Holder Intermediate Certificate of the Incorporated London Academy of Music. Competition judge.
Address: 87 Penwortham Road, Streatham, S.W.16.
Best photos: Claude Harris, London.

GEERE (Miss), Sheila; general teacher. Advanced Member of the Operatic Association; Fellow and Council Member of the Imperial Society (Operatic, Greek, Cecchetti and Ballroom branches); Member of the Association of Teachers of the Revived Greek Dance. Has own School of Dancing at Sutton.
Address: 1 Moray House, Worcester Gardens, Sutton, Surrey.
Best photo: Douglas Hooper, Sutton.

GENEE, Adeline, I. et A. (Mrs. Frank S. N. Isitt). Born at Aarhus, in Denmark, and received her entire dancing training from her uncle and aunt, M. and Mme. Alexander Genée, the latter having been a *première danseuse* well known on the Continent under her maiden name, Mdlle. Antonie Zimmerman. Her uncle studied in his youth with Petipa and Johanson, and her aunt received her training at Budapest and Hanover under Granzow, the father and teacher of his famous daughter, Adele Granzow. Madame Genée made her first public appearance at Oslo (then Christiania) when only nine years of age, and danced at her uncle's theatre at Stettin. Appeared in Berlin as guest *première danseuse* at the Royal Opera in 1896, and the following year in a similar capacity at the Opera House, Munich, whence she was summoned by Mr. George Edwards for a six weeks' Season at the Empire Theatre, London—an engagement that was extended until it had lasted over ten years. She made her London debut on November 22nd, 1897, in a revival of the " Treasure Island " tableau from the ballet *Monte Christo*, and achieved her first great success on February 14th, 1898, as the " Spirit of Liberty " in C. Wilhelm's *Press Ballet*. Then followed the long series of successful " Empire " ballets, in the course of which Madame Genée won the hearts of all Londoners by her brilliant dancing. Particular mention should be made of *High Jinks*, in which she first danced the famous Hunting Dance, *Coppelia* in 1906, and *The Debutante* and the *Belle of the Ball*, which followed. In January, 1908, she appeared in *The Soul Kiss* in New York, and returned to the Empire the same year dancing in *Coppelia* for ten weeks before returning to the United States for a second tour of thirty-two weeks. *Robert the Devil*, arranged by her uncle, followed the next year, and this was her last Empire ballet. After her second visit to America she returned to London, and at the Coliseum produced her own ballet entitled *Butterflies and Roses*, and subsequently produced the ballet *La Camargo* by C. Wilhelm, music by Dora Bright. Two more American tours and one Australian and New Zealand followed, in the course of which her own compilation, entitled *La Danse* (music arranged by Dora Bright, and costumes by C. Wilhelm), was produced at the Metropolitan Opera House, New York. On her return to London she appeared in a Repertoire Season of ballets—some revivals of her old successes—at the Coliseum, and also appeared in *Spring* at the Alhambra, the music specially written for her by Sir Frederic Cowen, who also conducted.

Since Madame Genée retired from the stage in 1917 with the reputation of being the most brilliant danseuse of her day, she has, by her indefatigable efforts, rendered enormous service to the Art of Dancing in the country of her adoption. She was brought once more into immediate contact with the dancing profession when she took the Chair at the first " Dancers' Circle

Dinners" in 1920, and her active interest made the foundation of the "Association of Operatic Dancing of Great Britain" on December 31st of that year possible. She was unanimously elected President of that body—an office which she still holds. In 1928 she was instrumental in securing the Patronage of Her Majesty the Queen for this Association, and in 1930 she presided at the Inaugural Dinner of the "Camargo Society." Ever since its foundation, Madame Genée has taken a very close and active interest in the "Operatic Association," and it is impossible to over-estimate the help she has been to its members.

GEORGI, Yvonne. Trained at the Wigman School, Dresden. Ballet Mistress in Gera; later at the town theatre in Hannover, where she produced numerous modern ballets. Partner of Harald Kreutzberg, with whom she toured the Continent and America with great success.

GERALD (Miss), Eily; operatic dancer and teacher. Born in Manchester in 1901. First studied dancing under Mr. Alfred Haines and afterwards with Mdme. Ware and Theresa Heyman. Has since received training from Alex. Goudin, Serge Morosoff, Astafieva, Cecchetti and others. Appeared at the age of 10 in Sir Joseph Beecham's pantomime, "The Golden Land of Fairy Tales" at the Aldwych Theatre, London. In 1915, at the age of 14, was engaged by Sir Thomas Beecham as one of the principal dancers of the Beecham Opera Company, and remained with it for five years. Then became *première danseuse* of the British National Opera Company and the International Opera seasons at Covent Garden for four years. After two years' touring of Egypt, India, Ceylon, Rhodesia, South Africa, Zanzibar, Kenya and Uganda, Miss Gerald is now teaching dancing at Nairobi, Kenya Colony.
Address: P.O. Box 1,000, Nairobi, Kenya Colony, B.E.A.

GERT, Valeska; well-known German dancer, famous for her grotesque satyrical interpretations. Appeared in all important towns.
Author of "Mein Weg" (biography).

GILBERT (Miss), Renee; teacher of ballroom dancing and children's work. Is co-Principal with Miss Doreen Cleare of the Purcell School of Dancing.
Address: Purcell School of Dancing, 95 Wigmore Street, London, W.1.

GILLIS (Miss), Moyra (Miss Bertha Vivian Pearce); operatic, tap and all-round dancer. Member of the Operatic Association, and holds Elementary, Intermediate and Advanced Certificates; also Elementary Certificate of the Cecchetti branch of the Imperial Society. Born in October, 1912, at Johannesburg, South Africa. Studied dancing with Mdme. Ravodna. Winner at several Eisteddfods. On Mdme. Anna Pavlova's advice came to England in 1926. In 1928 signed a three year contract with Mr. Andrée Charlot, and appeared in "Charlot's 1928 Revue." Danced later in cabaret at the Hotel Splendide and at Grosvenor House, doing speciality ballet work. Appeared in "Wonder Bar" at the Savoy Theatre, London.
Address: 22 Maxilla Gardens, North Kensington, London, W.10.
Best photos: Foulsham & Banfield, and Mannell, London.

GINNER (Miss), Ruby; Greek dancer, actress, mime, choreographer. Principal of the Ginner-Mawer School of Dance and Drama. President and Founder of the Association of Teachers of the Revived Greek Dance. Fellow of the Imperial Society of Teachers of Dancing. Member of the Academic Council of the Central School of Speech Training and Dramatic Art. Born in Cannes, 1886. Received dramatic training under Elsie Fogerty. Was a member of Sir Frank Benson's Company, and leading dancer in the Haymarket Company, Marie Brema Opera Company, Thomas Beecham's Opera Company. Created the art of the Revived Greek Dance, now standardized in the Association of Teachers of the Revived Greek Dance (founded

by her in 1923). Has done a great deal of research work in connection with this dancing. Founded the Ginner-Mawer School in co-operation with Miss Irene Mawer.
Address: The Ginner-Mawer School, Philbeach Hall, Philbeach Gardens, London, S.W.5.
Best photos: Navana, Claude Harris, London.

GLEDHILL, Robert; ballroom teacher. President of the International Association of Dancing Masters, and of the Universal Association of Teachers of Dancing, both of which latter Associations have been merged into the International Association. Winner of various competitions, etc. Has been connected with the Blackpool Dance Festival since its inception as competitor, M.C. and adjudicator. Has demonstrated at the Empress Ballroom, Blackpool, on special occasions every year since it opened. Was the instigator of Municipal Dancing in Bradford, and for a number of years was the professional M.C. and had charge of the dancing. Was appointed Manager of the Central Pier and Pavilion Ballroom, Morecambe, in May, 1930.
Address: Charlton Dancing Academy, 85-91 Westgate, Bradford.
Best photos: Webber, Morecambe.

GLENDINNING (Miss), Mary; general teacher. Principal of Glendinning's School of Dancing, Edinburgh, where all subjects are taught by a well-qualified staff, ballroom dancing being a special feature.
Address: 1 Chalmers Crescent, Edinburgh.

GLOVER (Miss), Mabel; general teacher. Intermediate Member British Ballet Organization (Full Teaching Diploma); Member International Dancing Masters' Association. Winner of 20 medals and certificates for stage dancing. Has a large dancing connection in Huddersfield.
Address: Maybelle School of Dancing, Brook Street, Huddersfield.

GODBY (Miss), Gladys; operatic, tap and general dancer. Advanced Member Operatic Association. Trained under Madame Ravodna, Johannesburg, and then under Madame Espinosa in London. Bronze Medallist in All England Competition, 1925, and appeared with George Royle's Concert Party, and as principal dancer with Arthur Hamilton in pantomime. Appeared with Fred Clement's Concert Party, trained by T. C. Askew; solo in "Shake Your Feet," London Hippodrome; one of Cochran's Young Ladies in "This Year of Grace" and "Wake Up and Dream," London Pavilion, taking Tilly Losch's part for six weeks. Toured in provinces on Moss tour, partnered by Errol Addison, and played also in Barcelona. Appeared as understudy in "Ever Green," Adelphi Theatre.
Address: 3 Cathcart Road, South Kensington, London, S.W.
Best Photos: Frank Mavis; Princess Yvonne, Newcastle.

GODFREY (Miss), Phyllis; general teacher and dancer. Advanced Member Operatic Association and holder of Espinosa's Advanced Certificate and Full Teaching Diploma. Examiner of Operatic Dancing for Royal Academy of Music, London. Dancing Mistress for Hasleton Operatic Society, and has a big dancing connection in Hastings and St. Leonards. Has arranged dances and played in *The Geisha, The Rebel Maid, The Gondoliers,* etc.
Address: San-Souci, Milward Road, Hastings.

GODWIN (Mrs.), Lilian; general teacher. Member British Ballet Organisation and Chairman of local branch and Examiner; Member Operatic Association; Member Midland Association, Vice-President and Examiner. Received training from Professor De Vene (ballet master of Lyceum Theatre, London) and Phyllis Bedells. Pupils are trained in all types of dancing, and dancers are supplied for local amateur dramatic societies and concert parties.
Address: 16 Dean Street, Portland Square, Bristol.
Best Photos: Alfred Wager, Bristol.

GORNOLD (Miss), Ivy; ballroom teacher. Licentiate Faculty of Dancing; Member of the Imperial Society (Certificate), and holds Casani Certificate. Entered the " World's Dancing Championship " in 1922-23, and in " Mixed " events obtained fourth place in all dances. In 1926 opened a branch of the Casani School at Brighton with Mr. Edward de Larun as partner. Miss Gornold is acknowledged as a successful organiser of charity balls and competitions; also as a judge and demonstrator.

Address: Casani School of Dancing, 2 Cambridge Road, Hove, Sussex.

Best photos: Margaret Ellsmoor, Worthing.

GOULD (Miss), Diana; classical ballet dancer. Pupil of Mdme. Marie Rambert. Member of the Ballet Club Company. Created the part of " The Vamp " in *Boxing* (Salaman-Berners); " Leda " in *Leda and the Swan* (Ashton-Corelli), Clara Vere de Vere in *My Lord of Burleigh* (Camargo Society); and has danced in *Carnaval* (Chiarina), *Les Sylphides*, *L' Apres Midi d'un Faune*, *Aurora's Wedding*, etc., both at the Ballet Club, and at all seasons at the Lyric, Hammersmith. Danced at special Farewell performance of Moscow Arts Theatre, January, 1932.

There is a section devoted to Diana Gould in the book by Arnold Haskell entitled " The Marie Rambert Ballet " (British-Continental Press, Ltd.).

Address: Mulberry House, The Vale, Chelsea, London, S.W.3.

Best Photos: Reprograph, London.

GRAHAM, Bert; teacher of stage work. Member Variety Artists' Federation. Worked the Music Halls as a tap dancer prior to the war, during which time he served with the Middlesex Regiment. After the war was Stage Manager and Ballet Master for Mr. Charlot, and later for Julian Wylie and at the Trocadero for Mr. Cochran. He then became Chief Instructor for Mr. Max Rivers, and produced eight shows in France. Appeared for Max Rivers at the Dominion Theatre, London. Opened his own school in April, 1931, which was at once successful, and has several troupes of dancers. Is also interested in production work.

Address: 116 Charing Cross Road, London, W.C.2.

GRAHAM (Miss), J. G.; ballroom teacher. Member of the Ballroom Branch of the Imperial Society. Is in charge of a branch of Mr. Maxwell Stewart's School at Winchester, and is also teaching at Southampton.

Address: South Western Hotel, Southampton.

GRAHAM (Miss), Janette; teacher of ballroom and general dancing. Member United Kingdom Alliance, and was awarded Diploma for solo dance at their Conference in 1929. Trained at the Thomson Schools, Glasgow, and for four years was assistant to Mr. Douglas Thomson at his Southern Academy. Opened own Academy of Dancing about three years ago. Has judged competitions and given demonstrations in Glasgow.

Address: The Vine Studio of Dancing, 494 Crown Street, Glasgow.

GRANADOS (Senorita), Asuncion; typic and classic Spanish dancer; teacher of the guitar. Born in Madrid in 1908. First public appearance was at the " Maravillas Theatre " in Madrid. After having danced and played the guitar in the best theatres of Spain, went to France, appearing with great success, and from there to Belgium and Holland. Then visited England, and has danced at the London Coliseum, Ciro's Club and the Piccadilly Hotel, and the Chiswick Empire, London, and also at Manchester, Leicester, Bristol.

Address: Abada 25, Madrid, Spain.

Best photos: Sobol, Paris.

GRANT (Mrs.), Freda; operatic, Greek, ballroom and general teacher. Advanced Member and on Sub-Committee of the Operatic Association; Advanced Member and Examiner and also on Committee of the Association of Teachers of the Revived Greek Dance; Fellow and Examiner of the

Greek, Operatic and Ballroom Sections of the Imperial Society, and Vice-President of the Greek Branch. Examiner of Children's Greek and Ballroom Examinations, and has judged at many Festivals. On the Committee of the Faculty of Dancing. Was first trained with Miss Belle Harding. Has been responsible for the London and district branch of Miss Hutton-Moss's connection since 1908.
Address: 30 Blackheath Park, London, S.E.3.

GREATRIX, Philip. Member of the Imperial Society. Principal of the Audley School of Dancing, London.
Address: Audley School of Dancing, 449 Oxford Street, London, W.1.

GREENE, Ronald; ballroom dancer. Member of Imperial Society of Teachers of Dancing. Winner of " Daily Sketch " Waltz Championship in 1922 ; British Professional Ballroom Charleston Championship ; runner-up in " Star " Professional Dancing Championship for 2 years ; second in World's Dancing Championship in 1928. Has danced at Murray's Club, Café de Paris and other well-known restaurants and clubs ; also at Westover Ballrooms, Bournemouth. Gave first exhibition of Ballroom Dancing for talking pictures, and has appeared at Plaza, London, etc. Organized " West of England Championships " for the Bristol *Evening World*.
Address: Westover, Stoke Hill, Stoke Bishop, Bristol.
Best Photos: Foulsham & Banfield.

GREENHILL (Miss), Dorothy; operatic and tap dancer; general teacher. Advanced Member of the Operatic Association. Pupil and Holder of Espinosa's Certificate. Fellow of the Imperial Society (Operatic Branch). Has had general stage experience at Daly's, the Gaiety and Winter Garden Theatres, London. Is Principal of the Dorothy Greenhill School of Dancing at Kensington and other branches.
Address: 81 Stafford Road, Croydon, London, S.E.

Best photos: Claude Harris, and Hana (now Navana), London.

GREENWELL, W. A.; ballroom and national teacher. President National Association, 1931-32 ; Past President Northern Professional Dance Teachers' Association and British Association Teachers of Dancing, and is Examiner for each ; Member Academie des Maitres de Danse, Paris. Winner of the Gold Medal and 100 Guineas Trophy, Blackpool, 1926, amongst other competitions.
Address: Royal Arcade Assembly Rooms, Pilgrim Street, Newcastle-on-Tyne.
Best Photos: Bainbridge, Gateshead.

GREENWOOD (Miss), Amy; teacher of ballroom dancing. Member of Imperial Society. Has adjudicated at a number of important competitions.
Address: 34 Bloomsbury Street, London, W.C.1.

GREGOROVA, Natasha; operatic and character dancer. Was placed by Madame Pavlova under the tuition of Laurent Novikoff, and later danced in the Pavlova ballet. Then became a pupil of Anton Dolin, and a member of his company. Was one of the soloists in the Balanchine Ballet at the London Coliseum and Alhambra, and recently worked for Leonide Massine.
Address: 31 Alfred Place, Bedford Square, London, W.C.1.

GREVILLE (Miss), Eva (Mrs. Percy Ogle) ; operatic dancer and general teacher. Principal dancer at Gaiety Theatre, London, with George Edwarde's Company, first appearance being in the original *Pas de quatre* in " Faust Up-to-date " in 1889 ; danced in Fred Leslie's Company in " Ruy Blas," etc., and appeared also at Strand Theatre and Alhambra ; played principal boy in pantomimes. Has taught in Pinner for twenty years, with connections in Northwood, etc.
Address: 1 The Parade, Pinner.
Best Photos: Downey & Barron.

GRIFFITHS (Miss), Maisie; operatic,

acrobatic, character, musical comedy and ballroom dancer. Speciality dancer for Julian Wylie's and Edward Dolly's Productions, 1926 and 1927, also dancing at Coliseum, Alhambra and Duke of York's Theatre, London; Ballet Mistress for Archie De Bear, Vaudeville Theatre, in 1928; summer seasons with Murray Ashford, Eric Ross and Rex Burchell. Recent engagements as spectacular dancer include London's principal hotels, clubs and restaurants and season with Medredett Balalaika Orchestra. Producer for Eric Ross's Cabaret "Dazzle" and choreographist for H.W. Productions. Trained by Euphan Maclaren.

Address: 36b Earlsfield Road, Wandsworth Common, London, S.W. 18.

Best Photos: Margaret Clarke, Southend-on-Sea; Reprograph, London.

GRIGORIEFF, Serge; stage manager and *Régisseur* of Serge Diaghileff's Russian Ballet. Completed his studies at the Petrograd Imperial Ballet School in 1900. Became a dancer in the ballet company of the Imperial Marinsky Theatre. At the same time took a course at the Imperial Dramatic School, which he completed in 1904. He did not stay on the dramatic stage, but remained in the ballet company as a mime artist. In 1909 entered Serge Diaghileff's Ballet Company as Stage Manager and *Régisseur*, and remained in this position (taking mime parts in some ballets) during the whole of its existence and until Diaghileff's death in 1929, *i.e.*, for 20 years. Was a collaborator in all the ballet's activities; rehearsed and prepared all the ballets of the repertoire; managed all the performances which were ever given by Serge Diaghileff. After the latter's death, he organised a small company consisting of Diaghileff's dancers, which worked temporarily at Monte-Carlo during the Opera Season in 1930.

Address: 16 Boulevard d'Italie, Monte-Carlo, Principauté de Monaco.

Best photos by Swaine, London.

GROOM (Miss), Gladys; operatic dancer. Advanced Member of the Operatic Association. Trained with Madame Cavalazzi and later with Edouard Espinosa and Madame Astafieva. With her partner, Ramon Ferrata, assisted by twelve girls from her own School, has played own act at all the principal London halls and cabarets, including the Coliseum, Alhambra and Palladium, and has toured the Moss and Stoll Halls in the Provinces. Their work is not confined to ballet only, but also includes acrobatic lifts and swings.

Address: "Lestelle," 63 London Road, Forest Hill, London, S.E.23.

GUNSTON (Miss), Gwendolen; general teacher. Member of the Imperial Society of Teachers of Dancing (Ballroom and Greek branches); Elementary Member of the Operatic Association; Member of the Association of Teachers of the Revived Greek Dance. Was bronze medallist in the "All England Duet Competition" in 1927, and finalist in the "All England Solo Competition" in 1928. Established her own School of Dancing in 1928.

Address: The Studio, 42 Granville Park, Lewisham, London, S.E.13.

H

HAAKON, Paul. Pupil of Michael Fokine. American-Danish dancer, brought to London by Anton Dolin, in whose Company he danced at the Coliseum and elsewhere. Danced at the last "Sunshine Matinee." Joined the Pavlova Company and was on their last tour. Appeared recently in the American production of *Job* by Vaughan Williams.

HAINES, Alfred; general teacher and dancer. Full Member Operatic Association. Principal with Miss Mabel Haines of the Haines School of Dancing. Inaugurated Haines English Ballet, 1915. Appeared at London Coliseum, Alhambra, Victoria Palace, Palladium, and other principal theatres in Great Britain. Still touring with great success.

Address: Westwood, Upper Chorlton Road, Manchester.
Best Photos: F. Ingham and Guttenberg, Manchester.

HAINES (Miss), Rosalie; general teacher. Principal of the oldest established school in Belfast. Was elected President of the Northern Ireland Dance Teachers' Society for 1931. Has won and also adjudicated at many competitions, and gives frequent charity performances in Belfast and district.
Address: 47 Donegall Pass, Belfast, Ireland.

HALL (Miss), Gladys; general teacher. Trained by a pupil of Paul Valentine and by Charles d'Albert.
Address: 12 Regent Street, London Road, Leicester.

HALLS (Miss), Joan; operatic, tap, Greek and acrobatic dancer. Intermediate Member of the Operatic Association, and holder of the Elementary Cecchetti Certificate and the Revived Greek Certificate of the Imperial Society. Trained by the Cone School of Dancing. Winner of the " All England Duet Competition " Junior Cup with Audrey King as partner in 1927, and in 1929 was the winner of the Senior Cup of the " All England Solo Dancing Competition." First professional engagement was with Sybil Thorndike in " Henry VIII." at the Empire Theatre. Since then has appeared with the Oumansky Ballet; in ballet at Drury Lane; solo dancer for two seasons for Messrs. Royle and Newman; for Charles Heslop, and is now working variety halls with Fiori and Chase. Has recently been appearing in cabaret at the principal West End hotels and clubs. Has danced at " Sunshine Matinees."
Address: 113 Bensham Manor Road Thornton Heath, Surrey.
Best Photos: Stilliard, London.

HAMILTON, Arthur (Arthur Moore Hamilton); ballroom, operatic and tap dancer and teacher. Member of Imperial Society of Teachers of Dancing (Ballroom Branch); Member of Operatic Association. Trained by Madame Judith Espinosa and Victor Silvester. Principal dancer in Haines' English Ballet at London Coliseum and provincial theatres. Cabaret and Ballroom demonstrations at leading hotels and dance halls in England and Ireland. Principal of the Hamilton School of Dance and Dramatic Art in Belfast.
Address: 19 Windsor Park, Belfast.
Photos: Hana (now Navana), London.

HAMMOND (Miss), Irene; general teacher, specializing in operatic work. Advanced Member of the Operatic Association, and also a Member of the Sub-Committee, and is a Children's Examiner. Advanced Member of the British Ballet Organization. Born and trained in Cheltenham, Miss Hammond's first teaching experience was gained at the Cheltenham Ladies' College. She has, in addition, studied at the Hutton-Moss School in London, and was trained in operatic work by Espinosa. In 1920 she became Miss Webster's successor in Chester, and has a most successful school.
Address: Grosvenor Hotel, Chester.

HAMMOND (Miss), Olive. Co-Principal of the Five Ways School of Dance, where all branches of dancing are taught, combined with own rhythmic method of musical interpretation. Won first prize in All England Solo Competition, Greek Section, 1927. Is Ballet Mistress to the Birmingham Grand Opera Society.
Address: The Five Ways School of Dance, Islington Row, Birmingham.
Best Photos: Walden Hammond, Leamington Spa.

HAMPTON (Miss), Eileen M.; operatic dancer and teacher. Advanced Member of the Operatic Association of Great Britain; Member of the Imperial Society (Cecchetti Branch). Winner of Silver Medals in Solo Competitions in London and Blackpool in 1930 for Operatic Dancing. Is a Member of the " Regional Revellers " (Midland Branch, B.B.C.).

HAN

Address: "Roxwell," Lichfield Road, Four Oaks, Sutton Coldfield, Birmingham.
Best photo: Speight, Sutton Coldfield.

HANFORD, Frank Leslie; ballroom teacher. Member of the International Dancing Masters' Association. Is the Winter Season Host at the Premier Dance Hall, Loughborough. Was finalist in the "Star" Professional Championship, 1930, and finalist in the North of England Championship at Blackpool in the same year. Acts as the Summer Season host at the Café Dansant, Skegness. Is Principal of the Style and Simplicity School of Dancing, Nottingham.
Address: 94 Sneinton Boulevard, Nottingham.

HARDING, Belle (Mrs. MacGregor); prominent teacher of ballroom dancing, who, with headquarters in London, has branches of her school in several provincial towns and in many places on the Continent. Was one of the first to hold Tea Dances in London before the War and to teach the tango, of which dance she has been a staunch supporter ever since. Organises the dances at many English and Continental hotels.
Address: 1 Gliddon Road, London, W.14.

HARE (Miss), May; general teacher. Co-Principal with Miss Mollie Thomas of the May Hare and Mollie Thomas School of Dancing.
Address: 209 Archway Road, Highgate, London, N.6.

HARRISON (Miss), Freda; general teacher. Member of the Association of Teachers of the Revived Greek Dance. Trained by Miss Ena Bartley, and was for a time assistant to Miss Eleanor Ratcliffe in Eastbourne. Since 1928 has been assistant to Miss Ena Bartley, in Birmingham, specializing in Greek Dancing.
Address: Bandon, Barnt Green, nr. Birmingham.

HASKELL, Arnold L.; writer. Member of Faculty of Dancing. Art Director of the Camargo Society, and together with Mr. P. J. S. Richardson, convener of the founding body. Organiser of the Diaghileff Memorial Exhibition held at Claridge Gallery in 1930, and was Editor of the Souvenir Catalogue. Director of the Ballet Club, 1930. Presented Thamar Karsavina and Company at the Arts Theatre Club, May, 1930, and Lydia Lopokova and Company at the same theatre in December, 1930.

Author of "Some Studies in Ballet" (Lamley, 1928); "Vera Trefilova," with foreword by Prince Wolkonsky; "Anton Dolin," with foreword by Mr. P. J. S. Richardson; "Tamara Karsavina"; "Penelope Spencer," with foreword by Gustav Holst; and "The Marie Rambert Ballet," with foreword by Tamara Karsavina. The last five books are of the "Artists of the Dance" series published by British Continental Press. Contributor to *The Dancing Times*, etc. Joint Editor of "Who's Who in Dancing."
Address: 22 Hornton Street, Kensington, London, W.8.

HATTON (Miss), Mary; operatic dancer. Intermediate Member Association of Operatic Dancing of Great Britain. Trained at the May Hatton School of Dancing, Hereford. Was *première danseuse* in the Sarah Siddons Centenary production at the Kemble Theatre, Hereford, in June, 1931.
Address: The Brooklands, Victoria Street, Hereford.
Best photos: Vivian, Hereford.

HATTON (Mrs.), May; general teacher. Elementary Member Operatic Association; Member Imperial Society of Teachers of Dancing (Ballroom branch). Ballet Mistress to Hereford, Ross and Ludlow Operatic Societies; producer of a ballet in Sarah Siddon's Centenary at Kemble Theatre, Hereford, in 1931. Has a large dancing connection in Herefordshire, etc.
Address: The Brooklands, Victoria Street, Hereford.

HAWKINS, A. J., and Miss B.; ballroom teachers. Members of Pro-

fessional Dancers' Association. Specialists in all modern ballroom dance movements since 1926.
Address: Studio of Ballroom Dancing, 42 Surbiton Road, Kingston-on-Thames.
Best Photos: H. P. Rider, Kingston, Surrey.

HAYLOR (Miss), Freda; ballroom dancer and teacher. Is an assistant to her sister, Miss Phyllis Haylor and Miss Molly Spain, at their School of Dancing at the Basil Street Hotel.
Address: Basil Street Hotel, Knightsbridge, London, S.W.1.

HAYLOR (Miss), Phyllis; teacher of ballroom dancing. Member and Examiner of the Imperial Society. Winner of the World's Championship (Mixed) in 1925 with Mr. Cedric Raphael. Winner of the "Star" Championship, 1926, with Mr. Alec Millar. Winner of the Quick-step Championship of Great Britain, 1927. Judge in the Columbia Amateur Championship, 1927 and 1928, and in the "Star" Championship in 1928, 1929 and 1930. Was a Principal with Miss Molly Spain of the Century Ballroom, Regent Street. Now teaching at the Basil Street Hotel, London.
Address: Basil Street Hotel, Knightsbridge, London, S.W.1.
Best photos: Yvonne, and Gregory, London.

HAYTON, Tom; ballroom teacher. Past Vice-President of the British Association of Teachers of Dancing. Founder of the United Kingdom Alliance, and is present Vice-President. Founder and Past President of the Manchester Association of Teachers of Dancing; also Examiner. Is a well-known teacher in Manchester, and has taught for many years.
Address: 210 Plymouth Grove, Rusholme, Manchester.
Best photos: Porter, Manchester.

HAYWARD, Mr. B. S.; ballroom teacher. Advanced Member, with Honours, and Teachers' Diploma; also Examiner of the Lancashire Dancing Association; Member of the Official Board of Ballroom Dancing. Born in Manchester, Mr. Hayward received his early training in that area. Transferring to Blackpool in 1920, he was immediately successful in organizing dances and classes, assisted by his wife and daughter. He relinquished his private practice in 1929 on his appointment to the position of M.C. and demonstrator at the well-known Empress Ballroom, Blackpool. Mr. Hayward does a great deal in the organization of the Annual Blackpool Festival.
Address: Empress Ballroom, Winter Gardens, Blackpool.
Best photos: Herbert Lord, Blackpool.

HAZLEWOOD (Miss), Marjorie; general teacher. Holder of Espinosa's Advanced Certificate and Intermediate Member Operatic Association. Principal of Derby School of Dancing, Derby, where all types of dancing are taught.
Address: 19 St. Peter's Street, Derby.

HEATH, William Henry; amateur ballroom dancer. Winner of Veterans' Championship, 1925; World's Amateur Championship, 1926-1928 and 1931; Veterans' Championship of Europe, 1927; Provincial Columbia Championship, 1929; and Championships of Germany, Italy, Switzerland, Central Europe, Middle Europe, etc., 1929-1931. Represented the Dancing World at luncheon for Amy Johnson at Savoy Hotel, given by *Daily Mail*.
Address: "Holmstall," Westleigh Avenue, Putney Hill, London, S.W.15.

HEATHER, George J.; ballroom and operatic teacher. Past President of and Examiner and Auditor for National Association of Teachers of Dancing; holder of certificate and diploma of this Association. Principal, with Mrs. Van Hepburn, of Heather's School of Dancing, which was founded in 1913, where all types of dancing are taught, the Tango being a special feature.
Address: 47 Upper Tulse Hill, Brixton, London, S.W.2.

HEAVEN (Miss), Eileen; teacher of operatic, ballroom, acrobatic and step dancing. Intermediate Member of the Association of Operatic Dancing of Great Britain. Holds Advanced Teaching Diploma of the British Ballet Organization and Operatic Dancing Teachers' Society. Member of the Imperial Society, Ballroom and Operatic Sections. Holds Advanced Certificate English Folk Dance Society. Is Teacher of Dancing at Clifton College, and is Branch Secretary of the B.B.O. and O.D.T.S. Trained in Operatic Dancing by Mr. Espinosa, and was assistant to Miss Phyllis Bedells when she was teaching in Bristol, afterwards taking on the School. Has been Principal there for the last five years. Was Ballet Mistress in the Bristol Opera Seasons, producing the ballets in *Dido and Aeneas*, *Travelling Companion*, *Fireflies*, etc., and has produced the dancing items for the *Times* and *Mirror* Comedy Club and Bristol Amateur Operatic Society. Teaches in Bristol and district, and also in Wells, Glastonbury and Cheddar in Somerset and Corsham in Wilts.
Address: West of England Academy of Dancing and Physical Training, Swedish Gymnasium, Lansdown Road, Clifton, Bristol.

HEAVEN, Evelyn and Gwen; operatic and ballroom teachers. Intermediate Members Operatic Association (local representatives); Members Imperial Society of Teachers of Dancing (Ballroom branch). Principals of the Court School of Dancing, Southend-on-Sea, which opened in 1925; branches in other districts.
Address: 153 Hamlet Court Road, Westcliff-on-Sea.
Best Photos: Margaret Clarke, Southend-on-Sea.

HELFERT (Miss), Peggy; ballroom teacher. Member Imperial Society of Teachers of Dancing. Trained with Josephine Bradley in 1927; went to Germany to teach with Fritz Conradi; taught at Berlin Academy of Dancing Teachers, being given a special certificate; has acted as Josephine Bradley's Students' Teacher, and has fulfilled positions as dance hostess at the Beresford Hotel, Birchington, and Montreux Palais Hotel; has taught for Madge Atkinson at Arley and Manchester.
Address: 23 Rylett Road, London, W.12.
Best Photos: Does, Berne.

HELLIWELL (Miss), Ethel; general teacher. Born in Blackpool. Captained the original Plaza-Tiller Girls from 1926 to 1928. Is now Ballet Mistress for all Francis A. Mangan's productions, which include the Plaza Tiller Girls, the 24 Mangan-Tillerettes, the 24 Mangan-Tiller Girls, the Paramount Tiller Girls, the Carlton-Tiller Girls, and the Mayfair-Tiller Girls. These presentations are produced in London (at the Plaza and the Paramount Astorias), in Paris (the Paramount), in Manchester, Barcelona, Bordeaux, Rome, and elsewhere.
Address: C/o Paramount Theatres, 104/108 Oxford Street, London, W.1.

HELSHAM, Purcell; masseur, limber and general trainer for dancing; inventor of pads for pirouettists.
Address: 72 East Hill, Dartford, Kent.

HENRY (Miss), Iris; operatic dancer. Advanced Member of the Operatic Association. Trained by Karsavina and Phyllis Bedells. Has appeared with Anton Dolin's Company, Balanchine Dancers, etc.
Address: Benhilton College, Sutton, Surrey.
Best Photos: Princess Yvonne, London.

HERBERT (Miss), Constance M.; general teacher. Specializes in Greek Dancing and Mime, and in the arrangement and production of dances and ballet.
Address: 66 Berkeley Street, Glasgow, C.3.
Best photos: Paterson's Studios, Glasgow.

HERITAGE (Miss), Evelyn Claire; general dancer and teacher. Member

Operatic Association (Intermediate Diploma). Trained at Pauline and Noreen Bush School of Dancing, and now Principal of the Evelyn Heritage School of Dancing, Sutton-on-Sea.
Address: The Evelyn Heritage School of Dancing, The Park, Sutton-on-Sea, Lincolnshire.
Best Photos: Short, Nottingham.

HESS, Günter; *maître de ballet, premier danseur*, and teacher. Member of the Deutsche Buhnengenossenschaft, and the Deutschen Chor and Ballet-Verband. Studied classical and "modern" dancing in Germany with Mr. Hanns Stork of the Opera, Zurich; Max Terpis (State Opera, Berlin), and the Laban School, Hamburg. Gave a number of solo dance recitals in Leipzig, Berlin, Hannover, Dresden, Osnabruck, and various smaller towns, and afterwards became Ballet Master in Osnabruck, Dessau, and Hagen in Westphalia, where he is now leading the Modern Chamber Dance Group. He has produced a number of successful ballets amongst which are *Facade* (music by William Walton), *Kreislauf* (music by Honnegger), *Hamburg* (music by Niemann), *Komodie in Himmelstadt* (music by Weissman), etc. One of his greatest successes was when he appeared as the guest artist in the part of "Joseph" in "Joseph's Legend" at the Opera in Leipzig.
Address: 40 Lutzowstr, Hagen i/Westphalia, Germany.
Best photos: Theresa Knietsch, Leipzig; Liebherr, Berlin; Kraft-Ehrenberg, Dessau.

HEYMAN (Miss), Therese; general teacher. Member of Council and Examiner for Imperial Society of Teachers of Dancing (Ballroom and General branches), and Examiner for Children's examination. Advanced Member Operatic Association; Intermediate Member Cecchetti Society; Advanced Member Revived Greek Association. Is Principal of the Operatic and Stage Section of the Italia Conti School.
Address: 52 Priory Gardens, Highgate, London, N.6.

HEYWORTH (Miss), Anita; teacher of natural movement dancing. Fellow, Member of Council and Examiner, Imperial Society of Teachers of Dancing, and Holder of their Advanced Certificate (Natural Movement branch). Was trained by Miss Madge Atkinson, of Manchester. Has danced and assisted in training for all Miss Atkinson's productions in both solo and group work for many years. During the Opera Festival Season in Manchester, danced in the Venusberg Ballet from "Tannhauser," "Aida," "Samson and Delilah" and "Faust." Appeared twice at the "Sunshine" Matinees. Has been especially successful for many years past in the "All England" "Sunshine" Competitions and at the Blackpool Festivals. For the past six years has been a principal teacher with the Atkinson-Suffield School, and has recently been taken into partnership.
Address: Studio School of Dancing, 259 Deansgate, Manchester.
Best Photos: T. Longworth Cooper, Sale, Cheshire.

HICK (Mdme.), Gertrude; general teacher. Pupil of Espinosa in 1905. Principal of school for children and students where all types of dancing are taught.
Address: 4 Baker Street, Hull.
Best photos: Lafayette, London.

HICKEY (Mdme.), Florence Eva; teacher in all branches of dancing. Member of the Imperial Society.
Address: Calabria, Newton Abbot, Devon.

HILARY (Miss), Ruby (Mrs. Ruby Rowsell); operatic, tap and ballroom teacher. Advanced Member Operatic Association. Associate of the Imperial Society (Ballroom Branch). Was trained by Miss Theresa Heyman at the Italia Conti School, and has taught there for the past eight years. Danced in C. B. Cochran's *Coppelia* ballet and at Covent Garden Opera ballets. Also danced in "The Tempest" ballet at the Royal command performance at Drury Lane Theatre. Acts as Ballet Mistress for Miss Conti

for "The Windmill Man" each Christmas at the Victoria Palace, London. Opened her own school at New Southgate in February, 1931.
Address: 365 Alexandra Park Road, London, N.22.

HITCHINS, Aubrey; operatic dancer. Studied with Mdme. Judith Espinosa, Enrico Cecchetti and Nicolas Legat. Danced in Fokine's ballets in "Hassan," 1923, and in Legat's ballet in "London Life." Following this he danced in "The Duenna," and then worked again for Fokine, playing Apollo in his ballet *The Frollicking Gods*. In the summer of 1925 danced with Nadedja Nicolaeva in *Le Lac des Cygnes*, and was then engaged by Madame Anna Pavlova, and subsequently toured with her for many years, and partnered her in *Russian Folk Lore, Autumn Leaves, Gavotte Pavlova* and *Valse Triste*. He also partnered Ruth French and Felia Doubrovska. Appeared with the Russian Opera and Ballet Company at the Lyceum Theatre in June, 1931.
Address: 79 Gower Street, W.C.1.
Best photos: Furley Lewis, Northolt Junction, and Mmes. Trude Geiringer and Dora Horovitz, Vienna.

HOARE (Miss), Mary; operatic and tap dancer. Advanced Member Operatic Association. Has appeared in Oumansky's Ballet in "Rio Rita," Anton Dolin's Company, Balanchine Ballet, and the Albertina Rasch Ballet of "Waltzes from Vienna."
Address: 11 Birch Grove, Lee, London, S.E.12.
Best Photos: Navana and Reprograph, London.

HOCTOR (Miss), Harriet; dancer. Began training with Louis H. Chalif at the age of 12, and later with Ivan Tarasoff. Her ambition was to be an interpretive dancer, using "toe dancing" merely to give the effect of lightness and daintiness, and with this idea began to work out various variations of the back bend on toes, which has been a special feature of her work. She first secured bookings for a year in Vaudeville with Nelson Snow and Charles Columbus, which experience gave her confidence. Her first production was with the Duncan Sisters in "Topsy and Eva," after which she did the *Fairy Doll* Ballet in Rosalie Stewart's "Revue a la Carte." Florenz Ziegfeld saw her in this, and immediately placed her under a long term contract. She has danced in "The Three Musketeers," "Show Girl" and "Simple Simon." Is at present appearing in "Bow Bells" at the London Hippodrome.
Address: 455 West 23rd Street, New York; and 78 Brook Street, London, W.1.
Best Photos: Steichen, Edward Thayer Monroe and Maurice Goldberg, New York.

HOGARTH (Mdme.), Jessie (Mrs. Eustace St. George Pett); general teacher. Fellow and Life Member Imperial Society of Teachers of Dancing, and Member of Council since 1920; Member Operatic Association 1922-1928. Pupil of Mr. Crompton, Brighton. Present at inaugural meeting of Imperial Society in 1904; began Teachers' Courses with Mr. Espinosa and Mr. Browning. Now teaches in London, and produces for amateur dramatic societies. While working in Brighton taught the Principals of the Cone and Robinson Schools, London.
Address: 32 Lynton Road, Acton London, W.3.

HOLBROW (Miss), Clarice M.; Head Branch Teacher and Organizing Secretary of the Mersey and Deeside Branch of the English Folk Dance Society.
Address: 13 Islington, Liverpool.

HOPKINS (Miss), Marie; general teacher. Advanced Member Operatic Association. Trained by Phyllis Bedells; gold medallist in Bristol Eisteddfod in 1927. Principal of Mercers Hall Academy of Dancing, Gloucester, which opened in 1928, where a thorough training for the stage or teaching profession is given.
Address: La France, Conway Road Hucclecote, Gloucester.

Best Photos: Richard Hall, Gloucester.

HORTON (Miss), Phyllis; ballroom teacher. Born in Ireland in 1902. Came to London in 1916 and trained under Miss Josephine Bradley. Finalist in the " Star " Dancing Championship, 1925. Was on the staff of the Hammersmith Palais de Danse for several years.
Address: 38 Shaftesbury Road, Ravenscourt Park, London, W.6.
Best photos: Dora Head, London.

HOUGH, Harry; Irish dancer and piper. Teacher of Irish step and round dances. Instructor to the Gaelic League of London, Irish Literary Society, Irish Club, the City Literary Institute (L.C.C.), and other societies.
Address: 93 Belgrave Road, London, S.W.1.

HOULDSWORTH (Miss), Ada; operatic dancer, general teacher. Intermediate Member Association of Operatic Dancing. Commenced teaching in 1927. Was a silver medallist in the Operatic Section at the Blackpool Festival in 1927. Is coach for the local Operatic Society.
Address: Dalkeith School of Dancing, 118 Whitham Road, Broomhill, Sheffield.
Best photos: Seaman & Sons, Sheffield.

HOWARD (Miss), Andree; classical ballet dancer. Pupil of Madame Marie Rambert. Member of the Ballet Club Company. Has appeared in *Carnaval* (Papillon); *Les Sylphides* (Mazurka); and in *Facade* (the Milkmaid and Tarantelle), etc., at the Ballet Club, and in all seasons at the Lyric, Hammersmith.
There is a section devoted to Andree Howard in the book by Arnold Haskell entitled " The Marie Rambert Ballet." (British-Continental Press, Ltd.).
Address: C/o The Ballet Club, 2a Ladbroke Road, London, W.11.

HUMBERSTONE (Miss), Vera; general teacher. Fellow Imperial Society of Teachers of Dancing (Operatic Branch), and Member of their General Branch. Member of Operatic Association. Has been teaching in Forest Hill and surrounding districts for the past twelve years, and has a large connection.
Address: 72 Woolstone Road, Forest Hill, London.

HUMPHREY (Miss), Joyce; general teacher. Member of the Imperial Society of Teachers of Dancing (Ballroom Branch).
Address: 3 Avenue Road, Sevenoaks, Kent.

HUSSAIN (Miss), Husna Jehan; Indian and Eastern dancer. Also holds the Casani certificate for ballroom dancing. Born in Bhagalpur, Behar, India, and is the daughter of a very old Muslim family. Began dancing career by having own studio in India and teaching dancing of all kinds. Afterwards toured that country with own small company. Since coming to England, has appeared at Covent Garden, and has also been filmed by the Gaumont Co. Has given a Recital and Lecture for the Faculty of Dancing. Has danced before the Prince of Wales and Prince and Princess Arthur of Connaught.
Address: C/o The Imperial Bank of India, 22 Old Broad Street, London, E.C.2.

HUSKISSON (Miss), C.; Branch Teacher for the Mersey and Deeside Branch of the English Folk Dance Society.
Address: Waterside Lodge, Barrel Well Hill, Chester.

HUTCHENS (Miss), M. L.; general teacher. Member Imperial Society of Teachers of Dancing (Ballroom and General branches); Member British Association of Teachers of Dancing, and on Executive Council since 1927; Glamorgan County Certificate for Physical Training; Drill Instructress under Southampton Education Authority. Began to teach dancing in 1900, and opened School at the Gordon Hall, Southampton, in 1913.

Address: Gordon House, 9 Carlton Road, Southampton.

HUTTON, Lois; danseuse and mime. Diplomée C.C.P.E. Senior dance teacher at Roedean School, 1918; principal dancer and teacher at Margaret Morris Theatre and School, 1920-1923; recital in Paris with Héléne Vanel and founded Studio, "Rhythme et Couleur." Opened classes for Greek dancing, decor, etc., at Saint Paul, Cannes; later in Paris. Ballets, "Rhythme et Couleur," performed in Paris, Belgium and Italy, 1926-1928; Théâtre, "Rhythme et Couleur," opened at Saint Paul, and inauguration of "Mardis de la Danse" in 1929, since when seasons have been given in Paris, Brussels, etc.
Address: Saint Paul, Alpes Maritimes, France.
Best Photos: Marant, Paris; Salerni, Nice; Bertram Park, London.

HUXLEY, Mr. and Mrs. Fred; teachers of ballroom dancing. Mr. Huxley is a Vice-President and Examiner of the Allied Dancing Association.
Address: 30a Oxton Road, Charing Cross, Birkenhead, Cheshire.

HYMAN, Prudence; ballet dancer. Holder of Cecchetti certificate. Studied under Marie Rambert. Appeared in the *Mars and Venus* Ballet in "Jew Suss." Has danced leading rôles at the Karsavina-Rambert seasons at the Lyric Theatre, Hammersmith, and at the Ballet Club. Was Columbine in Fokine's *Carnival*, Blue Bird in *Aurora's Wedding*, did waltz in *Les Sylphides*, and appeared in "Circus Girl" (Salaman-Bradford), etc. Danced at the Camargo Society's second and third performances, creating the rôle of Aurora in *Cephalus and Procris* (de Valois-Gretry), and of Cupid in *Valse Fantaisie* (Karsavina-Glinka). Première danseuse in Sir Nigel Playfair's *Aladdin*, 1931/2.
Books: A study of Prudence Hyman is included in "The Marie Rambert Ballet" by Arnold L. Haskell (British Continental Press).

Address: 24 Glebe Place, Chelsea, London, S.W.3.
Best photos by H. J. Whitlock & Sons, London.

I

IDLE (Miss), Doris; general teacher. Specialist in Greek Dancing. Advanced Member Association of Teachers of the Revived Greek Dance (Honours). Examiner for the Association, and also for Children's Examinations (Greek Branch). Trained at the Chelsea College of Physical Education, 1914-17, and gained a Distinction Diploma. Subsequently studied the Revived Greek Dance at the Ginner-Mawer School, whilst teaching at Roedean School, Brighton. Was one of the original members of the Association of Teachers of the Revived Greek Dance, passing both the Elementary and Advanced Examinations with Honours. Served on the Committee from its inauguration until 1928. Is now Principal of the Blackheath School of Dancing.
Address: Blackheath School of Dancing, "The Studio," 3 Blackheath Village, London, S.E.3.

IDZIKOWSKI, Stanislas; operatic dancer, teacher and choregraphist. Honorary Member Cecchetti Society. Born in Warsaw, and studied under Gilbert, Wiltzak and Enrico Cecchetti. First public appearance in *Ali Baba*, arranged by Auguste Berger, and first London appearance at Empire Theatre with Phyllis Bedells. Joined Pavlova's Company 1913, and Serge Diaghileff's Company at Lausanne, 1914. During 12 years with Diaghileff danced in many ballets, including Harlequin in *Carnaval*, Battista in *The Good Humoured Ladies*, Petrouchka in *Petrouchka*, the Cat in *Children's Tales*, the Snob in *La Boutique Fantasque*, the Spark in *The Three Cornered Hat*, etc., etc.; *pas de deux* in *The Blue Bird*, *Cimarosiana*, etc.; *pas de trois* in *Le Lac des Cygnes*, etc., etc. Appeared with Lydia Lopokova in a short season at the Coliseum, London, in 1924 in *The Soldier and Grizette* by Legat. Formed own Ballet Company and danced in *Les Roses*, produced by Massine at the Coliseum. Rejoined Diaghileff in Spain in 1926, later dancing with Lopokova at the Coliseum, London, in *The Postman*, by Legat. In 1928 appeared at His Majesty's Theatre, London, with Diaghileff's Company, and since then has toured England and Scotland, dancing, teaching and producing ballets, which include *The White Mask*, *Spring's Ecstasy* and *Divertissement*.

Author, with Cyril Beaumont, of " A Manual of Classical Dancing."

Address : 44 Bernard Street, Russell Square, W.C.1.

Best Photos : Numa Blanc, Monte Carlo.

IMPEKOVEN, Niddy; popular German concert dancer. Appeared first in Berlin, 1919, when only 15 years old, and became famous at once. Trained at the opera ballet school in Frankfurt, in Loheland, Dirlos u/Fulda. Works entirely alone. Very individual style. Has appeared in all important towns in Germany. Also abroad (India, Japan, etc.). In 1931 danced at the Arts Theatre Club in London.

Address : C/o Schiller Theatre, Berlin.

INYOKA, Nyota ; Oriental dancer. Born in Egypt of Egyptian-Indian parents. Has studied various techniques, ballet included, and has used them in the interpretation of Indian and Egyptian dances. Has danced at the Salon d'Automne, Théâtre de l'Oeuvre and in the festivals connected with the French Colonial Exhibition. Made two successful visits to London at the Arts Theatre Club. Her most famous dances are : The Nautch Girl, Krishna, Bedouin Girl, and Vishnou.

" Deux mots de l'avoir vue danser, me restent: simplicité, sourire . . ." says Fernand Divoire.

A study of Inyoka appears in Fernand Divoire's " Découvertes sur la danse."

IRVING (Mdme.), Ethel; director of dancing at the Irving Academy, Cheltenham, and at the Queen's Gate Hall, South Kensington, London. Madame Irving's Academy was primarily an Academy of Dramatic Art. Dancing was added to the curriculum in the year 1918.

Address : The Irving Academy, Cheltenham.

ISOBEL (Miss), Betty ; teacher of operatic dancing. Intermediate Member of the Operatic Association. Received her training from Miss Ruth French, and has recently opened her own School of Dancing at Thornton Heath.

Address : 44 Lyndhurst Road, Thornton Heath, Surrey.

IVANOVA (Mdme.), Rinka; operatic dancer and teacher. Trained in Brussels under Mdme. Cannes, of the Scala, Milan ; in Paris under Mdme. Mariquita at the Opéra Comique, and Mlle. Chasles from the Opéra. Danced in Brussels before the Queen of the Belgians. Booked by Mdme. Yvette Guilbert to dance in her Company in Paris and Brussels. Came to England and trained under Miss Lila Field. Toured England and Wales as *Prima Ballerina* and finally started a School of Dancing in Fulham.

Address : 55 Chelsea Road, Southsea, Hants.

Best photos : Elliott & Fry, and Hellis, London.

J

JACKSON (Miss), Eleanor M.; general teacher. Life Member of the Imperial Society. Commenced teaching in Cardiff in 1909 as successor to the late Miss Day.

Address : 37 Charles Street, Cardiff.

JACQUES, Henry; ballroom dancer and teacher. Member of the Imperial Society of Teachers of Dancing ; the National Association of Teachers of Dancing ; Allied Association of Teachers of Dancing ; and the Syndicat National des Professeurs de Danse et Danseurs Professionnels. Commenced his training under Madame

Calling of Southport, and afterwards was Head Assistant to the "Carl Muller School of Dancing," Southport. Later studied ballroom management, and has been manager of some of the principal Restaurant Ballrooms and Dance Halls in the Liverpool and Manchester district. Since 1930 has been Cabaret Manager of the Café de Paris, London. Was Finalist in the World's Championship, Paris, 1926; Winner of the " Pearce Shield " of the National Association of Teachers of Dancing, 1926 and 1927; Winner of the Northern Counties Professional Championship, 1926-7. Runner-up for the A.O.F.T. Championship in Liverpool, 1928-29. Runner-up for the Midland Counties Professional Championship and winner of the Waltz event, and of the Lancashire and Cheshire Tango Championship in 1930. In the " Star " Professional Championships for 1931 was fourth in the Waltz and Fox-trot, and third in the Quick-step competitions. Runner-up for the British Professional Championship in 1931 and 1932.

Address: 20 Adam Street, Portman Square, London, W.1.

Best Photos: Molloy, London.

JAMES, Leslie E.; ballroom teacher. Has arranged and acted as M.C. at a number of local dances.

Address: Newbridge House, Newbridge Road, Small Heath, Birmingham.

JAMES (Miss), Betty; general teacher. Holder of the First Class Certificate of the Ginner-Mawer School and their Teachers' Diploma. Winner of the Senior National Section in the All England Solo Dancing Competition in 1928.

Address: 81 Abington Street, Northampton.

Best photos: Navana, London.

JAMES, Phyllis (Mrs. E. Neasom Cluke); operatic, Greek and ballroom teacher. Trained at Liverpool Training College, and taught on the staff, 1923-1925; founded the Phyllis James School of Dancing and Physical Education, Northampton, in 1925, where all types of dancing, etc., are taught, and pupils prepared for examinations and competitions. Local Secretary for Children's Examinations of Operatic Association, 1929-1930. Runner-up *Dancing Times* Cup, All England Solo Competition, 1931.

Address: 81 Abington Street, Northampton.

JAMES, The Misses Doreen and Mavis; general teachers. Members of Operatic Association; Members of British Ballet Organization. Principals of the Mavdor School of Dancing.

Address: 13 Walliscote Grove Road, Weston-super-Mare.

JERMAINE (Miss), Lorna; operatic dancer. Advanced Member of the Operatic Association. Started as a child dancer in Percy Dunsford's Pantomimes at Exeter, her home town, in 1920 and 1921. Was afterwards trained by Madame J. Espinosa. Gained Senior Cup in the " All England " Solo Dancing Competition, and second prize in the *Dancing Times* Competition in 1925. Was pupil at the R.A.D.A. 1922-24 and was awarded a special prize for dancing by Lady Tree. After touring England, left for America in 1927 and toured in Keith and Orpheum circuits for twelve months. Afterwards appeared in Paris and Berlin. Has lately danced at London Clubs (Ciro's, etc.). She is one of the Paramount chief solo dancers. In August, 1930, had a six weeks' season as *première danseuse* in M. Santiago's ballet at the London Coliseum.

Address: 56 Upper Gloucester Place, London, N.W.1.

Best photos: Mannell, and Raphael, London.

JOHNS (Miss), Ena (Mrs. Richard Talmage); ballroom teacher. Member of the Imperial Society (Ballroom Branch). Passed Elementary and Intermediate Examinations of the Association of Operatic Dancing and the Elementary Cecchetti examination. Ballroom Examiner of the London Academy of Music. Commenced training at the Ruby Peeler School of

Dancing in 1924. Was " Star " finalist in 1928, 1929 and 1930.
Address: Ruby Peeler School of Dancing, Eccleston Hotel, Eccleston Square, London, S.W.1.
Best photos: Swaine, London.

JONES (Capt.), Charles B.; ballroom teacher. Host at the Pump Room, Bath. Has been a Member of the British Association of Physical Training.
Address: Cambridge House, Widcombe Hill, Bath, *and* 5 Connaught Place, Weston-super-Mare.
Best photos: " Bath Chronicle."

JOOS, Kurt; dancer, teacher and producer. Pupil of Rudolf von Laban. Member of the " Tanzbühne Laban," ballet master in Münster i. West. Ballet master of the " Städtische Bühnen, Essen " and director of the headquarters Laban School; Folkwang Schule, Essen, Abtlg. Tanz, where the Laban examinations are held. Produced numerous modern ballets at the theatre, and toured with his company. Some of his best known works are: *Larven, Die Brautfahrt, Koenig Drosselbarth*, Laban's *Gaukelei* at the Congress, Munich, 1930.
Address: Städtische Folkwangschulen, Essen/Ruhr.

JUAN and JUANITA; exhibition, acrobatic, ballet and character dancers. Appeared in the principal cabarets of Holland and Germany, and in Brussels and Paris. Also in many of the leading London hotels and clubs. Have danced at three Request Performances for Royalty for the Stage Guild.
Address: Albemarle Court Hotel, Leinster Gardens, London, W.2.
Best photos: Walden Hammond, Leamington Spa.

JUDSON, Stanley; operatic dancer and teacher. Member Operatic Association. Trained by Jeanie Smurthwaite, and was then seen by Espinosa, who offered him a tour of one year in Robert Courtneidge's production of " Catherine." Studied under Serge Morosoff, and in Paris under Volinine. In 1927 joined the late Anna Pavlova Company, later joining a musical production in London and playing at the Old Vic. Opened a school of dancing in London in 1929, but closed it to dance with the Chicago Civic Opera on tour in U.S.A. Has danced in pantomime with Molly Radcliffe, toured for Stoll and Paramount Films, Ltd., arranged ballets for Covent Garden Opera House, partnered Madame Lopokova, and is now with the Vic Wells Opera Company 1931-1932 as dancer and assistant stage manager. Appeared in the 1932 Camargo Season.
Address: " The Limes," Highgate Road, London, N.W.5.
Best Photos: Basil, London.

K

KARINA, Madame (Karina Janssen); *Prima Ballerina* Royal Opera, Copenhagen, and Covent Garden Opera, London. Educated at Royal Opera House, Copenhagen. Toured extensively in Europe. Appeared with Melba and Caruso at Royal Command Performance in London, May 14th, 1914. Opened School of Dancing in 1915.
Address: Royal School of Dancing, 29 King Henry's Road, London, N.W.3.
Best Photos: Elliot & Fry, London; Manuelle, Paris; Elfeldt, Copenhagen; Willinger, Berlin.

KARPELES (Miss), Maud; English Folk Dance teacher. Member of Committee, Examiner and late Hon. Secretary of the English Folk Dance Society.
Author of " The Lancashire Morris Dance " and " Twelve Traditional Country Dances," published by the English Folk Dance Society, and co-author with Cecil Sharp of the " Country Dance Book " (Part V), published by Novello & Co.
Address: 4 Maresfield Gardens, London, N.W.3.

KARSAVINA, Tamara (Mrs. H. J. Bruce); Prima Ballerina of the Imperial Ballet of St. Petersburg.

Educated at the Imperial Schools under Johanssen, Guerdt, Sokolova, Cecchetti, and in Milan under Beretta. Made her début with Fokine in *The Fisherman and the Pearl.* Danced leading rôles in all the classical repertoire. First tournée in Prague. First appearance in 1909 at the London Coliseum under the name of La Tamara. Prima Ballerina of the Diaghileff Ballet from its beginnings. For many years the Diaghileff contract depended upon Karsavina being its prima ballerina. Created such diverse and important rôles as The Young Girl in *The Spectre of the Rose* with Nijinski; the Dancer in *Petrouchka*; *Thamar*, the American Girl in *Parade*; the Miller's Wife in *The Three-cornered Hat*; *The Firebird*, etc. Her last creation was Juliet in *Romeo and Juliet*. Perhaps her greatest performance was in *Giselle* with Nijinski at the Paris Opera. Later, Karsavina made frequent appearances at the London Coliseum, in J. M. Barrie's *Truth About the Russian Dancers*, *Nursery Rhymes* (décor by Lovat Fraser), Handel's *Water music*, Strauss' *Galop*, etc. Made her last appearance with the Russian Ballet at Covent Garden, 1929, in *Petrouchka*. In 1930 gave a season at the Arts Theatre Club in *Le Spectre de la Rose* (with Harold Turner), *Mademoiselle de Maupin*, etc.; also appeared in *Carnaval* and *Les Syphides* with the Marie Rambert dancers at the Lyric, Hammersmith. Created and danced in *Valse-Fantaisie* (Glinka) at the third Camargo performance. Appeared with the Marie Rambert Ballet at the Lyric, Hammersmith, in June, 1931, creating the principal rôles in *Mercury* (Ashton-Satie) and *Waterloo and the Crimea* (Salaman-Berners).

"You are a great virtuoso," says the French critic, R. Broussel, "but the prestige of your technique is forgotten because of the charm of your art."

A. L. Haskell, in his study of her, says: "If Karsavina were unable to dance, she would still remain the world's greatest actress. It is only when we examine her achievements that we can realize her wonderful versatility: a young girl, dreaming of her first dance, a cruel oriental queen, a legendary bird of fire, a puppet, tragic, sentimental, mischievous, a Spanish miller's wife. Each rôle entirely different; each time a new and inspired Karsavina."

She has been a Member of the Council of the "Operatic Association" since the inception of that body, and is Vice-President of the "Camargo Society." She is the author of "Theatre Street" (Heinemann). Has been painted by Sargent, Glyn Philpot, Oswald Birley, Serov, Bakst, etc.

Books on Karsavina: in English, by Valerian Svetloff (Beaumont Press); by Arnold Haskell (British-Continental Press); in French by Jean Louis Vaudoyer, "Album dedie a T.K."; by Robert Broussel, "L'Heure dansante au Jardin du Roi"; in German "Der Feuervogel" by Grunenberg; in Russian by Andre Levinson, and is dealt with at length in all books on the Russian Ballet.

Address: 4 Albert Road, Regents Park, N.W.

KEEN (Miss), Hilda Cornock; teacher of English Folk Dancing. Is on the Headquarters Staff, and a Branch Teacher for the Birmingham District of the English Folk Dance Society, and is a representative of the Teaching Staff on the Branch Council of that society. In 1918-19 taught Folk Dancing and organised Demonstrations amongst soldiers in British Base Camps in France, and, after the Armistice, in Germany, under the auspices of the Lena Ashwell Concert Party. From 1920 to 1930 taught Folk Dancing in Cornwall, Devon, Sussex and Birmingham. In 1929 attended the Conference of International Congress of Folk Art at Rome, as representative of Great Britain.

Address: "Haresfield," Tuffley Crescent, Gloucester.

KEET (Miss), Pearl; teacher of operatic, national, Greek, musical comedy, tap and ballroom dancing, and elocution. Intermediate Member of the Association of Operatic Dancing; Fellow of the Imperial Society;

Holder of the I.L.A.M.'s bronze medal for Elocution. Teacher in various Schools, Clubs and Institutes, and also at her own School.
Address: 29 Loraine Mansions, Widdenham Road, London, N.7.

KEMP, Travis; operatic dancer. Intermediate Member Operatic Association. Trained at the Bush School, Nottingham. Was booked by Miss Ninette de Valois to appear in the Vic-Wells Ballets, and has danced in *Job, Regatta, Jew in the Bush*, etc. Has also appeared in Cabaret at the Trocadero Restaurant, Empress Rooms, etc., London, and in the provinces with Victor Leopold's Company. Appeared in *Rio Grande* at the first production of the Camargo Society, and on other occasions.
Address: C/o The Bush School of Dancing, 48 Forest Road West, Nottingham.

KENNEDY, Douglas; teacher of folk dancing. Director of the English Folk Dance Society, of which he is also a Lecturer and Examiner, and Member on the Board of Artistic Control. Was educated at George Watson's College, Edinburgh, and the Imperial College of Science. Has been Organising Director of the English Folk Dance Society since 1924 (on the death of its Founder, Cecil J. Sharp) and Director since 1928, also Founder Member since 1911.
Is *part editor* of "The Country Dance Book," Series I (E.F.D.S.), and has written various monographs and articles on folk dancing.
Address: Cecil Sharp House, 2 Regent's Park Road, London, N.W.1.
Best Photos: Bee Bolton, and Swaine, London.

KENNEDY (Mrs.), Helen; English folk dancer. Member, examiner, judge, teacher and demonstrator for English Folk Dance Society. Hon. Member and Professor of Folk Dancing at Royal College of Music. Began folk dancing in 1909, and became Hon. Secretary of small club, which was the nucleus of English Folk Dance Society, founded in 1911. Hon. Secretary for this society for eleven years; later a continuous member of Executive Committee. Fulfilled many appointments outside the Society, and was appointed Inspector of Folk Dancing for the Board of Education in 1920. Joint Editor of *Country Dance Book* (English Folk Dance Society).
Address: 10 Downside Crescent, London, N.W.3.

KILLEN, Joseph; general teacher, specializing in ballroom. Member and Examiner of the National Association of Teachers of Dancing; also the Allied Association. Has been President of the latter. Late instructor at the New Brighton Tower, Cheshire.
Address: Killen's School of Dancing, 85 Church Street, Egremont, Wallasey, Cheshire.

KINDERSLEY (Miss), A. H.; general teacher. Member of Association of Teachers of the Revived Greek Dance. Specialist in Children's work, Educational and Remedial. Adopts the D'Egville-Michau System of Physical Culture. Was Visiting Mistress at the Cheltenham Ladies' College 1918-19; at St. Margaret's School, Buxted, in 1918; at the Notting Hill High School in 1925, and at the North Middlesex School for Girls, Enfield, in 1927, etc. Principal of the Northern Heights School of Dancing since 1928, during which time the School has been awarded "The Pedlar's Fair" Shield for Group Dancing, 1929 and 1930, and the Silver Medal for Group Dancing at the "All England" Competition, 1930.
Address: The Northern Heights School of Dancing, The Gate House, Highgate, London, N.6.

KING (Miss), Estelle; teacher of all branches of dancing. Advanced Member Association of Operatic Dancing of Great Britain, and is also a "Children's Examiner" and "Local Organiser" for that Association. Received early training from the Gilmer School, and from Mdme. Louie, afterwards studying for some years with Espinosa.

KIN

Address: 159 Burngreave Road, Sheffield, and Winchester House, 44 Fargate, Sheffield.

KING (Miss), Lena (Lena Mayer King); operatic dancer and teacher. Advanced Member Operatic Association. Hon. Member Imperial Society of Teachers of Dancing. Made début as *première danseuse* at Empire Theatre, 1922; appeared in single turns at Palladium and in " Sally of the Sawdust," Empire Theatre, 1923; *première danseuse* at Plaza, in Trocadero Ballet, at Victoria Palace and Chiswick Empire, 1925-1926; toured as solo dancer in " Sunny," 1926-1928; solo dancer in Georges Carpentier's act, touring Great Britain and Roumania, 1928-1929; solo dancer at Coliseum, 1930, and at Le Paramount, Paris; has also toured Great Britain and South Africa as solo dancer and in single acts; appeared at all well-known cinemas, in pantomimes and in cabarets at London and provincial hotels, restaurants and dance halls.

Address: 49 Belsize Park Gardens, London, N.W.3.

Photos: Hana (now Navana), London.

KINNEY, Troy; painter, etcher and writer. Hon. Member Dancers' Club (N.Y.); American Society of Teachers of Dancing; Print Club of Philadelphia; Member Architectural League (N.Y.); Elihu (Yale University); Belta Kappa Epsiton; Brooklyn and Chicago Societies of Etchers. Trained at Yale Art School and Chicago Art Institute. Newspaper work until 1920, when he began to write articles on dancing, choregraphic art, etc.

Author (in collaboration with his wife), of " The Dance, its place in Art and Life " (Stokes).

Address: Falls Village, Connecticut, U.S.A.

KIRKWHITE (Miss), Iris; operatic, tap, and character dancer; general teacher. Advanced Member of the Operatic Association. Began to study dancing seriously at the age of 12, and passed the Advanced Examination of the Operatic Association at the age of 14, being at that time the youngest Advanced Member. Commenced stage career in the chorus of " The Blue Mazurka " at Daly's Theatre, and was afterwards chosen for the principal dancer in " Sunny " on tour. Then joined the cast of " Charlot's 1928 Revue," and afterwards danced solo in cabaret at the majority of the principal hotels and clubs in London. Joined the cast of " Follow Thru' " at the Dominion Theatre, London, and later became solo dancer in " Rio Rita " at the Prince Edward Theatre, London, going on tour with " Rio Rita " as principal dancer and juvenile lead. Led " The Moonlight Ballet " at the London Coliseum. Was principally trained by her sister, Miss Sylvia Kirkwhite, and is now teaching with her at their own school in London. Her recently formed partnership with Errol Addison in exhibition dancing has proved remarkably successful and they appeared at the Royal Command Performance at the Palladium in May, 1932.

Address: 16 Linden Gardens, Notting Hill Gate, London, W.2.

Best photos: Dorothy Wilding, London; Capstack, Blackpool.

KIRKWHITE (Miss), Sylvia (Mrs. Sylvia Fenwick); operatic and character dancer; general teacher. Member of the Imperial Society of Teachers of Dancing (Ballroom). Studied with Novikoff. Joined the Anna Pavlova Company, and toured with them for some years. Is now teaching with her sister, Miss Iris Kirkwhite, at their own school in London.

Address: 16 Linden Gardens, Notting Hill Gate, London, W.2.

Best photos: Sonya Solnitz, Berlin.

KIRSANOVA (Mdme.), Nina. *Première danseuse* Anna Pavlova Co. Born in Moscow. Studied dancing with Neledova. Was engaged by Novikoff at the age of 16 and worked with him. Studied for two years with Gorsky and Legat. *Prima ballerina* of Theatre of Musical Drama, Moscow. Left Russia in 1922. First dancer at Lemberg Opera. Toured Poland. *Première danseuse* at Opera at Belgrade. Went to France and danced

at Nice and at the Opera Comique. Toured South America. Joined Pavlova in 1921 at Rotterdam and remained with her until her death, touring Europe, Egypt, India, Burma, Straits Settlements, etc. Has taken the lead during her career in such ballets as *Coppelia, Lac des Cygnes, Magic Flute, Khovantchina*, etc.
Address : 40 Rue Poussin, Paris.
Best photos : Studio Iris, Paris.

KLAMT, Jutta; dancer, teacher and choreographer. Principal of the Jutta-Klamt School in Berlin, founded 1917. Own acknowledged system of training. Dance group since 1920. Filmed for first colour movietone (dance) film for UFA in Berlin, 1932. Married to her co-principal, Jo Vischer. Council Member of the "Deutsche Tanzgemeinschaft."
Address : Berlin-Grunewald, Gillstr, 10.
Best Photos : Robertson, Berlin.

KNUST, Albrecht; pupil and assistant of Rudolf von Laban, principal of the Laban School in Hamburg. Leader of the Hamburg Amateur Movement Chorus. Has done a considerable amount for the furtherance of chorus movement, and produced numerous compositions of this. Makes a special feature of the development of dance-writing, Kinetographie (for group-work) on which he has published various essays and practical suggestions. Founded the "Hamburger Tanzschreibstube" in co-operation with Miss Azra von Laban, where scores for all types of dances are being written and published. Demonstrated at the Imperial Society's Congress in London in 1930.
Address : Hamburg 24, Schwanenwik 38.

KOSLOFF, Alexis; stage dancer. Educated at the Moscow Ballet School, making his *début* in 1905 at the age of 17. Has toured Europe with his own company. First engaged by the Metropolitan Opera House, New York, for the season 1922-1923, and subsequently retained by them for every season. Has arranged many important productions in America, among them being "Chu Chin Chow," "Sinbad," "Le Coq d'or," "Sunny," and others. As a teacher of dancing he has had charge of Ann Pennington, Gertrude Hoffman, Marion Davies, Louise Eaton, Marilyn Miller, etc.
Book : "Russian Ballet Technique."
Address : Metropolitan Opera House, or 171 West 71st Street, New York City.

KRAUS, Gertrud; leading modern dancer in Vienna. Own school and dance-group, with whom she created great impression at the last Dance Congress in Munich, 1930. Special feature dance compositions on Jewish themes and with Jewish music. Great success on tour through Palestine.
Address : Mariahilfstr. 53, Vienna VI.

KREUTZBERG, Harald; concert dancer. Was born in Reichenberg, Czechoslovakia, 1902. After studying painting at the Academy of Arts, in Dresden, took up dancing at the Wigman School, and shortly joined the Ballet at the Opera House in Hanover under the direction of Max Terpis, going a year later with him to the Staats Opera, Berlin, where he stayed for three years, eventually becoming first solo dancer. Then appeared at the Saltzburg Festival for Max Reinhardt, and afterwards went with the latter to America, where he appeared in "A Midsummer Night's Dream" and other plays. A Dance Recital with Tilly Losch in New York followed. Later, with Yvonne Georgi as his partner, he created and danced in many successful ballets, including *Creation of the World* (Milhaud), *Merry Go Round* (Fr. Wilckens), *The Planets* (Holst), etc., appearing at the Opera Houses in Hanover, Leipzig and Berlin. Afterwards fulfilled a three years contract of Dance Recitals in America, Yvonne Georgi still as his partner, with Fr. Wilckens at the piano. During 1932 is again appearing in America with a group, but without Yvonne Georgi. During the months of July and August, 1932, will be giving

lessons at the Salzburg Orchestral Academy.
Address: C/o F. Wilckens, Hertzstrasse 1, Hanover, Germany.

KRUGER, Enrique; amateur ballroom, exhibition and character dancer.
Address: Avenida Alfonso XIII., 343, Barcelona, Spain.

KURYLO, Edward J.; ballet master. Hon. Member Imperial Society of Teachers of Dancing; Académie des Maîtres de Danse de Paris; Union Internationale des Chorégraphers, Paris; Magyar Tánctanitók Országos Szövetsége, Budapest, etc. Born in 1883, entered Government Ballet School, Warsaw, at an early age; later became solo dancer in Grand Opera Ballet Company, Warsaw; studied dramatic arts at the " War. Tow. Muz " and received honorary presents from H.I.M. the late Czar of Russia. Premier dancer and *Maître de Ballet* at Empire Theatre, London; Ballet Director of Government Theatres in Warsaw; toured the world with his company. Danced with Anna Pavlova, Adeline Genée and Lydia Kyasht. Was President of the " Society of Teachers of Dancing in Poland " and the " Association of Professional Dancers in Poland." Published and edited a revue called *The Dance and Pastime*. Correspondent of *The Dance, The Dancing Master, Variety*, etc., etc. Government Examiner of Teachers of Social Dancing. Author of " The Folk, Court and Social Dancing," " The Theory of Ballet Dancing," (Warsaw).
Address: 15 Piwna, Warsaw, Poland.
Best Photos: Jan Malarski, Warsaw.

KYASHT (Mdme.), Lydia (Mrs. Lydia Ragosin); operatic dancer and general dancer. Trained at the Russian Imperial School of Dancing. Left there in 1905 and was immediately promoted to the rank of *première danseuse*. Came to England in 1908 to appear at the old Empire Theatre succeeding Adeline Genée, and following her month's contract was re-engaged and stayed there until the end of 1913. Went to the United States and appeared at Schubert's Winter Garden Theatre for three months, then returned to England to appear at the Coliseum. Did the Stoll tour, and afterwards danced with the Russian Ballet at the Alhambra. During the War again danced at the Coliseum, and also in Petrograd. After the War opened a School of Dancing in London which was carried on most successfully until 1925, when Mdme. Kyasht commenced touring the country with her own company. The tours lasted for four and a half years, after which time the whole company was booked by another company. Is still touring the provinces
Author of " My Romantic Recollections " (Brentano).
Address: 12 Cavendish Road, St. John's Wood, London, N.W.8.
Best Photos: Bassano; Navana; Foulsham & Banfield, London.

L

LAKE (Miss), Molly; operatic dancer and teacher. Fellow Imperial Society. Member Cecchetti Committee and examiner for Cecchetti Branch. Holder of Cecchetti's original certificate. Pupil of Astafieva and Cecchetti. Also studied with Egorova, Trefilova and Sedalba. Toured (and became soloist) with Pavlova in the Far East, America, Canada, Mexico and Europe. Also danced in England with Karsavina and Kyasht. Was *première danseuse* for some time at the Marigny Theatre, Paris, and afterwards at the Deutches Theatre, Munich. Appeared for Grigorieff in Italy, Monte Carlo and Paris. Taught for some time with Ninette de Valois, and has also taken over Mdme. Karsavina's classes during her absence.
Address: 80 Lexham Gardens, London, W.8.
Best Photos: Anton Salm, Munich.

LAMBERT, Constant; composer and conductor. Born in London in 1905. Composer *Romeo and Juliet*, first English ballet produced by Diaghileff

at Monte Carlo in 1926. A second ballet, *Pomona*, was produced by Nijinska at Buenos Aires in 1927, being produced for the first time in England at the opening performance of the Camargo Society, with choregraphy by Frederick Ashton, who also did the choregraphy for his *Rio Grande* for the same Society. Is Conductor for the Camargo Society and for the Vic-Wells Ballet.
Address: 15 Percy Street, London, W.1.

LAMBERT (Miss), Lillian F.; general teacher. Intermediate Member Operatic Association; Member Imperial Society of Teachers of Dancing (Ballroom branch); Gold Medal of Incorporated London Academy of Music (Elocution). Trained for Operatic examinations at the Cone School and for Ballroom examination with Ruby Peeler. Founded the Lillian Lambert School of Dancing and Elocution in 1925, where students are trained in all branches of dancing.
Address: 2 Howard Terrace, Brighton.

LASCELLES, Robert; operatic and character dancer. Member of the Swedish Ballet 1921-3, and was with the Pavlova Company from 1923 to 1927. Danced in J. C. Williamson's Company's productions in Australia in 1927 and 1928. Has since come to England, and with Miss Thurza Rogers has produced an act known as " Rogers and Lascelles with Jean, Joan and Jill," which has appeared at all the leading Music Halls and the West End Cabarets.
Address: " Four Winds," Blue Anchor Bay, Somerset.
Best photos: Lenare, London.

LAWLESS (Miss), Pat; general teacher. Holder of Casani Certificate. Has studied Italian, Spanish and German dancing.
Address: The St. Margaret Academy of Dancing, 7 New Steine, Brighton.

LAWRENCE (Miss), Moreen (Mrs. Donald Cunary); general teacher. Advanced Member (Solo Seal) of the Operatic Association; also Examiner of the Children's Examinations. Council Member and Examiner of the Imperial Society (Operatic, Cecchetti, Ballroom, Greek and General). Advanced Member of the Association of Teachers of the Revived Greek Dance. Born in Scotland and received early training from Mr. J. B. McEwen. Studied in London with Mdme. Astafieva, Mr. Espinosa and Mdme. Karsavina. Is well known for her Scottish dancing.
Address: 53 Mansfield Road, Ilford, Essex.
Best photos: Claude Harris, London.

LAWSON (Miss), Joan; operatic dancer and choreographer. Studied with Margaret Morris and Mme. Astafieva, and appeared as a soloist in the Margaret Morris Troupe; also in the Carl Rosa Opera Company and B.N.O.C. Ballets. Played *The Jackdaw of Rheims* for Julian Wylie for two years, and was soloist in his pantomimes. Appeared with Anton Dolin's Ballet in London and on the Continent; also in many cabarets. Is now running own ballet, consisting of Elizabeth Allison, Rosemary Rees and Gwen Wilby, and with them has appeared in Robert Courtneidge's "Lavender" Company and Catlin's Royal Pierrots in own original ballets.
Address: 90 Oakwood Road, Hampstead Garden Suburb, London, N.W.11.
Best photos: Sasha, London; and Guttenberg, Manchester.

LAZENBY (Miss), Olive A.; general teacher. Principal of School of Dancing, which is the headquarters for Operatic Association Examinations in Newcastle.
Address: Lambton House, 28 Great North Road, Newcastle-upon-Tyne.

LEANING (Mrs.), E. E.; teacher of ballroom, Greek and mime dancing. Holder of Casani Certificate for ballroom dancing.
Address: 14 North Street, Gainsborough, Lincs.

LEE (Mdme.), Nancy; ballroom, step and operatic teacher. Past Vice-President of the British Association of Teachers of Dancing. Has adjudicated in a number of competitions. Had a studio for some time in Newman Street, Oxford Street, London.
Address: Melba House, St. Saviour's Road, London, S.W.2.
Best photos: Neame, London.

LEGAT, Nicholas. Professor of Russian Operatic Dancing. Member of Beaux Arts (France), and of the Imperial Society of Teachers of Dancing. *Born* 1873 at St. Petersburg. Received first dancing lessons from his father, Gustav Legat, then premier soloist of Imperial Theatre. At Imperial Ballet School studied first under Gerdt and then under Christian Johanssen. First solo *début* in Imperial Marinsky Theatre at age of 18 while senior pupil at Ballet School in *Pachita*. Subsequently danced principal rôles in over 70 ballets, including all chief productions of Petipa, Ivanoff and Volkoff. In 1904, at the Imperial command, staged *The Fairy Doll* at Hermitage private Imperial Theatre, and then succeeded Petipa as first *Maître de Ballet* of Marinsky Theatre, producing *Talisman, Crimson Flower, Blue Beard, Two Robbers, Four Seasons*, etc. Upon retirement of Christian Johanssen from post of Senior Instructor of Imperial Ballet School and Director of Class of Perfection, Legat, at Johanssen's request, succeeded to these posts, at same time remaining First Soloist and *Maître de Ballet* of the Marinsky Theatre. Among his pupils in the Class of Perfection and for private tuition were the following: M. Kseshinskaya, L. Egorova, L. Kyasht, O. Preobrazhenskaya, Vera Trefilova, Anna Pavlova, T. Karsavina, A. Vaganova, J. Sedova, M. Fokine, V. Nijinsky, M. Oboukhoff, T. Kosloff, A. Bolm, A. Gavriloff, A. Volinine, Andrianoff and many others. Legat served in the Imperial Russian Ballet for 25 years, was decorated by the Tsar, received the title of Soloist of His Majesty, and was granted a life pension. Leaving the Imperial Stage in 1914, he toured in Italy, France and England with his young pupil, Nadejda Nicolaeva. Returning to Russia, where Nicolaeva was engaged at the Moscow Grand Theatre, they undertook a tour throughout Russia, but were obliged to escape from the revolutionary régime in 1925. In 1926-1927 Legat was instructor to the Diaghileff Company, but severed this connection owing to differences over Diaghileff's later tendencies. Legat is direct transmitter of the Russian School in its purest form. Among the younger generation who have received tuition from him are: Nadejda Nicolaeva, V. Nemtchinova, A. Danilova, L. Lopokova, V. Novikoff, A. Oboukhoff, S. Lifar, and among English dancers Phyllis Bedells, N. de Valois, A. Dolin and many others. Legat has been married three times, his third wife being his pupil, Nadejda Nicolaeva. Besides his speciality as dancer and Professor, Legat is also a musician and artist. He was honorary member of the Russian Imperial Society of Watercolour Painters, and his drawings were exhibited at several exhibitions. He holds the Palme Académique des Beaux Arts (France), and is a Vice-President of the Imperial Society of Teachers of Dancing.
Book: "The Russian School of Dancing" (British Continental Press).
Studio Address: 46 Colet Gardens, London, W.14.

LEHMISKI (Mdme.), Helena; general teacher. Principal of the Studio School of Dancing, Birmingham.
Address: Shaftesbury Buildings, 61 Station Street, Birmingham.

LEOFFELER (Madame), Lilian; teacher of all branches of stage dancing, specializing in operatic work. Registered Theatrical Manager. First appeared as child dancer and toured the Continent. Later presented her own act. In 1909 took control of the dancing section of the well-known Stedman's Theatrical Academy, and remained there for 17 years. Has trained many successful dancers. Anna Pavlova and Serge Diaghileff repeatedly selected her pupils for their

Companies. Hilda Butsova, Lydia Sokolova and Vera Savina are three of her pupils. Has arranged the dancing for Royal Opera at Covent Garden, for the Coliseum, Alhambra, Victoria Palace, etc. Started her own School in 1926, presenting dance-scenas and film prologues (then a novelty) at cinemas. Has successfully launched a number of variety acts, and toured the " Leoffeler Dancers," who number 24.
Address: 91 Great Portland Street, London, W.1.
Best photos: Pearl Freeman, London.

LEOPOLD, Victor; tap dancer. A member of the well-known family of acrobats and dancers. In 1909, at the age of 10, appeared in pantomime at Glasgow, and has played juvenile dancing lead for Clayton and Waller, Walter Bentley, Fred Karno and Frank E. Franks amongst others, and worked music halls and cabarets with his own act. For eleven summer seasons appeared at Skegness for Mr. Fred Clements. Is now teaching tap dancing at the Bush School of Dancing, Nottingham, of which his wife is Principal.
Address: Stamford House, Forest Road West, Nottingham.
Best Photos: Capstack, Blackpool.

LESLIE, David; musical comedy and speciality dancer. Is partnered by his wife, Erica Leslie. They commenced their dancing career at the Claridge Hotel, Paris, by taking the place of Marjorie Moss and Georges Fontana. Continued under same management for two years (including Riviera, Paris and Vichy bookings). Returned to London and danced at the Piccadilly Hotel, afterwards making their first stage appearance at the Palladium, then dancing at Ciro's. Returned to the Continent, and fulfilled a very successful Paris season, followed by engagements in Brussels, The Hague, and Berlin. Again came to London, and during an engagement at the Coliseum, met Frederick Jackson, and as a result of the meeting played their first speaking parts in two of his plays.
Address: 22 Cliveden Place, Eaton Gate, London, S.W.1.
Best photos: Sasha, and Vaughan & Freeman, London.

LESLIE (Mrs.), Erica; musical comedy and speciality dancer. (*See David Leslie*.)

LEX, Maja; dancer and teacher at the Günther School, Munich. Leading dancer of the Günther Tanzgruppe, which was a special feature at the Dance Congress in Munich in 1930 and the Olympia della Grazia in Florence, 1931, through " Barbarische Suite," dance composition for group in five parts, with accompaniment of a special new percussion orchestra.
Address: Günther Schule, Munich, Luisenstr. 21.

LIFAR, Serge; *premier danseur* and *maître de ballet*. Born in Kieff, April 2, 1905. Began to study dancing in 1920 and was engaged by Serge Diaghileff three years later. His first important rôle was the " Assistant " in *La Boutique Fantasque*, but he made his *début* as *premier danseur* in *Zephyr and Flora* at Monte-Carlo, and in *Les Matelots* in Paris, 1925. Created the choreography for Stravinsky's *Renard*, Paris, 1929. Engaged by the Paris Opera as *premier danseur* and choregraphist, and created *Les Créatures de Prométhée* of Beethoven on December 30, 1929. In March, 1930, created Sauguet's *Night*, and appeared in Berner's *The Freaks* for Mr. C. B. Cochran. Serge Lifar possesses an important collection of pictures and designs by well-known artists connected with the ballet, and these have been exhibited in London and Paris. His rôles with Diaghileff include principal parts in *Barabau, Romeo and Juliet, Pastorale, Le Triomphe de Neptune, La Chatte, Le Pas d' Acier, Ode, Apollon, Le Bal, Le Fils Prodigue*, besides which he has danced in many of the rôles of the regular repertoire, such as *Swan Lake, Les Sylphides*, etc. Has danced with Spessiva in a revival of *Giselle* at the Paris Opera.

Address: Théâtre National de 'Opera, Paris.
Best photos: Lipnitski, Paris; Numa Blanc, Monte-Carlo; and Sasha, London.

LILLY (Miss), Gertrude; general teacher. Member of Operatic Association; Member Imperial Society of Teachers of Dancing (Ballroom branch). Gained Silver Medal for Operatic Dancing 1926-27 at competition held at Crane Hall, Liverpool. Principal of large school of dancing in Wallasey, where all types of dancing are taught.
Address: 27 St. James Road, Wallasey, Cheshire.

LINDOWSKA (Mdme.), Linda; operatic dancer and teacher; ballroom teacher. Trained under Enrico Cecchetti, Alexander Genée, Ivan Clustine and Michael Fokine. Was a soloist for eleven years with Mdme. Anna Pavlova.
Address: 154 Cranbrook Road, Ilford, Essex; also 43 Knightsbridge, London, S.W.1.

LINDSAY, Cecil Maylor; ballroom dancer and teacher, and writer. Associate Member of the Ballroom and Classical Ballet (Cecchetti) Branches of the Imperial Society of Teachers of Dancing. Previously principal of the Desnaux School, Malden, and chief ballroom instructor for Miss Belle Harding. Member of the Press Club, London, and Sub-Editor of the *Encyclopaedia Britannica*.
Address: C/o the Imperial Society of Teachers of Dancing, 113 Charing Cross Road, London, W.C.2.

LINES, Phil; general teacher; arranger of ballets and ensembles. Inaugurated the Phil Lines Theatrical Booking Offices in 1919.
Address: 151 Napier Road, Gillingham, Kent.

LITTLEWOOD (Miss), Letty; general teacher. Member of the Operatic Association; Member Imperial Society (Ballroom Branch). Trained at the Bostock and Brown School, and also by Miss Ninette de Valois. For some years has been associated with the Wimbledon Conservatoire of Music.

Has contributed articles on dancing to the press, and is part *author* of " The Bower Book " and " Our Nursery Rhyme Book " (Herbert Daniel).
Address: 220 Worple Road, Wimbledon, London, S.W.
Best Photos: Maud Shelley and Russell & Sons, Wimbledon.

LLOYD (Miss), Gweneth. Member of the Association of Teachers of the Revived Greek Dance, and also of the Greek and Ballroom Branches of the Imperial Society. Co-Principal with Miss Doris McBride of the Torch School of Dance, Leeds.
Address: 50 Wellington Street, Leeds.

LLOYD (Miss), Lillias; ballroom teacher. Member British Association Vice-President 1929-1930, and Examiner for Lancashire District; Member Nederlandsche Vereeniging Van Dansleeraren. Adjudicator All England Festival, Liverpool, 1930, and Blackpool Festival, 1931.
Address: 26 Wembley Road, Mossley Hill, Liverpool.

LLOYD (Miss), Maude; classical ballet dancer. Member Imperial Society (Cecchetti Branch) and on the Board of Examiners of that Society in South Africa. Member of the Marie Rambert Ballet, and has appeared with them at seasons at the Lyric Theatre, Hammersmith, the New Theatre and the Ballet Club, etc. Has also danced for the Camargo Society on various occasions. She has appeared in various roles of the classical repertoire, and has created parts in *Façade*, *Lady of Shalott*, and the leading role " Olivia " in Antony Tudor's *Cross-Gartered*. Created " Marianna " in Ashton's *My Lord of Burleigh* (originally produced at the " Midnight Ballet " Carlton Theatre).

There is a reference to Maude Lloyd in " The Marie Rambert Ballet " by Arnold L. Haskell (British-Continental Press, Ltd.).

Address: 49 Weltevreden Street Gardens, Cape Town, South Africa; and C/o The Ballet Club, 2a Ladbroke Road, London, W.11.

LOBEL (Miss), Sali; general teacher. A Roumanian artiste who has a big School of Dancing, Elocution, Physical Culture and the kindred arts in Manchester. Miss Lobel is well known as a lecturer on the history of dancing, as a danseuse, reciter and exhibition dancer. Has recently completed an extensive tour of the United States, and is organiser of the " First International Summer School " to be held at Buxton in 1932.
Address: 260 Oxford Road, Manchester.
Best photos: Warwick Brookes Studios, and Oxford Studios, Manchester.

LOPOKOVA, Lydia (Mrs. J. M. Keynes); *première danseuse*. Was educated at the Imperial School, St. Petersburg. Was a member of the original Diaghileff Ballet, and at one time *prima ballerina* of the Ballet. Partnered by Leonide Massine appeared in *The Midnight Sun, Children's Tales, The Good Humoured Ladies, Les Sylphides*, etc. Perhaps her greatest roles were her creations of the " Can Can dancer " in *La Boutique Fantasque* and "Columbine" in *Carnaval*. Danced the " Princess Aurora " and the " Lilac Fairy " in *The Sleeping Princess* at the Alhambra Theatre. Her last appearance with the Diaghileff Ballet was in the revival of *The Firebird*. Danced and acted at the Arts Theatre Club, December, 1930.
" Lydia Lopokova has contributed a series of unique portraits to the gallery of ballet memories. She may well be called incomparable. Her particular contribution has been the spirit of youth, freshness and mischief. The creator of Columbine in *Carnaval*, the spirit of Columbine is present in all her work; yet she is an actress of great subtlety, carefully choosing the degree and the quality of her mischief." (From an article by Arnold L. Haskell.)

There is a bust of Lydia Lopokova by Frank Dobson, and portraits by Duncan Grant.
Is on the Committee of the "Camargo Society " and has appeared in several of that Society's productions.
Address: 46 Gordon Square, Bloomsbury, London, W.C.1.

LORRAINE (Mdme.), Ethel; general teacher. Member of the Faculty of Dancing. Pupil of Santos Casani and Lillian Ware. First public appearance in pantomime in 1911; toured in revues and pantomimes for Harry Day and Bros. Hannaway. Since 1920 has taught in Chiswick, giving many displays, etc.
Address: 2 Bourne Place, Chiswick, London, W.4.
Best Photos: Messrs. Wakefield, Ltd., London.

LOSCH, Tilly; *première danseuse* of the Vienna State Opera. Made her London *debut* at the London Pavilion, and danced in two Cochran revues. Her greatest success was in *Gothic* (with Lauri Devine) and in *Hands* (Ravel). Danced at the Salzburg Festival, 1928. Has since been appearing in New York. Takes the part of the " Nun " in ' The Miracle " at the Lyceum revival of that play in 1932.
Address: 3 Culross Street, London, W.

LOWE (Mrs.), George; general teacher. Has been in the dancing profession for thirty years—at first in partnership with her husband, and since his death with her daughter, Mrs. Pearson. Both are well known in Scotland, and are recognised authorities on Highland dancing. They hold appointments in a number of the best schools in and around Edinburgh.
Address: 6 Ethel Terrace, Edinburgh.

LUCAS (Miss), Margaret; teacher of ballroom dancing. Trained by Miss Josephine Bradley. Licensed by the University Authorities to teach dancing to members of Oxford University. Specialises in private lessons,

which are given at Stewart's Restaurant, Cornmarket Street, Oxford.
Address: 281 Woodstock Road, Oxford.
Best photos: Tegner, Oxford.

LUDMILA (Miss), Anna; operatic dancer. Trained in the United States by Bolm, Pavley, Oukrainsky, Tarasoff, etc. Made her debut as a soloist at the age of 13 at the Carnegie Hall with the New York Symphony Orchestra. Appeared in "Greenwich Village Follies," and was principal dancer to the Chicago Opera Company. Danced at the Colon Theatre, Buenos Aires, with Bolm, and was a soloist with the Ida Rubenstein Company in Paris. Was about to join his company when M. Diaghileff died. Partnered Anton Dolin at the London Coliseum and elsewhere, and has appeared in cabaret and revue. Her outstanding success in this country has been in the name part in the ballet *Pomona* for the "Camargo Society." Has adjudicated at several important Dance Festivals including the "Sunshine" and "Blackpool."
Address: 27 Gower Street, London, W.C.1.

LUDWIG, Frank; ballroom teacher. Member International Dancing Masters Association, and on Executive. Member Midland Association of Teachers of Dancing. Past President English Association of Dancing Masters and was General Secretary of that Association during the negotiations for amalgamation with the International Association. Has promoted several dances in North London. Principal of the Enfield School of Dancing, Parsonage Lane, Chase Side, Enfield, founded in 1921.
Address: 68 Falmer Road, Enfield, Middlesex.

M

MAC (Mrs.), Hildora; ballroom teacher. Member Imperial Society of Teachers of Dancing (Ballroom Branch). Head of the Ballroom Branch at the Cone School of Dancing, London. Winner of the Imperial Society's Competitions and others.
Address: 10 Arkwright Mansions, Finchley Road, London, N.W.

McBRIDE (Miss), Doris; teacher of the Revived Greek Dance, and Character Dancing. Advanced Member (Honours Certificate), and also Examiner of the Association of Teachers of the Revived Greek Dance. Received training from the Ginner-Mawer School, gaining Diploma. Member of the staff of that School 1922-27, after which opened "The Torch School of Dance," Leeds, in September, 1927.
Address: Torch School of Dance, 50 Wellington Street, Leeds.

McCARTHY (Miss), Sheila; operatic and character dancer. Advanced Member of the Operatic Association. Is a prominent member of the Vic-Wells Ballet Company, and danced "Procris" in *Cephalus and Procris* with them. Was principal dancer in *Danse Sacrée and Danse Profane* at the Camargo Society's first production at the Cambridge Theatre.
Address: 38 Wickham Road, London, S.E.4.
Best Photos: Pearl Freeman, London.

MACDONALD, Edward William; ballroom teacher. Principal of Macdonald School of Dancing.
Address: 71 Balham High Road, London, S.W.12.
Best Photos: Wykeham Studios, Balham High Road, London, S.W.12.

MACFARLANE-MOORE (Miss), May; teacher of Scottish solo dances, hornpipes and jigs. Danced in U.S.A. before coming to England in 1926. Winner of the Lancashire and Cheshire Federation of Scottish Societies' Championship 1929-1930, and present holder of the Challenge Trophy 1931. Gold Medallist at Morecambe, Southport, Douglas Highland Gatherings, and at Cowal Games, Argyllshire. Recently opened Scottish School of Dancing, Blackpool.
Address: 267 Promenade, Blackpool.

McINTOSH, Alex; teacher of all branches of dancing. Member of the Council; Examiner for the General Teachers' Branch; and Member of the Greek, Cecchetti, General Teachers, and Ballroom Branches of the Imperial Society. Is also a Fellow of their Operatic Branch. Intermediate Member of the Association of Operatic Dancing of Great Britain. Holds full Teachers' Diploma of the British Ballet Organization. Has passed the Examinations of Teachers of the Revived Greek Dance—both in theory and practical work. Late Ballet Master to the Theatre Royal, Edinburgh. In 1930 and 1931 was engaged as Sole Instructor for the Congress of the Dutch Society—Ned. Genootschap van Beroepsdansleeraren.
Address: 3 Lansdowne Crescent, Glasgow, N.W.

McKAY (Miss), Jean; ballroom teacher. Secretary of the Ballroom Dancers' Association. Was a pupil of Mrs. Wordsworth from the age of 3, becoming a pupil teacher at the age of 14, and doing a great deal of solo stage work. Studied voice production and the organ, and sung a great deal just before and during the war, taking the solo in several big oratorios, but completely gave up singing in 1919. Trained in exhibition dancing with Moss and Fontana in 1920, and later in ballroom dancing with Mr. and Mrs. Alec Mackenzie, and Mr. T. C. Askew in speciality work. Started own School of Dancing with Charles de Cerjat in 1923, joining Mr. Maxwell Stewart in London in September, 1930.
Address: 37 Overstrand Mansions, Prince of Wales Road, London, S.W.11.
Best photos: Brights, Bournemouth.

McKENZIE (Miss), Frances; dancer and general teacher. For three successive seasons since 1926 produced revues, musical comedies, ballets and ensembles at a number of important Continental theatres. Is now in charge of the teaching at the Frank Perry School of Dancing, London.
Address: 48 Carnaby Street, Regent Street, London, W.1.
Best photos: Basil, London.

MACKENZIE, Alec. (Alexander MacKenzie); teacher of ballroom dancing. Fellow of the Imperial Society; Member of the New York Society Teachers of Dancing; Member Ballroom Dance Special Research Committee, U.S.A. Opened the MacKenzie School of Dancing in Queen's Road, Bayswater, London, in 1912, which he conducted there, and subsequently at Holland Park Avenue; Duke Street, St. James's; the Hotel Washington; the St. James's Palace Hotel and 99 Regent Street until 1928, with the exception of the War period, when the School was conducted by Mrs. Mackenzie. During the War he was wounded and captured in 1917, when he taught many of his brother officers, who were also prisoners of war, to dance. Adjudicated at the Finals of the World's, National and other outstanding ballroom dancing competitions until 1928, in which year he opened his School of Ballroom Dancing in New York, U.S.A. He instituted, under the auspices of the *Dance Magazine*, the first American Open Conference on Ballroom Dancing, from which a special Research Body was elected. In 1922 he brought from Paris the Tango exponent, Carlos Cruz, to be associated with the MacKenzie School in London. He holds the Carlos Cruz Cup, contested for at the Queen's Hall Competitions on January 9th, 1925, awarded to the producers of the Champion Amateur Tango couple.
Address: 812-815 Steinway Hall, West 57th Street, New York City.
Best Photos: Lenare, London: Mitchell, New York; Sobel, Paris.

MACLAREN (Miss), Euphan; teacher of all branches of stage work. Is the Principal of one of the most important schools in London. *Maitresse de Ballet* of the Lyceum Theatre pantomimes, and arranges the dances for a number of other London theatres. Choregraphist for the annual production of "Hiawatha" at the Royal Albert Hall. The "Euphan MacLaren Dancers," "The Piccadilly Six," "The Dancing Daffodils" and "The Henriette Fuller Dancers" are some of the

well-known troupes produced at her School. Adjudicates at many important Festivals.
Address: 10 Scarsdale Villas, Kensington, W.8.

MACLENNAN, D. G. Member of the Council of the Operatic Association since 1923. As a boy was trained by his brother (the late William MacLennan, who had been a pupil of Cecchetti), and specialised in National Dancing, first gaining amateur championships, and afterwards, as a professional, being acclaimed the "Premier British National Dancer," winning the Champion Cup for the sixth consecutive time in 1910, after which he retired from competitions. He studied for a time under Alexander Genée, sharing the lessons given to Madame Adeline Genée, and also with Victor Chiado, who produced Kiralfy's colossal ballets at Olympia. Held an annual summer course in New York before the war, where he was appointed Foreign Instructor to the American National Association. He was the first to show the fox-trot and other American dances in this country. Has arranged several dances for Madame Adeline Genée, including her "Sailor's Hornpipe" and "English Jig," and some of the dances in "The Pretty Prentice." Is now teaching in Scotland.
Address: Albert Hall, Shandwick Place, Edinburgh.

MADDOCKS (Miss), Kathleen L.; general teacher.
Address: 79 Cotham Brow, Bristol.

MAKAND (Miss), Ruth; operatic and tap dancer. Began training at an early age at the Belle Harding School at Edinburgh, and, later, at the De Vos School, Weymouth, and the Max Rivers School, London. When 17 joined the De Vos School in London to study more advanced operatic and tap dancing under Mr. Fred Lord. At her first audition for professional work was chosen to partner Harold Turner in "Bow Bells" at the London Hippodrome.

Address: "Annesville," Alexandra Road, Weymouth, Dorset.

MANGAN, Francis A.; producer of dance presentations. Born in Pennsylvania, U.S.A. Has been Presentation Director for the Paramount Company in Europe since 1926. Previous to that, organized stage presentations for Paramount in New York, Cleveland, Detroit, St. Louis, Los Angeles and Canada. Dancing troupes include the Plaza-Tiller Girls, the 24 Mangan-Tillerettes, the 24 Mangan-Tiller Girls, the Paramount-Tiller Girls, and the Carlton-Tiller Girls and Mayfair-Tiller Girls. These troupes are the outstanding features of the Mangan productions, and the presentations are built round them.
Address: C/o Paramount Theatres, 104-108 Oxford Street, London, W.1.

MARKHAM (Miss), Agnes; general teacher. Member of the Imperial Society (General Branch).
Address: 18 Spring Mount, Harrogate.

MARKOVA (Miss), Alicia; ballet dancer. Studied with Seraphine Astafieva. Joined the Diaghileff Ballet at the age of 13. Danced the adagio from *Lac des Cygnes*; Red Riding Hood in *Aurora's Wedding*; *pas de trois* in *Cimarosiana*; *The Cat*; created The Nightingale in Balanchine's version of *The Story of the Nightingale* (Stravinsky), etc. Danced with Frederick Ashton in *Marriage à la Mode*. Created rôle of *Procris* in *Cephalus and Procris* (De Valois and Gretry), and also the Polka in *Façade* (Ashton and Walton) for the Camargo Society. Appeared as a guest artist at the Ballet Club, creating *La Péri* (Ashton and Dukas), and appearing in *Aurora's Wedding*; adagio from *Lac des Cygnes*, *Facade*, etc. Danced as guest artist during the 'Vic-Wells" special season, 1932.
Book: "Study of Alicia Markova" (British Continental Press).
Address: 48 St. Quentin's Avenue, North Kensington, London.
Best photo: Raphael, London.

MARSH, Gordon; general teacher. Member Imperial Society of Teachers of Dancing. Producer of Concert Parties and Musical Productions. Producer for Concert Party for Margate Corporation. Proprietor of the Cabaret "Gordon Marsh and the Marshmallow Girls." Has performed before Their Majesties The King and Queen, and also before T.R.H. The Prince of Wales and The Duke of York in the winter 1930-31.
Address: 128-130 High Street, Kensington, London, W.8.

MARSHALL (Miss), Mary W.; general teacher. Member of the Association of Operatic Dancing; Fellow of the Imperial Society. Received her early training from Miss Ruby Flatow. Is a well-known teacher and dancer throughout Cumberland and Westmorland and the Southern Counties of Scotland.
Address: 11 Eldred Street, Warwick Road, Carlisle.
Best photos: F. W. Tassell, Carlisle.

MARSTON, John S.; ballroom teacher. Member and examiner National Association Teachers of Dancing. Secretary and examiner of the Northern Counties Dance Teachers' Association.
Address: 80 High West Street, Gateshead, Co. Durham.

MARTELL (Miss), Flo; stage, operatic, acrobatic, tap and musical comedy dancer; producer for professionals, etc. Began career at Empire, Leicester Square, appearing in ballets for 23 years, being Ballet Mistress for George Edwarde's at the Gaiety and Adelphi Theatres. Appeared as Rip in *Rip Van Winkle* with Genée; the Reaper in *The Reaper's Dream*, with Lydia Kyasht; Diana in the ballet *Sylvia*. Appeared as name part in *Faust* in America, and produced *The Girl from Utah* for Frohman. School was opened during the last years of Ballet at the Empire, many well-known artistes having been trained there.
Address: 20 Fitzroy St., London, W.1.
Best Photos: Navana, London.

MARTIN (Miss), Desiree. Certificated teacher of Dalcroze Eurythmics. Member of a Plastic Group of Dancers. Is the composer of Chamber Music and Music for Movement. Holds Remedial Classes.
Address: 21 Holland Park, London, W.11.

MARTIN, John; dance critic of the *New York Times*. Faculty Lecturer at the New School for Social Research. Has contributed articles on dancing to the "Encyclopaedia of the Social Sciences," the "National Encyclopaedia," the "Drama Magazine," the "Theatre Arts Monthly," the "Theatre Guild Magazine," "Schrifttanz" (Vienna), etc.
Address: 3742, 84th Street, Jackson Heights, New York, U.S.A.

MASSINE, Leonide; classical ballet dancer and choreographer. Educated at the Imperial Schools in Russia. Succeeded Fokine and Nijinsky as *premier danseur* and choregraphist of the Diaghileff Ballet. His most famous works are *Joseph's Legend, Midas, Coq d'Or, The Midnight Sun, Children's Tales, Parade, Good Humoured Ladies, Boutique Fantasque, Three Cornered Hat, Pulcinella, Cimarosiana, Chout*. Left the Diaghileff Ballet and returned later to produce *Zephyrs and Flora, Les Matelots, Mercury* and *Le Pas d'Acier*. As a dancer perhaps his greatest roles have been as "The Miller" in *The Three Cornered Hat*, for which he made a thorough study of Spanish dancing; as the "Can-Can Dancer" in *Le Boutique Fantasque*. Was Ballet Master of the Roxy Theatre in New York for many years. In 1932 produced *Jeux d'Enfants* at Monte Carlo and the dances in "Helen" and "The Miracle" for Mr. Cochran in London. In the last-named gave a striking performance as the "Spielmann."
All works on the Russian Ballet contain studies of Massine.

MAWER (Miss), Irene; mime, actress and verse speaker. Member Association of Teachers of Speech Training; Hon. Member Association of Teachers of Revived Greek Dance. Co-Principal of Ginner-Mawer School of Dance and Drama. Training and Dramatic Art. Appeared with Ruby Ginner's Company in mime play " Et Puis Bon Soir " ; produced choric dances for Sybil Thorndike productions of " Trojan Women " and " Medea " at Old Vic, Queen's Theatre, etc. With Ruby Ginner specialized in verse dancing and the writing of poetry and dance, carrying out research work in Greece and Sicily. Became Professor of Mime at Central School of Speech Training in connection with Diploma in Dramatic Art, London University. In 1928 revived " L'Enfant Prodigue " at Arts Theatre Club, Everyman Theatre, etc.

Author of " The Dance of Words " (Dent) and " Rhymes and Plays for the Bobblies."

Address : 79 Clarendon Road, London, W.11.

Best Photos : Pollard Crowther ; Navana, London.

MAY (Miss), Helen; dancer and Teacher. Pupil of Pavlova and Cecchetti. First appearance was with Pavlova at Palace Theatre. Created " Sunshine " Ballet for the late Mrs. Percy Dearmer's Children's Theatre Scheme. Was principal dancer at Aldwych Theatre, and appeared at Garrick Theatre with Ruth Draper. Has written various ballets and given recitations in New York and in London ; arranged dances for Lady Diana Manners in " The Miracle."

Address : 68 Holland Park, London, W.11.

Best Photos : Dorothy Wilding ; Lenare ; Hoppé, London.

MEDWYN-OWEN (Miss), G.; general teacher. Life Member of the Imperial Society and on Executive Council 1908-12 ; Member British Ballet Organisation ; Member of the Faculty of Dancing. Has an old-established visiting connection of over 25 Girls' Schools and Colleges.

Address : 7 Haven Green, Eaton Gardens, Ealing, London, W.5.

MELLOR (Miss), Phyllis; general teacher. Member Operatic Association of Great Britain ; Member Imperial Society ; Member British Normal School (Espinosa's) ; Member Operatic Dancing Teachers' Society ; Member British Ballet Organization, and Local Organizer for their Examinations. Started training for dancing at the age of 9, and when 12 years old joined the Compton Comedy Company and had several good children's parts. Was also with Mr. Harold V. Neilson and Mr. Bannister Howard. Obtained Elementary and Intermediate Certificates of the Association of Operatic Dancing in 1924, and was for a time a Local Organizer of Children's Examinations. She established her own school some six years ago.

Address : 89 Forest Road West, Nottingham.

MENCE, Gene (Miss Jean Mence) ; dancer and teacher of ballroom dancing. Has won several " All Ladies " Competitions. Has taught on Mr. Santos Casani's staff for over five years, and has recently partnered him in his demonstrations and his films for Pathé Studios.

Address : 7 Colosseum Terrace, Albany Street, London, N.W.1.

Best Photos : Dernier Cri, London.

MENDELSSOHN, Felix; dance organiser. Has organised a number of successful events. For two years was dance organiser at the Gloworm Studios in Wigmore Street. He is a grandson of the late Richard Warner, theatrical agent, and is a direct descendant of the celebrated composer Mendelssohn.

Address : 35 Woodstock Road, Golders Green, London, N.W.11.

Best Photos : Molloy, London.

MENZELI (Miss), LOLA (Mrs. Sonia Solomonoff) ; *première danseuse*. Toured the world with Senia Solomonoff, who created her best dances. Originator of heeled toe slipper, patented in Germany, etc. ; created part written for her by Sacha Guitry in " Lindbergh," and was presented with Lindbergh Medal by Aero Club of France for having danced at

celebrations in his honour; has appeared in vaudeville and concerts in Australia, U.S.A., South America, European towns, including Coliseum, London. Now teaching with Solomonoff in Atlanta, U.S.A., and making short concert tours.
Address: 243, 14th Street, N.E. Atlanta, Georgia, U.S.A.
Best Photos: Sobel, Paris; Goldberg, New York; Scherl Verlag, Berlin.

MEREDITH (Miss), Winifred; operatic teacher. Member Operatic Association. Principal of School, specializing in operatic and character dancing; received early training from Alfred Haines of Manchester.
Address: Rivoli Studio, Oxford Road, Manchester.
Best Photos: Oxford Studios, Manchester.

MERI, La (Signora Russell H. Carreras); concert dancer, specializing in research and reproduction of ethnologic dances. Member Diplome d'Honneur de la Societé Academique d'Histoire Internationale, Paris. First professional appearance as soloist at inauguration of Auritorium of San Antonio, Texas, 1926, later appearing as star dancer in *Sevilla* on Keith vaudeville circuit, and in Schubert's production, "A Night in Spain." Toured Central America with Theatre of the Arts, 1927, and made début as soloist at John Golden Theatre, New York, 1928. Engaged by Guida Carreras for extensive South American tour, and in 1930 made European début at Reinhardt's Theatre, Vienna, followed by engagements in Germany, Scandinavia, Belgium, France and Italy. Has written articles on dancing for *The Dancing Times*, London; *The Dance*, New York; *Home and Abroad*, Paris, etc.
Address: 22 Via Guerrazzi, Florence, Italy.

MERTON (Miss), Jessica (Jessie Fredricksen); operatic dancer. Holds Intermediate Certificate Operatic Association. First appeared on the stage in Variety at the age of 11. Studied operatic dancing under Madame J. Espinosa, and appeared in several touring shows as solo dancer. Whilst appearing at the Gaiety Theatre in one of Jack Hulbert's productions, "Lido Lady," she met R. W. Willey, and together they evolved the act "Balliol and Merton."
Address: 17 Carleton Road, London, N.7.
Best photos: Lenare, London; Schreider & Robertson, Berlin.

MIDDLETON, T. Milward. Business and Managing Director of Dancing Times, Ltd., since 1910.
Address: 25 Wellington Street, London, W.C.2.

MILES, Barbara (Mrs. Maxwell Fisher); ballroom teacher. Member and Examiner of Imperial Society of Teachers of Dancing. First appearance in public in Italia Conti's "Where the Rainbow Ends" in 1916. Began ballroom dancing at Queen's Hall Roof Garden. Winner of World's Ballroom Dancing Championship with Maxwell Stewart in 1924 and 1926; winner of Yale Blues Championship 1929. Has danced at London Coliseum and Alhambra, appeared in cabarets at well-known hotels, and toured in South Africa. In 1930 became Dance Hostess at the Savoy Hotel, London, a position relinquished on her marriage in 1932.
Address: Rosary, Ormond Road, Richmond.
Best Photos: Dorothy Wilding; Elwin Neame; Hana (now Navana), London.

MILLER (Miss), Florence S.; general teacher. Examiner and Member of Council of Imperial Society of Teachers of Dancing; Fellow Operatic Branch and Member Ballroom Branch; Member Operatic Association; Fellow British Association Physical Training. Principal of Elyssa School of Dancing, Forest Gate, which opened in 1910; branches at Upminster, Ilford, Upton Park, Bow and Hanover Street., W.1. Students trained for the profession and for the stage; special attention to children's work.

Address: Elyssa School of Dancing, 53 Hampton Road, Forest Gate, London.
Best Photos: Hana (now Navana), London; F. Clark, Forest Gate, London.

MILLS (Miss), Annette (Mrs. Robert Sielle); exhibition dancer with Robert Sielle. Starred in many famous cabarets in London, New York and on the Continent. They were the first couple to introduce light comedy into exhibition dancing. Introduced the Charleston and the Moochi.
Address: 18 Belsize Park, Hampstead, London, N.W.3.
Best Photos: Claude Harris, London.

MILNER, Arthur; ballroom dancer and teacher. Member of the Ballroom Branch of the Imperial Society of Teachers of Dancing. Partnered by Miss Norma Cave was winner of the Championship of Switzerland in 1930; winner of the International Championship at Nice in 1931; finalist in the " Star " Professional Championship, 1929-30-31; and winner of the Worlds Championship in Paris, 1931.
Address: 69 Wigmore St., London, W.1.
Best photos: Molloy, London.

MINIFIE (Miss), Violet (Mrs. Violet G. Fussell); operatic teacher. Intermediate Member of the Operatic Association. Received her first training from Miss Susie Boyle, and completed her training with the Edith Shotter School. Her connection extends over a wide area of North London.
Address: 15 The Ridgeway, Enfield, Middlesex.

MITTY (Miss), Germaine (Mitty and Tillio); operatic, acrobatic and character dancer. Began stage career at the age of 15 by doing a song and dance act with Mayol, the well-known French *fantaisiste*. In 1919 she met Tillio, and appeared with him as partner at the Folies Bergere in Paris in 1920—with exceptional success in acrobatic adagio dancing. They have danced in all the countries of Europe and visited the United States four times. Danced before the King of Spain in 1925.
Address: 162 Rue Ordener, Paris.
Best Photos: De Barron Studios, New York, and Valéry, Paris.

MONTAGU - NATHAN, Montagu; Secretary of the Camargo Society and author of several books on music.
Address: 5/42 Campden House Court, London, W.8.

MOODY, Mr. and Mrs. Ralph; ballroom teachers. Members Imperial Society of Teachers of Dancing. Received early training from Charles D'Albert, later from Josephine Bradley and Mrs. Lisle Humphries. Began professional dancing at " Murray's," Brixton Palais de Danse, 1920; then at Cricklewood Palais de Danse, 1922-1926. Opened Moody School of Dancing, Palace Hotel Ballroom, Lancaster Gate, in 1926. Finalists and prize winners World's Dancing Championship, 1924. Adjudicators and demonstrators for " Star " Dancing Championships, Croydon Dance Festival and other provincial Championships. Demonstrated Ballroom Dancing for synchronised sound films in 1925; appeared in exhibition dances and principal hotels and clubs in Great Britain, including special engagement to dance on Spanish Royal Yacht, Cowes Week, 1929. Awarded second place in " Star " Spectacular Exhibition Dance contest in 1930 for " Danse Exotique."
Address: Palace Hotel, Lancaster Gate, London, W.2.
Best Photos: Claude Harris, Le Dernier Cri.

MOORE, Alex; ballroom dancer and teacher. Member Imperial Society of Teachers of Dancing (Ballroom branch); Examiner and Technical Instructor to National Association of Teachers of Dancing. Took managerial post at Richmond, 1920; superintending dancing at Nuthall's Restaurant, Kingston - on - Thames, where a School of Ballroom Dancing was opened in 1922, Avis Moore being partner. With Miss Moore was winner of Blues Championship, 1923; Pearce Trophy at conference of National Association of Teachers of Dancing, 1924 and 1925; runner-up in World's Championship and finalist in "Star" Championship, 1926. Judge for "Star" and provincial championships. Produced first cabaret act in 1927, followed by many others at dance halls, hotels, etc., in London and provinces; also Burlesque of Old-time Dances, which was featured until marriage of Avis Moore in 1929. Original Member of Official Board and introducer of "Six-Eight" to members at meeting in 1929. Partnered Phyllis Haylor at Gleneagles Hotel during summer season, 1930, and appeared with her in demonstrations during following year. Organized Surrey Motor Dance Club.

Author of "Technical Analysis and Description of Modern Ballroom Dances."

Address: Nuthall's Restaurant, Kingston-on-Thames.

MOORE (Miss), Avis (Mrs. R. C. Reid); ballroom teacher. Member of the Imperial Society's Ballroom Branch (*see* ALEX MOORE).

Address: 53 Chancery Lane, London, W.C.2.

MOORE (Miss), Ralphia; general teacher. Member of the Imperial Society of Teachers of Dancing. Has a School of Dancing in Baker Street, London.

Address: 50 Baker Street, London, W.1.

Best Photos: Alexander Corbet, London.

MORETON (Miss), Ursula; operatic dancer and teacher. Holds personal certificate of Enrico Cecchetti. Advanced Member of the Operatic Association. Studied under Cecchetti from March, 1919. First appearance with Karsavina in J. M. Barrie's fantasy, *The Truth about the Russian Dancers*, at the Coliseum in 1920, at the age of 16. Joined the Diaghileff Russian Ballet in 1921, and danced *The Porcelain Princesses* with Hilda Bewicke and Kremnoff in the first production in England of Tchaikowsky's *Sleeping Princess* at the Alhambra. Appeared with Leonide Massine's Company at Covent Garden in 1922; also with Lopokova in *The Masquerade* at the Coliseum. Played the part of "Twin" in J. M. Barrie's "Peter Pan" at the St. James', and the following year at the Shaftesbury Theatre. Was *première danseuse* in Fokine's ballet in Basil Dean's production of "Hassan" at His Majesty's Theatre in 1923; also, under the same management, was *première danseuse* in Legat's ballet in Arnold Bennett's play, "London Life," and in Fokine's ballet in "A Midsummer Night's Dream" at Drury Lane Theatre, 1924. Next appeared with Anton Dolin's Company as soloist in the ballet *A Flutter in the Dovecote* at the Palladium, and in *divertissement* at the Coliseum, 1925. In 1926 appeared in "Aloma" at the Adelphi Theatre. Joined Ninette de Valois as assistant teacher in her school, since when she has appeared in her productions at the Festival Theatre, Cambridge, and the Old Vic., London. For the 1930 season was appointed ballet mistress and *première danseuse* to the Old Vic. Opera Company. She is now Assistant Teacher to Miss Ninette de Valois at the Vic-Wells School of Ballet, and first soloist in the Vic-Wells Opera Ballet Company. Danced in the first and second Camargo performances.

Address: 12 Argyll Mansions, London, W.14.

Best photos by Antony, London.

MORFIELD, Susette; operatic dancer. Associate of the Classical Ballet Branch of the Imperial Society of Teachers of Dancing, and Holder of their Elementary Certificate. Member of the Ballet Club Company. Trained by Madame Rambert.

Address: 40 Rowan Road, London, W.6.

Best Photos: Pearl Freeman, London.

MORRIS (Miss), Margaret. Founder and Principal of Margaret Morris School.

Member of the Chartered Society of Massage and Medical Gymnastics. Born in London in 1891, appeared in pantomime as a child, and studied under John D'Auban and Raymond Duncan; toured with Ben Greet's and Benson's Companies; danced in " Orpheus " at the Savoy Theatre; " the Blue Bird " at the Haymarket, etc.; toured in England and appeared in Paris; held special seasons at Court Theatre. Began School in 1910; in 1914 founded own Theatre and Club for original dancing; began remedial application of dancing in 1925, and evolved the " Margaret Morris Movement." After qualifying as a masseuse in 1930 founded the Margaret Morris Movement Association in connection with which yearly matinées are given.

Author of " Margaret Morris Dancng " (Kegan Paul), and " The Notation of Movement " (Kegan Paul).

Address: 1 Glebe Place, Chelsea, London, S.W.3.

MORTON, Arthur; ballroom teacher and demonstrator. Associate Imperial Society of Teachers of Dancing. Exhibition Dancer for several years; now principal of School of Ballroom Dancing.

Address: 43 Knightsbridge, London, S.W.1.

MOSELEY, L. Douglas; ballroom dancer and teacher. Member of the Imperial Society. Winner of the first prize for Teachers of Dancing at the International Dancing Championships at Interlaken in 1930 partnered by Miss Aimee Netter. And also again in 1931 partnered by Miss Violet Farrington, in partnership with whom he teaches at Hove. Trained by Miss Josephine Bradley.

Address: 3 Hove Lodge Mansions, Hove Street, Hove, Sussex.

Best Photos: Reprograph, London, and Ladislow, Eastbourne.

MOSS, Madame; ballroom teacher. Member of the British Association of Teachers of Dancing. With Mr. T. Moss is Principal of the Central Dance Studio in Wigan, and in 1930 they were the winners of the Chester Shield and the Bennett Medal at the B.A.T.D. Conference.

Address: 24 Swinley Lane, Wigan, Lancs.

Best Photos: Foley, Southport and Wigan.

MOSS, Marjorie (Mrs. Edmund Goulding); brilliant exhibition dancer and partner of Georges Fontana (q.v.). Previously had appeared in some of the later " Empire " ballets, and was understudy to Phyllis Bedells.

MOSS, T. (*See* MDME. MOSS).

MOSSETTI, Carlotta (Mrs. Sydney V. Etheridge); operatic and character dancer and general teacher. Born of an Italian father and Irish mother. Apprenticed to the School of Dancing at the Alhambra Theatre when 10 years of age, and made first appearance there in the ballet *Paquita* in 1908. Danced in " Carmen " and a number of shows before becoming Ballet Mistress at the Alhambra. Also acted as Producer. Was afterwards at the old Empire Theatre, and danced in *Ship Ahoy*, *Sylvia*, *Vive l' Europe*, *On the Square*, and arranged dances, etc., in " Lilac Time," " Angelo " and " Beloved Vagabond." Danced at the Coliseum with Adeline Genée in *La Camargo*, *Butterflies and Roses*, etc. Is incidentally very fond of outdoor sports.

Address: 14 Aberdeen House, Kenton Street, W.C.1.

Best Photos: Stage Photo Co., London.

MOUFLET (Miss), Gem; ballroom dancer and teacher. First opened a school in Wigmore Street, moved to the Strand, and then to the present address. Has demonstrated at a number of the leading West End hotels, and has judged and demonstrated a very great deal in connection with various charities.

Address: 11 Albemarle Street, London, W.1.

MULL (Miss), Stranraer (Mrs. Atkins); general teacher. Pupil of

Pavlova, Karsavina and Miss Toye, of Hove, and Santos Casani for ballroom dancing. Began teaching in India in 1926. Danced at the first concert which introduced the Faculty of Arts into India.
Address: C/o Lieut. J. C. Atkins, c/o Lloyd's Bank, Hornby Road, Bombay.

MUNRO, Malcolm; ballroom, exhibition and stage dancer and teacher. Member British Association. Opened the first dance hall in Liverpool; organised heats for World's Championships, Lancashire and Cheshire Championships, Charleston Ball, first A.O.F.T. Festival in provinces. Judge for World's Championship in 1927 and 1928, and Professional Championship of Great Britain in 1928. Revived " Olde Tyme " Dances with great success. Now at Grafton Rooms, Liverpool.
Address: Grafton Rooms, West Derby, Liverpool.
Best Photos: Walden Hammond, Leamington Spa.

MURRAY (Mrs.), Bianca; teacher of elocution and acting. Sister of Miss Italia Conti, and teaches at the Italia Conti Stage School.
Address: 14 Lamb's Conduit Street, London, W.C.1.

MUTCH, Albert H.; ballroom teacher. Was Floor Manager and Instructor of the Princes' Park Assembly Rooms, Liverpool, 1920-21. Opened his school in Bedford Street, Liverpool, in 1920, and has also taught in the Isle of Man and at Scarborough.
Address: Bedford School of Dancing, 125 Bedford Street South, Liverpool.
Best Photos: Harry Mac & Son, Liverpool.

N

NADJA (Beatrice Wanger); dancer and teacher of physical development. Danced in *Lysistrata*, Théatre Mogador, Paris; *Babylone*, Theatre Esoortique and Theatre de l' Exposition, Paris; Revue, 1927, at Palace Theatre, Paris, and in various concerts, etc. Founder of Noyl's School and Beatrice Wanger School, New York; writes dance news and articles for *Dancing Masters' Magazine*, Chicago, etc.
Address: C/o Guarantee Trust Co., Place de la Concorde, Paris.
Best Photos: Maurice Goldberg, New York; Maurice Beck, London; Henri Manuet & Watery, Paris.

NAIRN (Miss), Edith M.; general teacher. The first President of the Northern Ireland Dance Teachers' Association. Her School has been established thirty years. Specializes in children's work.
Address: Central Hall, Rosemary Street, Belfast.

NEWELL-JONES (Miss), Freda; ballroom teacher. Trained under Miss Hammond of Chester, Miss Tynegate-Smith and Mr. Casani. Holder of Casani Certificate.
Address: 5 Sheen Gate Gardens, East Sheen, London, S.W.14.
Best Photos: Navana, London.

NEWMAN, Claude; operatic dancer. Advanced Member Operatic Association. Trained by Miss Phyllis Bedells. First engagement was with Fokine's Ballet in " A Midsummer Night's Dream " at Drury Lane in 1924. This was followed by an engagement with Phyllis Bedells in " By the Way " at the Apollo in 1925. In 1926 was engaged by Espinosa for his " Three Graces " tour. Then went into musical comedy and appeared in " Tip Toes " at the Winter Garden Theatre. In 1927 joined the ballet in C. B. Cochran's Trocadero show, and at the same time appeared in " One Dam Thing After Another " at the Pavilion. Afterwards was booked by Jack Hulbert for " Lady Mary " and " Song of the Sea." Again appeared for C. B. Cochran in " Wake Up and Dream " in 1929, then went to New York and danced with Tilly Losch in " Coppelia." Returned to England in 1930 and joined Idzikowsky for a few weeks before appearing in "Evergreen" at the Adelphi. Has recently been appearing for Ninette de Valois in the Vic-Wells Ballets. Now in "Helen" at the Adelphi Theatre.

Address: 41 Arundel Gardens, London, W.11.

NEWTON (Miss), Joy; operatic and character dancer. Advanced Member Operatic Association. Associate Imperial Society (Cecchetti Branch). Prominent member of the Vic-Wells Ballet. Danced "Aurora" in *Cephalus and Procris* at the Old Vic and Sadler's Wells. Danced lead in *Homages aux Belles Viennoises*, and one of the daughters in *Job*. Has appeared in all the productions of the Camargo Society.

Address: 86 Marryat Road, Wimbledon, London, S.W.19.

NICHOLSON (Miss), May (Mrs. May Gradwell). Teacher of all branches. Intermediate Member of the Operatic Association. Her School is very well known and has won a considerable number of successes in various competitions, including "*The Dancing Times* Cup," at the Blackpool Festival in 1930 and 1932. Specializes in original character numbers and stage productions of all kinds.

Address: 38 Rowsley Road, St. Annes-on-Sea.

Best photos: Cooper Bros., Blackpool.

NICOLAEVA (Mdme.), Nadejda; operatic dancer and teacher. Member of the Imperial Society. Ballerina of the Moscow Grand Theatre. Studied first under Geyten, Kulichevsky, Gorsky, Tinomiroff, but principally under Nicolas Legat (q.v.). Appeared with Legat in Moscow, Petrograd, Russian tours, Persia, Algiers, and all European countries. Earliest London appearance, 1914 (*Passing Show*—Palace). 1926-7 with Serge Diaghileff. 1928 soloist with Mdme. Ida Rubinstein. Assistant to Legat as teacher Grand Theatre, Moscow, Diaghileff Company, and Paris and London studios. Danced principal roles in *Coppelia, Bayaderka, Swan Lake,* *Giselle, Magic Flute, Two Robbers, White Lily, Petroushka,* etc.

Address: St. Paul's Studios, Collet Gardens, London, W.14.

NIELSON (Miss), Marie (Miss Queenie Robertson); operatic dancer. Studied with Astafieva, Novikoff, Legat and Fokine. At the age of 13 appeared at the London Coliseum in Astafieva's Swinburne ballet. Danced at a series of performances produced by Komisarjevsky, and later joined (as Queenie Robertson) Anna Pavlova's company. Danced in John Murray Anderson's first London production, "The League of Notions," presented by C. B. Cochran, and in the three following Cochran productions. Studied with Fokine for a year in New York, and returned to London to be principal dancer in his ballets in the Drury Lane production of "A Midsummer Nights Dream." Appeared in several Julian Wylie productions, and is now a member of the Sadler's Wells ballet. Has danced for the Camargo Society.

Address: C/o Sadler's Wells Theatre, Rosebery Avenue, London, E.C.1.

Best Photos: Vaughan & Freeman, and Hana (now Navana), London.

NIJINSKA, Bromislava; dancer, choregraphist. Trained at the Imperial Schools. Sister of Vaslav Niminski. Succeeded Massine as choregrapher of the Diaghileff Ballet, her most successful works being *Les Noces* (Stravinsky), *Les Biches* (Poulene) and *Le Train Bleu* (Milhaud) and "The Three Ivans" in *The Sleeping Princess*. As a dancer she appeared in *The Sleeping Princess* (Lilac Fairy), *Les Biches* (the Hostess), *Le Train Bleu* (Tennis Champion), *Les Facheux* (Dancing Master). *Maitre de ballet* for Ida Rubinstein for whom she created: *Bolero* (Ravel), *Le Bal* (Ravel), *Noces de Psyche et de l'amour, La Bienaimee* (Milhaud), etc. Appeared at Covent Garden, 1931.

NIJINSKY, Vaslav; dancer and choregraphist. Educated at the Imperial Schools, principally under Michael

Obouchoff. *Premier danseur classique* of the Diaghileff Ballet from its *début*. Appeared in *Le Pavilion D' Armide* (with Pavlova and Karsavina), *Les Sylphides*, *The Spectre of the Rose*, *Carnaval*, *Jeux*, *The Blue God*, *Giselle*, *Sheherazade*, *Petrouchka*, *L'après Midi d'un Faun*, etc. Composed *Le Sacre du Printemps* and *L'après Midi d'un Faun*.

Karsavina, with whom he principally danced, says of his *début* :—

" Recognition of Nijinsky's wonderful gifts could not fail to be unanimous from the moment he came on the stage ; there was some reserve, however, in the appreciation of his personality. The troupe as well as the audience misjudged the unique quality of his talent ; had he tried to follow an approved pattern of male perfection, he would never have given the full measure of his genius. In later years, Diaghileff, with that clear conception of his that was almost uncanny, revealed to the world and to the artist himself the latter's true shape. At the expense of his better self, Nijinsky valiantly tried to answer the requirements of the traditional type till Diaghileff the wizard touched him with his magic wand. The guise of a plain, unprepossessing boy fell off—a creature exotic, feline, elfin completely eclipsed the respectable comeliness, the dignified commonplace of conventional virility."

His contribution to choregraphy is the use of angular movement " *en dedans* " as opposed to open movements and more especially an entirely fresh conception of the relations between movement and music in which he was influenced by Jacques Dalcroze.

Books : Mentioned in all leading works on the Russian Ballet.

Best photos : Sargent, Flandrin, and Extean.

NIKITINA (Mlle.), Alice ; classical ballet dancer. Studied in Russia. Joined the Diaghileff Ballet and danced in the leading roles of the classical repertoire ; also in *The Cat, Les Biches*, etc. Created the role of " Flora " in *Zephyr and Flora*. Danced with Serge Lifar in Charles B. Cochran's " 1930 Revue " at the London Pavilion.

NORTON (Miss), Lorraine ; operatic dancer and teacher ; also features musical comedy and national dancing. Holder of the Solo Seal of the Operatic Association, and is an Examiner and Member of the Sub-Committee of that Association. Holder of the Solo Seal of the British Ballet Organisation. Fellow of the Imperial Society. Holder of the Gold Medal of the I.L.A.M. for Elocution. Was trained at the " Florence Etlinger Dramatic Academy," and then had five years experience on the " boards," appearing in the Grand Opera Ballet at Covent Garden, as speciality dancer in J. L. Slack's Drury Lane production, " Shanghai," and as a solo dancer in a variety act on the Gulliver Circuit. Also played in many " straight " parts, including that of juvenile lead in Percy Hutchinson's " Luck of the Navy " company. Is Principal of a well-known School in Birmingham, which has passed a large number of pupils through the examinations of the Operatic Association, and many pupils have achieved considerable success on the stage.

Address : 38 John Bright Street, Birmingham.

Best Photos : Walden Hammond, Leamington Spa.

NORTON-COLLINS (Miss), Kathleen general teacher. Intermediate Member Operatic Association, Licentiate Imperial Society of Teachers of Dancing (Operatic branch) and Member (Ballroom branch). Trained at South Norwood School of Dancing. Appeared in Lena Ashwell's production " The Starlight Express " at Kingsway Theatre ; also in ballets in London and provinces as solo dancer. Became head assistant and partner in South Norwood School of Dancing ; now sole principal. Ballet Mistress for Croydon Operatic Society, Croydon Stagers' Society, Pearl Assurance Dramatic Society, etc.

Address : The Studio, 205 Selhurst Road, South Norwood, S.E.25.

NOVIKOFF, Laurent; ballet dancer. Trained at the Imperial School, Moscow, under Tichomiroff, and made his *debut* there. Danced all the leading roles of the repertoire. Toured as *premier danseur* to Anna Pavlova, perhaps his best known role being with her in Glazounov's *Bacchanal*. Danced in *La Fille mal gardee*, etc. Had an important School in London for several years.

O

OAKENFOLD, Leonard; ballroom dancer and teacher. Member of Imperial Society. Commenced his dancing career in 1924 at Birmingham, when, partnered by his wife, he was runner-up for the "Midlands Championship." In 1926-27 and 1927-28 was semi-finalist in the "Star" Championship, and finalist in that competition in the two following years. Has been very prominent in several other competitions, both in this country and on the continent. Mr. Oakenfold has been on the instructional staff of the King's Hall Rooms, Bournemouth, since 1926, and in 1930 was appointed Chief Instructor there.
Address: 127 Old Christchurch Road, Bournemouth.
Best photos: Brights, Bournemouth.

OAKENFOLD, Mrs. Leonard; ballroom dancer and teacher. On the instructional staff of the King's Hall Rooms, Bournemouth. (*See also* LEONARD OAKENFOLD.)

OAKESHOTT (Miss), Lilian. Intermediate Member of the Operatic Association. Member of the Operatic Branch of the Imperial Society. Member of the Association of Teachers of the Revived Greek Dance. Teaches at the Guildhall School of Music, London.
Address: c/o The Guildhall School of Music, Victoria Embankment, London, E.C.

OLENEWA (Madame), Maria; *Première danseuse*. Was trained by Nelidova in Moscow. First engagement at Marie Kousnetzoff's Opera Russe at the Champs Elysées, Paris. Was Soloist with Mme. Anna Pavlova in North America. In 1923 appointed *première danseuse* and *Maîtresse de Ballet* at the Theatre Colon, Buenos Aires. In 1926 went as *première danseuse* to the Theatre Municipal, Rio de Janeiro, where she now has a School of Dancing.
Address: Theatre Municipal, Rio de Janeiro.

OLIVER (Miss), Betty; operatic and tap dancer; general teacher. Born in South Africa, where she first studied dancing. Was a favourite with Cape Town audiences. Came to England and studied under Enrico Cecchetti, Leonide Massine and Marie Rambert. First appeared in Massine's ballets in "C. B. Cochrane's Revue" at the London Pavilion; was later *première danseuse* in Andre Charlot's productions, and also danced in cabaret at Grosvenor House and the Hotel Splendide. Ballet Mistress for Andre Charlot. Has arranged dances for the films.
Address: C/o The National Bank of South Africa, 111 St. Martin's Lane, London, W.C.2.
Best photos: Sasha, Hoppe, Mannell, London.

ORANGE, Wilfred; ballroom teacher. Vice-President of the International Dancing Masters' Association. Started dancing career as an assistant to Miss Dorothy Wright, of Sheffield. Became Member of the Yorkshire Association of Dancing Masters in 1927. Is an accomplished musician, and for some years was harpist to Sir Henry Coward's Orchestra. Appointed Musical Director to the Y.A.D.M. in 1929. Was one of the Yorkshire delegates who brought about the amalgamation of the English, Premier, Universal and Yorkshire Associations, now known as the I.D.M.A. Was elected Vice-President of the new Association in 1930. Established his School in 1927. Also runs the Wharncliffe Club in Sheffield.
Address: 16 Birch Farm Avenue, Meadow Head, Sheffield.

OOSTERVINK, J. H.; ballroom teacher. Member of the Imperial Society. Member of the Union des Professeurs de Danse de France. Member of the Syndicat National des Professeurs de Danse et Danseurs Professionnels. Member of the Ned. Genootschap van Beroepsdansleeraren. Studied in London and Paris. First gave lessons in September, 1926, and opened a school of his own in September, 1927, which is now one of the largest in Holland. Introduced the positions of " Host " and " Hostess " in Holland. Was the originator of the " Midway Rhythm," and taught it to the Committee of the Ballroom Branch of the Imperial Society, who adopted it.

Address: Leidschekade 102, Amsterdam C., Holland.

OUKRAINSKY, Serge; ballet master and concert artist. Born in Odessa of Russian parents; now a naturalized citizen of the United States. Educated at the Condorset College in Paris. Studied fine arts at the Juliah Academy, Paris, and was instructed in dancing by Ivan Clustine, ballet master. First appearance as a dancer was at the Châtelet Theatre with the Lamoureaux Orchestra. After a successful engagement in London, went to America and toured the principal cities. Then followed a European tour, during which he gave a special performance for the ex-Kaiser Wilhelm, then Emperor of Germany. He then became associated with Andreas Pavley, and shortly afterwards both were engaged by Cleofonte Campanini to organize the Chicago Opera Ballet. They then organized the Pavley-Oukrainsky School, and for eight years arranged the ballets of the Chicago Opera Company. They appeared at a special gala performance at the Metropolitan Opera House in New York given in honour of Marshal Foch, and following this engagement Mr. Oukrainsky made an extended tour with his company of forty dancers throughout South America, Mexico and Havana. In Buenos Aires they had a long and successful season, and gave special performances for the Crown Prince of Italy at the Colon Theatre. On their return, an engagement was given at the Hippodrome in New York City, which was followed by their appearance at the Theatre Etoile, Paris. Mr. Oukrainsky has produced the ballets for the San Francisco and Los Angeles Opera Companies for three seasons. Has also arranged the dances for Fox and Warner Brothers' Studios, and gave a performance at the Hollywood Bowl in 1928. His ability as an artist has obtained for him numerous commissions to design scenery and costumes for such organizations as the Chicago Grand Opera Company and Anna Pavlova, whose costume for her popular *Gavotte* he created. As choregraphist he created the ballets *La Fête à Robinson*, for which Mary Garden ordered special music written by Gabriel Grovlez, conductor of the Paris Opera, and *Boudour* with music by Felix Borowski. Both ballets were presented at the Manhattan Opera House in New York City.

Address: 64 E. Jackson Boulevard, Chicago, Ill., U.S.A.

Best photos: Charlotte Fairchild, New York, Ray Huff, Chicago; and Curtis, Los Angeles.

OWEN (Miss), Meredyth; ballroom teacher. Member Imperial Society. Was for some time partner to Monsieur Pierre. Now on the staff of the Audley School of Dancing.

Address: C/o Audley School of Dancing, 449 Oxford Street, London, W.1.

P

PAISLIEU (Miss), Jeanette; dance hostess, demonstrator, and ballroom teacher. As a child she studied operatic dancing, but in later years took up ballroom dancing seriously, and is a popular hostess in the West of England. Miss Paislieu has undertaken many hunt and theatrical balls, and was official dance hostess for the British-French Week.

Address: C/o Mr. B. J. Nichols, Bourne House, Winterbourne, near Bristol.

PALMER, Timothy; ballroom dancer and teacher. Started dancing at the age of 13, and was winner of a number of competitions before leaving School. At 16 won the South Coast Amateur Championship. In 1915 was fifth in the "Star" Amateur Championship. Following that left dancing for two years, after which he became a Professional, and in 1930 reached the Finals of the "Star" Professional Championship at his first attempt. In 1931, partnered by Miss Kathleen Price, was Runner-up for the "Star" Professional Championship, and a Finalist in the "Star" Professional Tango Championship. In that same year, again partnered by Miss Price, was placed fourth in the British Professional Championship at Blackpool, which important Competition these two won in 1932.
Address: 59a Maida Vale, London, W.9.

PALUCCA, Gert. A well-known German dancer and a pupil of Mary Wigman. Has her own School in Dresden, and has toured as solo dancer with her group in all the principal towns of Germany, and many other countries.
Address: Dresden, Bürgerwiese 6.

PARKIN (Miss), Sallie, M.A.O.., I.S.T.D.
Address: 36a Bridlesmith Gate, Nottingham.
Best Photos: F. Smith, Nottingham.

PARSONS (Miss), Barbara. Co-Principal of the Five Ways School of Dance, where all branches of dancing combined with own rhythmic method of musical interpretation are taught. Winner of the Gold Medal and Challenge Trophy in 1927 and 1929 at the Bristol Eisteddfod. Winner of the Midland Championship in Greek and National, 1929. Now Ballet Mistress to the Children's Theatre, Birmingham.
Address: The Five Ways School of Dance, Islington Row, Birmingham.
Best Photos: Walden Hammond, Leamington.

PASTRAT, Professor; ballroom and general teacher. Was responsible for the introduction of modern dances into Spain. Is the author of several small books for students.
Address: Rosellón 254, Barcelona, Spain.

PATERSON (Miss), Margaret R.; operatic and ballroom teacher. Intermediate Member Operatic Association and Associate Imperial Society (Ballroom Branch).
Address: 61 Beresford Rd., Oxton, Birkenhead, Cheshire.

PATON-SMITH (Miss), Hilda; general teacher. Member of the Imperial Society of Teachers of Dancing. Co-principal with Miss Vera Robartes of School of Dancing specializing in remedial work.
Address: School of Dancing, 8 Royal Parade, Harrogate.

PEARCE, A.; ballroom teacher. Past President, Trustee and Member of Executive Council National Association of Teachers of Dancing. Principal of School of Dancing with Mrs. A. Pearce. Promoted Dances at Cecil Hotel and Cannon Street Hotel. Donor of Silver Shield, to be competed for annually by professional inventors of new steps and rhythms.
Address: 244 Trinity Road, Wandsworth Common, London, S.W.18.

PEARSON, Mrs.; general teacher; a well-known authority on Highland Dancing. (See Mrs. George Lowe.)
Address: 42 George Street, Edinburgh.

PEELER (Mrs.), Ruby; ballroom dancer and teacher. Fellow, Council Member and Examiner of the Ballroom Branch of the Imperial Society. Trained by Miss Eve Tynegate-Smith, and in 1922-3 took charge of her School whilst Miss Tynegate-Smith was in Africa. In 1924 opened her own School in London, and two years later, whilst touring in Switzerland, opened several branches out there. In 1926-8 visited Spain, and gave lecture-demonstrations partnered by Mr. Frank Rodwell. Whilst there, demonstrated before and was presented to H.M. the Queen of Spain at the Embassy Ball. In 1929 a branch of her School was established in Madrid by Miss Daisy Romer, at which the Infantas and other members of the Royal Family were pupils. In that same year Mrs. Peeler visited Shanghai, and with Miss Helen Romer as her partner, established the Romer-Peeler School of Dancing there. In 1930 removed the headquarters of her School in London to the Eccleston Hotel, Victoria. Branches in this country are at Windsor and Cambridge, and the dancing at numerous schools and convents is under the direction of the School. Annual recitals are given at the Rudolf Steiner Hall, London. A number of big competitions have been won by pupils. For the past two years Mrs. Peeler has been Hostess at the Beresford Hotel, Birchington-on-Sea.

Address: Eccleston Hotel, Eccleston Square, Victoria, London, S.W.1.

Best Photos: Dorothy Hickling, London.

PERUGINI, Mark Edward; critic and historian of Dance and Ballet. Fellow of the Institute of Journalists; Member of the Critics' Circle; Hon. Member of the Association of Teachers of the Revived Greek Dance. Born in London and was educated at the City of London School; became Secretary to late Justin McCarthy, M.P.; was for some years Assistant Editor, and subsequently for four years, Editor of *The Lady's Pictorial*. During the war served as Lieut., R.N.V.R. Published in *The Dancing Times* in 1911-12 first extensive series of historical " Sketches of the Dance and Ballet," followed by others on " Mime," " Victorian Stars," and has since given many contributions to the same magazine, as well as supplying numerous signed articles on the Dance, Drama and Films in the British and American Press. Produced a one-act play " The Flame " (dedicated to Mme. Adeline Genée) at the Court Theatre, and " The Drum " at the Savoy Theatre in 1912. Was invited to lecture on the history of the Dance by the Musical Association (1920) and by the Operatic Association in 1928. In 1929 became Editor of *The Link*, the quarterly organ of the Association of Teachers of the Revived Greek Dance.

Author of " The Art of Ballet " (Secker), " Mime " (*Dancing Times*, Ltd.); " Victorian Days and Ways " (Jarrolds).

Address: C/o Institute of Journalists, Tudor Street, London, E.C.4.

PETER (Miss), Borneque; general teacher, specialist in ballroom dancing. Gold medallist in operatic dancing, silver medallist in gymnastics and calesthenics.

Address: 50 Poole Hill, Bournemouth.

PFUNDMAYR (Miss), Hedy; solo dancer. Has been a member of the Vienna State Opera since childhood, first as a toe-dancer, then as pantomime dancer, playing all big pantomime parts in well-known ballets, including *Potiphar, Scheherezade*, etc. Later the modern German method of expressionist dancing was developed, recitals with a special ensemble being given in Vienna, Berlin, Madrid, etc.

Address: J. Schottengasse 10, Vienna.

Best Photos: Professor Koppitz, Vienna.

PHILLIPS (Miss), Ailne; operatic dancer. Holder of the Advanced Cecchetti Certificate of the Imperial Society, and is an examiner and member of the Committee of the Cecchetti Branch. Principal dancer and producer in the Carl Rosa Opera Company. Appears with the " Vic-Wells " Ballet.

Address: 61 Ladbroke Grove, London, W.11.

Best Photos: Sasha, London.

PHILLIPS (Miss), Audrey; ballroom teacher. Member of Imperial Society of Teachers of Dancing (Ballroom branch). Principal of the Audrey Phillips School of Dancing, where all subjects are taught by a highly-qualified staff. Judge of heats for " Star " and Columbia Championships, 1926-1929; demonstrates at London

and provincial hotels, and while in Switzerland demonstrated for the Crown Prince of Italy and Queen Wilhelmina of Holland. Members of the staff fulfil many positions as dance hostesses in hotels in France, Belgium and Switzerland during summer and winter seasons.
Address: The Ballroom, Knightsbridge Hotel, London, S.W.1.
Best Photos: Janet Jevons, London.

PHILP, Robert H.; ballroom dancer and teacher. Winner of the West of Scotland Championship from 1925 to 1929, and of the East of Scotland Championship in 1929. Won the Scottish Championship in 1930 and 1931, the "Star" All-England Championship in 1931 and also the European Championship in 1931.
Address: 177 Renfrew Street, Glasgow.
Best photos: Navana, London.

PHIPPS (Miss), Aimee; teacher of operatic (Russian and Cecchetti), musical comedy, tap dancing, limbering, ballroom, etc. Associate of the Imperial Society (Cecchetti Branch).
Address: 2 Harrington Gardens, South Kensington, London, S.W.

PICKERING, J. Russell; general manager, Royal Opera House Dances, Covent Garden, and the Olympia Dance Hall, London. Managing Director of Sherrys, Brighton. Has done a great deal for co-operation between Dance Teachers and Dance Hall Managers, and organized the founding of the "Association of Ballrooms and Dance Halls" of which he is the Chairman.
Address: The Conifers, Clapham Park, London, S.W.
Best photos: Mannell, London.

PIERRE, Monsieur; ballroom teacher, and teacher of tap dancing. Fellow and Member of Committee; also Examiner of the Imperial Society; Member of Committee of the Faculty of Arts; Member of Official Board of Ballroom Dancing. Made his first appearance in the West End as an Exhibition Dancer in November, 1913, with Senorita Bebita Bayo, fulfilling engagements at the 400 Club (now Embassy Club), Lotus Club, etc. In April, 1914, became co-principal of the Harewood Dancing Academy with Miss Clayton, of "Marqnis and Clayton," the Tango and Maxixe dancers. Gave the first demonstration of the modern Ballroom Tango at Murray's Club in March, 1922, with Countess Gioia, the Italian *danseuse*. Was the first teacher to teach the "Blues" in England. Introduced the "Paso Doble" in 1926. Inventor of the "Stop Trot," "Off Trot" and "Valse Pierette." From 1923 to March, 1930, demonstrated and gave exhibitions with Miss Meredith Owen (late of George Edwards Theatrical Co.), making a feature of eccentric syncopated dancing. Judge for some of the most important Dancing Championships held in recent years, including the World's Championship, "Star" Championship, "Daily Sketch" Championship, etc. Now teaching and demonstrating with Miss Doris Lavelle.
Author of "How to Jazz" (Larby & Co.).
Address: 28 Heddon Street, Regent Street, London, W.1.
Best photos: Swaine, London.

PLESTCHEEF, Alexandre; critic and historian. Son of the famous Russian poet, N. A. Plestcheef.
Author of the most complete history of the Russian Ballet. Has recently celebrated his fiftieth jubilee as a writer.
Address: C/o Vozrasjdenia, 12 Rue de Sèze, Paris.

POSPISIL, Prof. Doctor Frantisek; Curator of Ethnographical Department of Government Museum, Brnǫ. Foreign Member English Folk Dance Society, London; Member Danish Folk Dance Society, Copenhagen, etc. A follower of Cecil Sharp. Responsible for the first films of folk, sword, war and Morris dances of all European nations. Lectured extensively in Europe and also in Canada and U.S.A., where he is at present studying Indian dances in reservations.

Author of various leaflets on Folk Dancing, etc.
Address: Ethnographical Dept., Government Museum, Brno, Moravia, Czechoslovakia.
Best Photos: Atelier Lehky, Brno.

PREOBRAJENSKAYA, Olga; *Prima Ballerina* of the Imperial Theatre, St. Petersburg. Educated at the Imperial Schools and studied under Cecchetti. Danced in all the leading rôles of the classical repertoire. Perhaps her greatest rôle was in *Les Caprices de Papillon*, which she chose for her benefit performance. Like Kshessinskaya, she is chiefly known in Russia, where she was noted for the wit and vivacity of her interpretations. Svetloff talks of her "elegant manner," and Karsavina says in "Theatre Street": "Her road to success had been a hard one. She began as a *corps de ballet* dancer and gradually worked her way to the top. Her virtuosity she owed to Cecchetti, her master, and perhaps even more to her own undaunted courage."
She appeared in London in *The Swan Lake*. There has been a study of her in Russian by André Levinson.

PRESTON (Miss), Ursula; teacher of all branches of stage dancing. Trained by Zelia Raye in stage and acrobatic dancing; managed Miss Raye's School during her South African tour; has appeared in many cabarets as solo dancer.
Address: 16 Irvine Court, Porchester Terrace, London, W.2.

PRICE (Miss), Kathleen M.; ballroom teacher. Winner of several "All Ladies" Championships. Finalist in the "Star" Professional Championship in 1929. Runner-up for "Star" Championship in 1931, and winner of the Quick-step Competition. With Timothy Palmer won the "British Professional Championship" at Blackpool in 1932. Is teaching at the Bradley School of Dancing, 6 Basil Street, Knightsbridge, London.
Address: Myrtle Wood, Oxshott Road, Leatherhead, Surrey.
Best photos: Molloy, London.

PURROTT (Miss), Dorothy; general teacher. Member of the Operatic Association (Intermediate Certificate); Fellow of the Imperial Society. Has a School at Beach Haven, Bexhill. Has held the position of Dance Hostess at the Palace Hotel, Mengen, for five years.
Address: Beach Haven, Bexhill-on-Sea.

R

RADCLIFFE (Miss), Molly; operatic and character dancer and teacher. Advanced Member of the Association of Operatic Dancing of Great Britain. Started dancing at the age of 4. Trained under Serge Morosoff for six years, Phyllis Bedells for three, and also under Espinosa and Legat. Is at present a pupil and an assistant of Madame Karsavina. In 1920 appeared both at Chiswick Empire and the Coliseum as a single turn. Toured with Morosoff as his partner and has had considerable experience in pantomime and vaudeville in general. Was Ballet Mistress and soloist in *Song of the Sea* at His Majesty's Theatre. Danced in Jack Hulbert's *House that Jack Built*. Danced a leading rôle in the second Camargo performance.
Address: 65 Biddulph Mansions, Maida Vale, London, W.9.
Best photos by Claude Harris, Marion Lewis and Staby, London.

RAMBERT (Mdme), Marie (Mrs. Ashley Dukes); operatic dancer and teacher. Fellow of the Imperial Society of Teachers of Dancing and Examiner of the Cecchetti Branch. Member of the General Committee of the Camargo Society. Director of the Ballet Club. Studied dancing in State School in Warsaw. Joined Diaghileff's Company in 1912; chosen by him from the Dalcroze School to assist Nijinski in his creation of *Le Sacre du Printemps*. Appeared under Mr. Cochran's management in "Pomme d'or," where she created the part of "Madonna"; also in *Fêtes Galantes*, creating the "Marquise"; in *Tragedy of Fashion*, by Frederic Ashton, as the "chief mannequin"; and in *Our Lady's Juggler* as the "Virgin." Amongst her pupils are Frederic Ashton, Harold Turner, Prudence Hyman, Andrée Howard, Diana Gould, Pearl Argyle, etc., etc. Presented and performed in seasons of Ballet at the Lyric Theatre, Hammersmith, in June and December, 1930, and June, 1931, Karsavina being the guest-artist.

Book: "The Marie Rambert Ballet," by Arnold L. Haskell (British Continental Press).

Address: 19 Campden Hill Gardens, London, W.8.

Best photos: Whitlock, London.

RANDELL, John Holland; ballroom teacher. Was President of the British Association of Teachers of Dancing 1904-5, and General Secretary of that Association from 1905-21; is now a Trustee.

Address: 28 Quex Road, West Hampstead, London, N.W.6.

RASCH, Albertina (Mrs. Dimitri Tiomkin); dance producer and general teacher. At an early age entered the Imperial Opera Ballet School at Vienna, where she was seen by R. H. Burnside and engaged as solo dancer for the New York Hippodrome, and at the age of 16 was *première danseuse* there. A few seasons later was engaged by Otto H. Kahn as *première danseuse* of the Century Opera Company, appearing in "Aida," "Carmen," "International Ballet," etc. After one year there and another at the Chicago Opera, she became *première danseuse* and Ballet Mistress of the American Opera Company at Los Angeles, where she staged Parker's "Fairyland" during the summer. Then in the winter joined the Ellis Grand Opera Company in the same capacity and toured the country with Geraldine Farrar and Lucien Muratore. At this time began training her own company, and toured the Keith Circuit. Was then asked by Sarah Bernhardt to join her in a concert tour through Cuba. Returning to the States, she took her own company on extended tours of the Vaudeville Circuits. Then made an extended concert tour through most of the larger cities of Germany and Holland, also visiting London and Paris, remaining in Europe for two years in all. In August, 1923, opened a permanent school in New York with the idea of forming an American Ballet, and her troupes of dancers, known as the Albertina Rasch Girls, are a tremendous attraction wherever they appear. During the past few years Mdme. Rasch has supplied dancers and arranged the dances for innumerable successful revues, musical comedies and films, particularly the latter, in connection with which she has received contracts from all the big houses. In 1930 she staged the most spectacular ballet ever attempted at the Hollywood Bowl, with over 70 of her pupils, to the music of her husband, Dimitri Tiomkin. It is she who is responsible for the dances in the successful London show, "Waltzes from Vienna."

Address: 113 West 57th Street, New York City, U.S.A.

RATCLIFFE (Miss), Eleanor; general teacher. Her School has been successful in a number of competitions, and in 1931 won the Senior Group Section of the All England Competition. Miss Ratcliffe visited Athens in 1914 to give lessons to the Royal Family.

Address: Eastbourne School of Dancing, The Lodge, Blackwater Road, Eastbourne.

RAVODNA (Mdme.); teacher of operatic dancing. Advanced Member of the Operatic Association. Youngest daughter of Leon Espinosa. Made her *debut* in 1904 with her sister Lea. Some time later worked with Stanislas Idzikowsky. In 1912 was Principal Dancer at the Lyceum, then joined her brother Edward, and worked with him until 1915 when they both visited South Africa, and Mdme. Ravodna remained there. She is recognised out there as the principal teacher of Operatic Dancing, and most of the leading teachers in South Africa have been to her for tuition.

Address: Crown House, 77 President Street, Johannesburg, South Africa.

RAYE (Miss), Zelia; general teacher. Formerly principal dancer and dance producer at the Adelphi and Gaiety Theatres, and the Piccadilly Revels, London. Has a Studio at 77 Dean Street, W.1. Has visited America and is a recognised authority on Stretching and Limbering, and the modern American "Tap" work. Is the author of "Rational Limbering" (C. W. Beaumont).
Address: 18 Thurlow Road, Hampstead, London, N.W.3.
Best photos: "Reprograph," London.

READE (Miss), Eleanor de C.; general teacher. Member British Association of Teachers of Dancing; Member of Executive Council and Examiner. Certificates for Ballroom and Operatic Dancing. Trained under Henry Whiteside. In charge of the dancing department of the Perry School of Dancing and Theatrical Agency, London, 1926-1927, and is now principal of the Wallington School of Dancing.
Address: 23 Elgin Road, Wallington, Surrey.

READER, Ralph; dance producer. Has produced dances for "Virginia," "Hold Everything," "Merry Merry," "Dear Love," "Silver Wings," "Cochran 1931 Revue," "Sons o' Guns," "Hour Glass," "Viktoria and Her Hussar," "Bow Bells," "Song of the Drum," "Tommy Tucker," etc. Has also danced in and produced revues at the Winter Garden, New York, and played in "Good News," London.
Address: 90 Galpins Road, Thornton Heath, Surrey.
Best Photos: Capstack, Blackpool.

REPHAEL, Lala (the Rajah Rham Singh); teacher of ancient and religious Eastern and classical dances, dramatist and composer-musician. As Rajput Brahmin, has toured the world as dancing equestrian in a circus. Produced "The Kashmeeri Girl" at Brighton; played heavy lead in "The Great Ruby" at Drury Lane; wrote libretto, lyrics and music of "The Belle of India," in which Kashmeeri nautch girls danced for the first time on the British stage. Principal of International Academy, Russell Square, and teaches Opera, Concert, Dramatic Voice-Culture, Violin, Eastern Music and Dancing. Is a disciple of Yogi Sathyavan, and as a psychiatrist specializes in Eastern philosophy and psychology. Has given recitals, concerts, lectures, etc., at Queen's Hall and Bechstein Hall, London; provincial theatres; Moss, Stoll, Gibbons, vaudeville theatres, etc., etc.; has toured Europe and the East.
Author of "The Moral Destiny of British Music, Society and Arts of the Stage" (L. V. Hatt).
Address: 1 Guildford Place, London, W.C.1.
Best Photos: Parkes & Co., London.

RICHARDS (Miss), Dorothy; ballroom teacher. Member of the International Dancing Masters' Association. Was a Finalist in the North of England Championship at Blackpool in 1930, and also the 1930 "Star" Championship. Winter Season Hostess at the Premier Dance Hall, Loughborough, and Summer Season Hostess at the Café Dansant, Skegness. Is a Principal of the Style and Simplicity School of Dancing, Nottingham.

RICHARDSON, Philip J. S. Editor of *The Dancing Times*, which, in partnership with Mr. T. M. Middleton, he founded in 1910, having purchased all rights in the title from Mr. Walter Humphrey, whose father, Mr. Edward Humphrey, had many years previously published the original *Dancing Times* as a "house-organ" of the "Cavendish Rooms" in Mortimer Street, London. Associate Editor (with Mr. Arnold Haskell) of this book. Has been Treasurer-Secretary of the "Association of Operatic Dancing of Great Britain" since the founding of that body (in 1920). He played a prominent part in its institution, and was elected a member of the Council in 1930. Is an Honorary Member of the "Association of Teachers of the Revived Greek Dance" and of the "Imperial Society

of Teachers of Dancing." Is Chairman of the "Faculty of Dancing" and of the "Official Board of Ballroom Dancing," which body he was instrumental in founding in 1928. Is Chairman of the Committee which controls the Annual "All England Solo Competition," and is Chairman of Judges at the annual Blackpool Dance Festival. Was Chairman of Judges at the three "World's Dancing Championships" held in London, and has adjudicated at innumerable ballroom and stage dancing competitions. Was a co-founder with Mr. Arnold Haskell of the "Camargo Society," and is a member of the Committee of that body. On the occasion in 1931 of the twenty-first anniversary of the founding of *The Dancing Times*, received the Prize of the "Ministry of Fine Arts" of France. Has organised ten "Sunshine Matinees" at which many of the most famous dancers of the day have appeared, in aid of the "Blind Babies' Homes." Contributor to many newspapers and periodicals on the subject of dancing.
Address: 25 Wellington Street, London, W.C.2.

RICKINSON (Miss), Dot; operatic dancer and teacher. Member Imperial Society (Cecchetti Branch) and member Ballroom Branch (Intermediate Certificate with Honours). Holder of Student's Certificate, with Honours, of the A.T.R.G.D. Advanced Member of the Association of Operatic Dancing and holder of the Solo Seal. Teacher at the Cone School of Dancing since 1926. Winner of the Senior Cup in the All England Solo Dancing Competition, 1926. Danced in the Fokine Ballet at Drury Lane Theatre, and also with Madame Karsavina at the London Coliseum. Solo dancer at the Scala Theatre, Christmas, 1928. Acted as under-study to Miss Phyllis Bedells at the Savoy Theatre, Christmas, 1930. Now taking Scholarship Children's classes at the Association of Operatic Dancing of Great Britain.
Address: 20 Stratford Place, Oxford Street, London, W.1.

RIDEN (Miss), Muriel; general teacher. Specializes in ballroom dancing, and is a Holder of the Casani Certificate. Has given many ballroom demonstrations and cabaret numbers in Exeter and Devon.
Address: Exonia School of Dancing, Gandy Street, Exeter, and 26 South Avenue, Exeter.

RIDER (Miss), Bridget; teacher of the Revived Greek Dance. Assistant at the Northern School of Dance and Dramatic Expression, of which Miss E. Irene Sample is Principal.
Address: C/o Northern School of Dance, Oxford Galleries, Newcastle-on-Tyne.

RIFFLER, Rod (Rudolf Heinz Ungar); dancer, producer and teacher. Member of the Vienna Academy and Conservatorium. At the age of 6 was already appearing in some of the largest theatres in Vienna, and was engaged for an acting and dancing part at one of Max Reinhardt's theatres. Then appeared in revue in Vienna and Munich. Later went to Paris, where he was starred in revue at the Casino de Paris, where he was noticed by Mistinguett and taken by her on her world tour, during which time he received favourable press notice as a dancer of unusual ability with a dramatic sense of the tragic as well as the lighter and comedy elements of the art of the stage. Has appeared before Royalty.
Address: Bloasstr. 33, bei Liatscheff, Vienna XIX.
Best Photos: Baccarini and Porta, Milan.

RILEY (Miss), Muriel; general teacher. Intermediate Member of the Association of Operatic Dancing of Great Britain. Is of Irish descent on her father's side and Russian on her mother's. Commenced dancing at an early age, and for a time toured. Is Principal of a large School of Dancing in Hull.
Address: 109 Linnæus Street, Anlaby Road, Hull.
Best photo: Turner & Drinkwater, Hull.

RIPMAN (Mrs.), Olive; general teacher. Member of the Imperial Society (General, Ballroom and Greek branches); Member and holds Advanced Certificate of the Association of Teachers of the Revived Greek Dance. Is also Examiner for these Societies, and holds office on various Committees. Principal of the Ripman Schools at the Welbeck Palace Hotel, London, and the Queen's Hall, Croydon. Commenced teaching career in Germany before the war. Trains students in all branches of dancing, to become teachers or for the Stage. Specializes in children's work. Is specially interested in Rhythmic work being taken in conjunction with Ballet. Has produced several successful groups. Was first to introduce a teacher of the Central European method into London. Winner of the *Dancing Times* Cup in 1930, and trained the winner of the Senior Cup at the All England Solo Dancing Competition in the same year. Gives frequent recitals and performances. Has own theatre at her London school.
Address: 12 Park Square West, London, N.W.1.

RITCHARD, Cyril; general dancer for musical comedy. Since coming to London in 1925 has played leading dancing juvenile parts with Dorothy Dickson for André Charlot; with Mimi Crawford in " R.S.V.P."; for Archibald de Bear in the Co-Optimists; with Madge Elliott in " The Love Race "; with Gilda Gray in the film " Piccadilly "; and in " Lady Luck," " So This is Love," " Love Lies," etc.
Address: 31a Connaught Street, London, W.2.
Best Photos: Dorothy Wilding, London.

RIVERS, Max; ballet master and producer. Born in London and began career as call-boy at Holborn Empire, where he began to study dancing. Toured abroad, and in 1923 staged dances for " Carte Blanche," Court Theatre, London. Became Dancing Master for Dion Titheradge, De Courville, Julian Wylie, Mrs. John Tiller, C. B. Cochran, etc. Produced dances for " Toni," Shaftesbury Theatre; De Courville's Revue, " Whirlwind "; Dion Titheradge's "Puppets," Vaudeville Theatre. Staged first full cabaret in Paris at the Frolics. Produced for Andre Charlot at Grafton Galleries, De Bear's " Punch Bowl," ' Co-Optimists," " Patricia," etc.; " The Wishing Well " for Tom Walls. Arranged ensembles and dances for C. B. Cochran's " On with the Dance," " Still Dancing " and " Clo Clo," Shaftesbury Theatre; " Cochran's 1926 Revue," " Lady Luck " for Laddie Cliff," " One Dam Thing After Another," " Shake Your Feet," " Up With the Lark," " This Year of Grace," " So this is Love," " The Girl Friend," " Mr. Cinders." Produced dances for " Hit the Deck," Paris and Marseilles; " This Year of Grace," New York; " Mr. Cinders," Berlin; " The White Horse Inn," Berlin, and at Coliseum, London. Has also produced many cabarets, including Cochran's Trocadero Cabarets and cabarets at Piccadilly Hotel, London. Has appeared on the Continent and in U.S.A., etc., staging revues at Palace Theatre, Paris, and dances for Folies Bergere, Paris; Deutche Theatre, Munich. Has been dancing partner to Dorothy Dickson, Phyllis Monkman, Jessie Matthews, Mimi Crawford, etc., etc., and has staged special dances for many well-known dancers, actors and actresses. In 1928 opened a large School of Dancing for all branches of dancing in London, and later a School in Berlin.
Address: 3/6 Rupert Street, London, W.1.

ROBARTES (Miss), Vera; general teacher. Member of the Imperial Society of Teachers of Dancing. Specializes in remedial work, and has had great success with both children and adults suffering from various physical weaknesses. Is co-principal with Miss Hilda Paton-Smith of a School of Dancing at Harrogate.
Address: School of Dancing, 8 Royal Parade, Harrogate.

ROBERT (Mr. R. O. Edwards); ballroom and exhibition dancer. Trained by Felix Demery in 1919. Was formerly on the staff of Miss Belle Harding and also that of the Tynegate-Smith School. Has appeared in Cabaret at well-known clubs in London and the provinces, and held positions of host at various hotels, etc., since 1920. Has also toured for Gaumont Films, Ltd. Now owns the Victoria Dance Hall at St. Albans.
Address: Victoria Dance Hall, Victoria Road, St. Albans.
Best Photos: Reprograph, Hana (now Navana), Rapho, Foulsham & Bamfield, Peter North, London.

ROBERTS, John; general teacher, specializing in operatic and ballroom dancing. Member of the Operatic Association; Operatic Examiner of the National Association of Teachers of Dancing, and Chairman of their Northern Council, 1931; Member Manchester Association of Teachers of Dancing. Holds Teachers' Certificate, British Ballet Organisation. Winner of the National Association Trophy for non-sequence dancing, 1930. Opened school with the late Mabel Roberts in 1920.
Address: Mabel Roberts' School of Dancing, 602 Stretford Road, Old Trafford, Manchester.

ROBERTSON (Miss), Elsie; teacher of all branches of dancing.
Address: 3 Cranbury Terrace, Southampton.

ROBINSON (Miss), Honor; general dancer and teacher. Advanced Honours Certificate of the Natural Movement Branch of Imperial Society; also Member of Ballroom, Operatic and General Branches. Committee Member Natural Movement Branch. Advanced Member Association of Operatic Dancing. Until the change of management at the Locarno Dance Hall in Streatham, London, she, with her sisters, had complete control of the dancing arrangements there.
Address: 200a High Road, Streatham Hill, London, S.W.16.

ROBINSON (Miss), Mabel; general dancer and teacher. Member Association of Operatic Dancing. Member of the Imperial Society (Ballroom, Cecchetti, Revived Greek, and Natural Movement Branches). Until the change of management at the Locarno Dance Hall in Streatham, London, she, with her sisters, had complete control of the dancing arrangements there.
Address: 200a High Road, Streatham Hill, London, S.W.16.

ROBINSON (Miss), Nancy; general dancer and teacher. Advanced Member Operatic Association. Intermediate Member Natural Movement Branch of Imperial Society. Until the change of management at the Locarno Dance Hall, Streatham, London, she, with her sisters, had complete control of the dancing arrangements there.
Address: 200a High Road, Streatham Hill, London, S.W.16.

ROGERS (Miss), Janet; general teacher. Intermediate Member of Operatic Association. Associate of Imperial Society (Cecchetti, Greek and Ballroom Branches). Advanced Member of Association of Teachers of the Revived Greek Dance. Was trained at the Cone School, London, for three years ending December, 1929, and opened her own School in Eastbourne in January, 1930.
Address: 2 Jevington Gardens, Eastbourne.
Best photo: Ladislaw, Eastbourne.

ROGERS (Miss), Thurza; operatic dancer. Had her first engagement with Karsavina at the Coliseum, London. From 1921 to 1927 appeared with Madame Anna Pavlova's Company; was *première danseuse* with that Company in the last year. Also danced in J. C. Williamson's Musical Comedies in Australia, and played the leading rôle in "Tip-Toes." Is now with an act known as "Rogers and Lascelles with Jean, Joan and Jill," playing at the leading variety halls and West End cabarets.
Address: 33 Penywern Road, Earls Court, London, S.W.
Best photo: Lenare, London.

ROSCOE (Miss), Adela (Mrs. Cyril Farmer); general teacher. Member Imperial Society of Teachers of Dancing; Examiner of London Incorporated Society. Winner Blackpool Dance Festival, 1920, and in 1930 won the Fifty Guinea Trophy for Best Sequence Dance (the Tapper) with Cyril Farmer; winner of North of England Professional Championship at Blackpool in 1930 and 1932 and of other competitions in the North. Has fulfilled many engagements in hotels in England and in Holland, and has judged many important competitions. Pupil of Espinosa.
Address: The Palais de Danse, Leeming Street, Mansfield, Notts.

ROSCOE (Mrs.), A. E.; general teacher and music teacher. Member of the Imperial Society (General Branch); Member and Past Vice-President, Musical Director and Examiner of the British Association; also Member and Musical Director of the International Dancing Masters' Association. Has been a teacher of music and dancing since the age of 15, and has trained many now successful Teachers of Dancing. Arranged many sequence dances when they were in vogue.
Author of "Music and Theory of Modern Ballroom Dancing by Questions and Answers," 1928 (Ball & Wareham, Mansfield).
Address: 3 West Hill Avenue, Mansfield, Notts.

ROSSLOVA (Miss Millicent Rosslare); operatic dancer and teacher. Trained under Lydia Kyasht, with whom she appeared, making her *début* at the Palace Theatre, London, as *première danseuse*, and subsequently at the Alhambra, Lyric Theatre, etc. Toured with Alice Delysia, Harry Tate, Nelson Keys, George Mozart, Gresham Singers. Appeared before H.M. The Queen of Norway and H.R.H. the Princess Victoria. In 1929 founded the Rosslova School of Ballet and Dance, with Headquarters at 13 Vernon Terrace, Brighton.
Address: 13 Vernon Terrace, Brighton.

Best photos: Hana (now Navana); E. W. Pannell and Navana, London.

ROWE (Miss), Iris; operatic and acrobatic-adagio dancer. Appeared as a child with Margaret Morris. Trained for Operatic with Robert Quinault, and partnered him during six years with great success all over Europe and America. Were the first couple to develop the possibilities of " Acrobatic-Adagio" work, *i.e.*, the combination *groupes enlevées* with classic adagio. " Miss Rowe is an amazingly pure and tractable instrument for the choregraphist "—Andre Levinson.
Address: 98 Redcliffe Gardens, London, S.W.10.
Best Photos: Cigarini, London.

ROWE (Miss), Joan Q.; ballroom teacher of dancing. With Mr. George C. Cousins was finalist in Columbia Amateur Ballroom Dancing Championship of Great Britain, 1929. Had teacher's course of training at the Rumsey School of Dancing, London.
Address: The Rhythm School of Ballroom Dancing, 8 Market Place, Rugby.
Best photos by Speight, Rugby.

RUAULT (Miss), Cecil; ballroom teacher. Member of the Imperial Society; Holder of Certificate from the Vernon Castle School of Dancing and was Head Assistant there for two years. Joined Mrs. Cynthia Humphreys in 1922 and remained with her until her marriage in 1927. In April, 1927, became co-principal of the Humphreys School of Dancing with Miss Galloway.
Address: 41 New Bond Street, London, W.1.

RUBEL (Miss), Margaret; specialist in National and Historical dancing. Teaches at the Court Players' School.
Address: 3 Stanford Road, London, W.8.

RUBINSTEIN (Mdme.), Ida; ballet dancer and actress. Appeared with the Diaghileff Company in *Cleopatra*, and was also presented in *Le Martyr de Saint Sebastien*, especially written for her by D'Annunzio and Debussy. Has been touring with her own Company in *Amphion, Bolero, Valse, Princesse Eugene, Nocturne, David,* etc. Made London *debut* at Covent Garden, July, 1931.

RUMSEY, H. St. John, M.A. (Cantab.); Holder of the Advanced Certificate, and is an Examiner of the Incorporated London Academy of Music. Also Holder of the Certificate of the Imperial Society, and the Bavarian Dance Teachers' Gold Medal. Member of the L.I.G. Member International Dance Academy, Zurich. Choral Scholar of Kings College, Cambridge. Assistant Master and Choir-Master Epsom College. Instructor for Speech Defects at Guy's Hospital from 1923 to present time, and was their representative and speaker at International Speech Conference. Has judged and demonstrated at many important competitious at home and abroad, and has contributed articles on ballroom dancing to several papers. Has now discontinued teaching.
Author of " No Need to Stammer," " Ballroom Dancing," and " Ballroom Dancing Explained " (Methuen).
Address: 10 Bristol House, Southampton Row, London, W.C.1.
Best photo: Rapho Studios, London.

RUMSEY (Mrs.), H. St. John (*née* Katie Smith). Examiner and Holder of Advanced Certificate Incorporated London Academy of Music (Ballroom Dancing). Studied the pianoforte for three years in Dresden. Demonstrated English Dances at Munich International Competition, January, 1929. Has now discontinued teaching.
Author of "The Art of Dancing" (Methuen).
Address: 10 Bristol House, Southampton Row, London, W.C.1.
Best photos: Navana and Rapho Studios, London.

RUSSWURM (Miss), Molly; general teacher; specializes in musical comedy, operatic and ballroom work. Elementary Member Operatic Association, and holder of their General Certificate, as also that of the British Ballet Organisation. Originally trained by Mr. Felix Demery. Had a small school in Bedfordshire for six years, moving to present address in 1930.
Address: "Arleedon," 16 Bushey Grove Road, Watford, Herts.

RUTHERSTON (Miss), Jeannette; teacher of rhythmic gymnastics, Central European dance, anatomy, and theory and practice of teaching. A dancer of the Central European method. Member of Ling Association, English Folk and Dance Society; holder of Elementary Folk Certificate and Advanced Country Dancing and Sword. Holds full College certificate of the Bedford Physical Training College and Old Students' Association. Had three years' training at the Bedford Physical Training College and two years at the Margaret Morris School as student and then on the staff; one year's course at the Bodenwieser School of Dancing, Vienna. Danced with Bodenwieser Ensemble in Poland and in Vienna. Started the " Rutherston Dubsky School of Rhythmic Movement " in October, 1930, in London with Miss Trudl Dubsky, with whom she has appeared in recitals at the Rudolf Steiner Hall and at the Faculty of Arts, London.
Address: 33a Cheyne Place, London, S.W.3.
Best photos by Zimbler, Vienna, and V. Dimitriew, Paris.

S

ST. DENIS, Ruth; teacher of classical dancing. Visited Europe in 1906/8 and appeared under the management of Henry B. Harris. Returned to the United States in 1908 and toured there under the same management. In 1914 married Mr. Ted Shawn, and in 1915 founded, jointly with Mr. Shawn, the " Denishawn School " in Los Angeles, California. In 1926-7 toured the Orient with Mr. Shawn and Company of twenty-five. Toured the United

States with Mr. Shawn almost every year for about twelve years. Finally moved business and school headquarters to New York City. At present the School is under her sole management, and is known as the Ruth St. Denis School of Dancing and its Related Arts, Mr. Shawn touring with Company.

Is the Author of " Lotus Light," a collection of poems.

Address: 67 Stevenson Place, New York City, U.S.A.

Best photos: Arthur Kales, Los Angeles; Nicholas Muray, N.Y.C.; Hoppe, London.

ST. LO (Miss), Peggy; classical dancer. Was trained at the Bagot-Stack Health School. Was Ballet Mistress at the London Hippodrome for the production of " Lucky Girl " when only 17. Her photograph was adopted by the Women's League of Health and Beauty as the picture from which their league badges were struck.

Best photos: Keystone View Co., London.

SALAMAN, Miss Susan; choregraphist and designer. Stage Manager of the Ballet Club. Produced and designed *The Tale of a Lamb* in 1929; *Our Lady's Juggler* and *Le Rugby* for the Marie Rambert dancers in 1930. Also Lord Berner's *Boxing* for the Ballet Club's first season, February, 1931.

Books: a chapter is given to Susan Salaman's choregraphy in " The Marie Rambert Dancers " by Arnold L. Haskell (British Continental Press).

Address: Ruckmans, Oakwood Hill, Dorking.

SAMPLE (Miss), E. Irene; ballroom and general teacher of dancing and elocution. Principal of Northern School of Dance and Dramatic Expression with Miss Nora Fearn and Miss Bridget Rider. The School was established in 1919.

Address: 1 Grange Crescent, Sunderland, Co. Durham.

SAVINA, Vera (Miss Vera Clark); operatic dancer. Member of the Operatic Association. First trained in 1911 at Stedman's Academy under Mdme Leoffeler. Has also studied for considerable periods under Edouard Kurylo, Enrico Cecchetti, Alexandre Volinine, Nicolas Legat and Leonide Massine. Her first engagement was with Mme. Anna Pavlova in " Snowflakes " (Palace Theatre, 1911). Appeared in revue, " Come Over Here " (London Opera House, 1913). In 1914 was *première danseuse* in " Cinderella " (H. Rallend's Tour), and also won Open Competition for engagement at Olympia as *première danseuse*. From 1915 to 1917 was *première danseuse* in " Alice in Wonderland " and in the latter year also appeared in " Mischievous Minn " (Victoria Palace). In 1918 appeared in " A Bunch of Violets " (Coliseum). In 1919 was engaged by Diaghileff Company and appeared at the Alhambra, and in 1920 appeared with the same Company at the Royal Opera House, Covent Garden. Owing to success in the *pas de deux*, *Poodles Dance* in *Boutique Fantasèue*, her name was changed by M. Diaghileff to Vera Savina. Was billed as a *première danseuse* for Paris season at Champs Elysées and took principal part in *Les Sylphides* and *Cimarosiana*. In 1921 left the Diaghileff Company, and at the beginning of September joined Leonide Massine and Company as *première danseuse* for six months tour of South America. In 1922 appeared as solo dancer in *The Cockatoo's Holiday*, arranged by Massine (Royal Opera House, Covent Garden); also toured England and Scotland and appeared at the Coliseum as a member of Leonide Massine's Quintette, which consisted of L. Lopokova, L. Sokolova, V. Savina, L. Massine and L. Woizikowsky. In 1923 was *première danseuse* in *Zephyr*, arranged by Massine (Coliseum, Alhambra and Victoria Palace). In 1924 was *première danseuse* with S. Idzikowsky and Company in *Les Roses*, arranged by Massine (Coliseum). Rejoined the Diaghileff Company and remained with them until 1928. During this engagement danced *L'Oiseau Bleu* (*pas de deux*) from *Aurora's Wedding*, *pas de trois* from the same ballet, *pas de trois* from *Le Lac des Cygnes*, and the little girl in *Children's Tales*. In 1929 toured England and Scotland as *première danseuse* with S. Idzikowsky and Company.

Address: 143 Dorset Road, Merton Park, London, S.W.19.

Best photos: Navana; Pierrot and Florence Vandamn, of London.

SCHLEE, Alfred; dance author. Member of the "Verband Deutscher Tanzkritiker" (association of German dance-critics). Studied music and theatre history; worked practically with Kurt Joos and Yvonne Georgi. In co-operation with Rudolf von Laban organised the German Dance Congress in Magdeburg, 1927. Since 1928 chief editor of the dance magazine *Schrifttanz* (Universal Edition, Vienna). Contributor to various German and American dance and theatre magazines.

Address: Baden bei Wien, Franzensring 27.

SCHOLLAR, Ludmilla; ballet dancer. One of the original members of the Diaghileff Ballet, who shared in the triumphs of the Paris *debut*. Created the role of "Estrella" in *Carnaval*, and also a role in Nijinsky's *Jeux*. Danced "The White Cat" in *The Sleeping Princess* at the Alhambra Theatre, London. Has danced a variety of roles in the classical repertoire.

Photos in Svetloff's "Le Ballet Contemporain."

SCHOOLING (Miss), Elizabeth; operatic dancer. Associate of the Imperial Society. Member of the Marie Rambert Ballet. Danced with Madame Karsavina at the Lyric Theatre, Hammersmith, and the New Theatre in *Sylphides*, *Le Cricket*, etc., and at the first performance of *Pomona* for the Camargo Society. Danced in *Lord of Burleigh* at the Midnight Ballet at the Carlton Theatre.

Address: The Ballet Club, 2a Ladbroke Road, London, W.11.

Best Photos: H. J. Whitlock & Sons, Ltd., London.

SCORER (Miss), Betty; operatic and tap dancer. Was trained by the Mayfair School, Anna Pruzina, Novikoff, Karsavina and Miss Phyllis Bedells. Appeared in a Russian Season for Novikoff at the Duke of York's Theatre, 1920; in ballet at the Old Vic, 1924; in Fokine's "Midsummer Night's Dream" ballet, 1924-25. Was a student at the Royal Academy of Dramatic Art for two years. Appeared in an Anton Dolin season, and also in *Santiago* at the London Coliseum, 1930, and has since danced in Balanchine's Company at the Coliseum and Alhambra Theatres, 1931, and in "Bow Bells" at the London Hippodrome.

Adress: 17 Cheniston Gardens, London, W.8.

Best Photos: Dorothy Wilding and Douglas, London.

SCOTT-ATKINSON, E. L. (Lennox Scott); exhibition and tap dancer. Won the World's Professional Tango Championship in 1924. Was at the Empress Rooms for four and a half years, and afterwards went to the Carlton Hotel, Haymarket, and then to the Kit-Kat Club. Visited New York in 1930-31, and is now doing exhibition dancing with Lunina. Has appeared with her in cabaret at leading West End hotels and restaurants.

Address: 5 Matheson Road, West Kensington, London, W.14.

SCOTT, Edward; general teacher, lecturer and author. Began career as an ornamental artist, but later began to teach dancing. Has now been teaching for over forty years, during the whole of which time he has waged unceasing war against all kinds of vulgarity in dancing, whether exhibited on the stage or in the ballroom. Has been a most prolific writer on the Art.

Author of "Dancing in All Ages" (Sonnenschien); "Dancing as it should be" (Routledge); "Dancing, Artistic and Social" (Bell); "Dancing for Strength and Beauty" (Allen & Unwin); "300 Hints on Modern Dancing, Recreative and Theatrical";

" Better Ballroom Dancing " (Nash & Grayson), etc.
Address : Rochester House, Holland Road, Hove.

SCOTT, Lennox. (*See* E. L. SCOTT-ATKINSON.)

SCRIMSHAW, Charles; ballroom dancer and teacher. Commenced professional career in Southport in 1926, and in that year won the World's Charleston Championship in Paris partnered by Miss Bunty Denham, and also was placed fourth in the Ballroom Charleston Championship held by Mr. C. B. Cochran at the Royal Albert Hall. In 1928-29-30 spent six months of each year teaching for Miss Jennie Brenan in Melbourne, Australia, and at the end of that time joined the Haylor-Spain School of Dancing at the Century Ballroom, Regent Street, London. In March, 1932, with Miss Phyllis Haylor as partner, gained third place in the " Amateur Dancers' " Championship, and in the summer of that year was Dance Host (with Miss Phyllis Haylor) at Gleneagles Hotel, Scotland, where he will again be during the summer of 1932. Is at present teaching at the Haylor-Spain School at the Basil Street Hotel, London.
Address : The Ballroom, Basil Street Hotel, Knightsbridge, London, S.W.1.

SCUTTS (Miss), Helen M.; ballroom teacher. Winner of " Star " All England Championship 1931, European Championship 1931, Scottish Championship 1930 and 1931, and other Scottish Championships (*See* PHILP, R. H.).
Address : 177 Renfrew St., Glasgow.
Best Photos : Navana, London.

SHACKLETON, Harold; ballroom teacher. Principal of School of Dancing at Keighley, Yorkshire. Member of International Dancing Masters' Association; President of Premier Association, 1927, and Examiner, and holder of Certificate of the Northern Dance Teachers' Association.
Address : Savoy School of Dance, 11 North Street, Keighley, Yorks.
Best Photos : Bruce Johnston, Keighley.

SHANLEY (Miss), Tony; general teacher. Member Operatic Association. Trained by Madame Judith Espinosa. Gives classes for Miss Conti and Madame Espinosa in acrobatic dancing, in which she specialises. Has her own School in Clapham.
Address : 3 Elms Road, Clapham Common, London, S.W.

SHARON (Miss), Ula (Ula Sharon Robinson); ballet and character dancer. Born in America, where she studied ballet dancing, but was prevented from professional work by the Child Labour Laws. Played in her own single act in Australia, and appeared first in New York at Aeolian Hall; played in Le Maire's " Broadway Brevities," Winter Garden, New York, and then danced for three years with the Greenwich Village Follies; appeared in Music Box Revue, " Song of the Flame," etc. *Prima Ballerina* in " Sunny " in London, 1926, and danced at Command Performance at Drury Lane; in " The Three Musketeers " at Drury Lane; at the Coliseum. Created the Lightning act in Oscar Wilde's " Nightingale and the Rose " while with Greenwich Village Follies.
Address : 122-87th Street, Jackson Heights, New York.
Best Photos : Sasha, London.

SHAWN, Ted; dancer, choreographer and producer. Founder with Ruth St. Denis of " Denishawn School " in Los Angeles in 1915. Principal with Ruth St. Denis of School in New York, where all types of dancing are taught, special subjects being dances of the Orient and Spain and Music Visualization. With " Denishawn Dancers " toured U.S.A., Canada and Far East. Appeared at Coliseum, London, in 1922; individual solo appearances in Germany and Switzerland in 1930 and 1931, being chosen to dance lead in Orpheus Dionysos with Margarete Wallman at Munich

Dance Congress, 1930. Creator of many original dances, dance-scenes and ballets, including *The Thinker*, *The Divine Idiot*, etc. Has produced well-known ballets, including *Job*, by Vaughan-Williams. With an ensemble of sixty dancers gives regular seasons of dancing at Lewisohm Stadium, New York.

Author of following books:—" Ruth St. Denis, Pioneer and Prophet," J. H. Nash & Co.; "The American Ballet," Henry Holt Co.; "Gods Who Dance," E. P. Dutton Co.

Address: 67 Stevenson Place, New York City, U.S.A.

Best Photos: Charlotte Rudolph, Dresden; Soichi Sunami, New York.

SHEEN (Miss), B. W.; general teacher. Associate London Academy of Music (Elocution), Licentiate Royal Academy of Music (Elocution). Trained in elocution by Ernest Pertwee and Acton Bond, in dancing by the Misses Hutton Moss and Laurent Novikoff. Taught for the Misses Hutton Moss 1913-1918; opened own school in 1918, and has a large connection in boys' and girls' schools in London and South of England.

Address: 40 Wigmore St., London, W.1.

Best Photos: Olive and Isabel Ray, London.

SHELLEY (Miss), Hazel; tap dancer. Born and studied at Philadelphia, U.S.A., and toured U.S.A. and Canada with Mildred Shelley and Ann Pennington as "Shelley Trio." Came to England and toured the Halls with own band. Entered cabaret as single, appearing in Metropole Midnight Follies, and Prince's, Piccadilly, and Archie de Bear's "Punch Bowl." Appeared at Hippodrome, New York, and in "Bunk of 1926" at Broadhurst Theatre, New York. Keith and Orpheum Tour with J. C. Flippen, and studied under Buddy Bradley. Appeared in "Folly to be Wise" at Piccadilly Theatre, London.

Address: 56 Delaware Mansions, Maida Vale, London.

Best Photos: Mitchell, New York.

SHEPPARD, Frederic Kaye; ballroom dancer. Member of the Ballroom Dancers Association. Was a District Finalist in the Columbia Amateur Championship of 1929, and commenced dancing professionally in 1930.

Address: 33 Croft Gardens, London, W.7.

SHORROCKS, H.; teacher of art, music and dancing. Holder of Certificates of the Manchester and British Association of Teachers of Dancing. Principal of Shorrocks Academy, Manchester, established in 1895. Also runs a public dance hall known as Shorrocks Palais Royal Ballroom, which is one of the principal halls in Manchester.

Address: Brunswick Street, Oxford Road, Manchester.

SIDES (Miss), Gertrude; general teacher. Advanced Member Operatic Association; Member Imperial Society of Teachers of Dancing (Operatic and Ballroom branches); Member Examination Committee and local representative for British Ballet Organization and holder of their Advanced Certificate. Principal of Gertrude Sides' School of Dancing, where all branches of dancing are taught.

Address: 5 Menlove Avenue, Mossley Hill, Liverpool.

SIDES (Miss), Norah W.; ballroom teacher. Member International Dancing Masters' Association. Began as assistant to Wilfred Orange, I.D.M.A., in 1929; became a member of Y.A.D.M. and I.D.M.A. in 1930. Is well known as co-Principal of Norton School of Dancing, and Hostess of the Wharcliffe Dance Club, which is run by the School.

Address: 418 Firth Park Road, Sheffield.

SIELLE, Robert; exhibition dancer with Annette Mills. Starred in famous cabarets in London, New York, Berlin, Copenhagen, Paris, Cannes, Monte Carlo, Nice, Aix les Bains and Juan les Pins, etc., etc. First couple to introduce light comedy into exhibition

dancing. Introduced the Charleston and the Moochi.
Address: 18 Belsize Park, Hampstead, London, N.W.3.
Best Photos: Claude Harris, London.

SILVESTER (Miss), Gwendolyn; ballroom and general teacher. Member Imperial Society of Teachers of Dancing. Having specialized in teaching children, has a good connection among Girls' Schools, including Ancaster House, Ancaster Gate, Bexhill-on-Sea; Battle Abbey, Sussex, etc.
Address: 20 New Bond St., London, W.1.
Best Photos: Navana; Swaine; Lafayette, London.

SILVESTER, Victor; ballroom dancer and teacher. Fellow of Imperial Society of Teachers of Dancing; First Vice-President of Ballroom Branch and Examiner for the Society. Winner of World's Dancing Championship 1922-1923, " Dancing World " £200 Waltz Championship, Ostend Waltz Championship,"Dancing Times" Waltz Championship, " Dancing Times " Tango Competition and " Frolics " All-Round Dancing Championship. Runner-up in World's Dancing Championship 1924 and 1925. Technical adviser to Columbia Gramophone Company. Vice-Chairman of " Star " All England Dancing Championships.
Author of " Modern Ballroom Dancing " (Jenkins); " Theory and Technique of Ballroom Dancing " (" Dancing Times "); " Bestway " Dancing (Amalgamated Press); " Gesellschaftstanz " (Germany and Austria—Der Tanz); " Modern Ballroom Dancing Up-to-date " (Jenkins); " Ubungen " (Germany and Austria—Der Tanz).
Address: 20 New Bond Street, London, W.1.
Best Photos: Claude Harris; Navana; Molloy, London.

SILVESTER (Mrs.), Victor; ballroom dancer and teacher. Fellow of, Examiner and Member of Ballroom Committee for Imperial Society of Teachers of Dancing. Runner-up with Victor Silvester in World's Dancing Championship 1924-1925; voted the best All England demonstration couple with Victor Silvester in the *Dancing Times* Competition. Adjudicator and demonstrator for the " Star " and Columbia Dancing Championships.
Address: 20 New Bond Street, London, W.1.
Best Photos: Claude Harris; Foulsham & Banfield; Swaine, London.

SIMMONDS (Miss), Millicent; general teacher and exhibition dancer. Member of the Imperial Society (Ballroom Branch). Trained by the " Gilmer " School, Nottingham, and Mons. Pierre. Has own school in Derby, with branches in Burton, Repton, Loughborough, etc.
Address: The Millicent Simmonds School of Dancing, 7a Victoria Buildings, London Road, Derby.
Best Photos: Winter, Derby.

SIMMONS (Miss), Muriel; ballroom teacher. Fellow, Examiner and Member of Committee Imperial Society of Teachers of Dancing (Ballroom branch). After training in London, became head assistant for Monsieur Robert in Paris, later starting own School of Dancing in London. Adjudicator for all leading Championships and Competitions; is one of the five original Members of Teachers of Dancing who standardized theory and technique of modern ballroom dancing.
Address: 13 Stratford Place, W.1.
Best Photos: Edmund Harrington, London.

SITZES, Fernando Castells; general teacher. Principal of the first Dancing Academy to be opened in Barcelona.
Author of book on the Black Bottom.
Address: Barcelona, Spain, calle Viladomat 140-30.

SKINNER (Miss), Ethne; general teacher. Member Operatic Association; Member Imperial Society of Teachers of Dancing; Member Committee Operatic Association; Examiner for Home Office competitions, private societies, etc. Principal of

School of Classical Dancing, London, including a large private connection in London and provinces, and teacher in well-known girls' schools and colleges, including Battersea Physical Training College, Sherborne Girls' School, etc.
Address: Logan Hall, Kensington, W.8.
Best Photos: Sawara.

SMART (Miss), Joyce E.; general teacher, specializing in Greek, National and Ballroom dancing. Holder of the Teachers' Certificate of the Ginner-Mawer School of Dance and Drama. Associate of the Imperial Society of Teachers of Dancing (Ballroom). Was trained at the Ginner-Mawer School, and the Victor Silvester School. Acts as a Visiting Teacher. Was Stage Manager to the Ginner-Mawer School for their Season of Performances in the summer of 1931.
Address: Oak Tree House, Redington Gardens, Hampstead, London.
Best photos: Molloy, London.

SMITH, Mr. (and Mrs.) Alf; ballroom teachers. Past President National Association; Past Vice-President and present Hon. Secretary Manchester Association of Teachers of Dancing. Both Mr. Smith and his wife have served the Northern Council of the National Association as Examiners, and Mr. Smith served the Council as Chairman for several years.
Address: 202 St. Mary's Road, Moston, Manchester.
Best Photos: Guttenberg, Manchester.

SMITH (Miss), Sissie W.; general teacher. Advanced Member Operatic Association; Member Imperial Society of Teachers of Dancing (Ballroom branch). One of the advanced members chosen to display ensemblé work at the first reception of the Operatic Association in 1928. Danced in Alexander Genée's production of *Coppelia* at a matinée organised by the Operatic Association at the Gaiety Theatre in 1929. Now conducting a successful School in Nottingham.
Address: 36a Bridle Smith Gate, Nottingham.
Best photos: F. Smith, Nottingham.

SMURTHWAITE (Mdme.), Jeanie; general teacher. Advanced Member Operatic Association, and Member of Sub-Committee. Fellow Imperial Society of Teachers of Dancing, and Vice-President Operatic Branch; Member of Cecchetti, Revived Greek and General Teachers' Branches; Member Association of Teachers of Revived Greek Dance. Examiner for Children's Examinations. Adjudicator at principal Festivals and Eisteddfods. Pupil of Professor Felix Gravé for Fencing.
Address: Devon House, 173 Great Portland Street, London, W.

SOKOLOVA, Lydia. Received her early training with Pavlova and Mordkin, and toured America with the latter. Played Zobriede in *Sheherazade* at the age of 15 as understudy to Baldina.
Karsavina says of her in " Theatre Street ":
" There was a new recruit to our ranks that season for whom the intricate difficulties of the music had unusually few terrors, and Lycession (Daphnis and Chloe-Ravel) was the first rôle that Hilda Munnings, hitherto a modest figure in the *corps de ballet*, interpreted. . . .
" . . . Hilda Munnings alone possessed that indefinable spirit that made her one of us. Like the Russians, she possessed that humility of heart, and a fervour almost religious in its intensity that gave her the same attitude towards her work as we had.
" From the day she entered our ranks she became artistically naturalized, rapidly learning Russian, and what is more important, thinking in Russian, and that, added to the fact that she had had a serious musical education, gave her an artistic experience similar in scope to what we had had at the Imperial School."
Since then Sokolova has danced a great number of the leading rôles in

the repertoire, both classical and character. Perhaps her finest are Columbine in *Carnaval*, the Rag Mazurka in *Les Biches*, Kikimora in *Children's Tales*, The Sailor's Wife in *Les Matelots* and The Miller's Wife in *The Three-Cornered Hat*. She scored a great triumph as the Virgin in *Le Sacré du Printemps* at Covent Garden, 1928, the final Diaghileff season.

" Lydia Sokolova is without the slightest doubt the finest dance artist this country has yet produced, and one of the great dancers of the world. She is a great actress as well as a great dancer, in every way an outstanding personality. I have yet to see her give an indifferent performance."—A. L. Haskell, in an article.

Address: 2 Vauxhall Villas, Birchington, Kent.

Best photos: Lenare; Antony; Sasha; Claude Harris, London.

SOLOMONOFF, Sonia; *maitre de ballet* and teacher. Began stage career at the age of four in dramatic work in New York. Appeared with Sir Ben Greet, Robert Mantell, Ernst von Possart and Rudolph Schildkraut. Commenced studying dancing at the age of nine under Mdme. Elizabeth Menzeli. Together with his wife, Miss Lola Menzeli, has toured the world with great success. Now teaching in Atlanta, Georgia, U.S.A.

Address: 243 14th Street N.E., Atlanta, Georgia, U.S.A.

SOMERVILLE (Mrs.), F. C.; general teacher. Principal of the Somerville School of Dancing, Yeovil, where all types of dancing are taught. Displays given by pupils have given substantial sums to local hospitals, etc.

Address: The Studio, Church St., Yeovil.

SONNE, Doris (Miss Doris Sonn); operatic dancer. Started training at the age of fourteen with Mdme. Lucia Cormani, afterwards with Nijinska and other well-known teachers. Started her career at the Lyric Theatre, Hammersmith as one of the Spanish dancers in *The Duenna*, 1924. Danced in La Nijinska's Ballet in her tour round England, 1925, and with Vera Nemchinova in her tour of France and Switzerland in 1929. Joined Anton Dolin in 1925 as member of *corps de ballet*, becoming a soloist, and later dancing with him as *première danseuse*. Soloist and leader with George Balanchine's Troup. Joined Monte Carlo Ballet, January, 1932.

Address: 77 Melrose Avenue, Cricklewood, London, N.W.2.

Best Photos: Lenare; Raphael, London.

SPAIN (Miss), Molly; ballroom teacher. Member of Committee of Official Board of Ballroom Dancing. Partner of Phyllis Haylor in School of Ballroom Dancing. With Frank Ford won " Star " Championship in 1927; runner-up in 1929. Judge of " Star " Championship in 1928.

Address: Basil Street Hotel, Knightsbridge, London, S.W.1.

Best Photos: Dorothy Wilding; Yvonne Gregory, London.

SPARGER (Miss), Celia; masseuse and remedial expert. Member Chartered Society of Massage and Medical Gymnastics. Trained at Chelsea College of Physical Education and taught several schools Swedish gymnastics and dancing. Later, specialized in remedial work, substituting operatic technique for Swedish remedial exercises, and is now treating orthopaedic cases by this method. Lectured to Chartered Society of Massage and Medical Gymnastics, Ling Association, etc., etc.

Author of " Rhymes and Dances for Little Folk," and " Dancing Time for Little Folk " (Nisbet)

Address: 16 Nottingham Place, London, W.1.

SPENCER (Miss), Penelope; dancer and choreographist. Ballet Mistress to Royal College of Music, League of Arts. Adjudicator of dancing at several musical festivals. Dancer and dance producer for the Glastonbury Players, and solo dancer and dance producer for the British National Opera Co., for Miss Sybil Thorndyke,

and for Sir Nigel Playfair ; solo dancer for the Royal Opera, Covent Garden, and has given a number of dance recitals and ballets in London and the Provinces. Has appeared at the London Coliseum. Danced in the Camargo Society's first performance.
Book : " Penelope Spencer " (Creatic Artist), by Arnold Haskell, ' Artists of the Dance Series (British Continental Press).
Address : 11 Brechin Place, London, S.W.7.
Best Photos : Herbert Lambert, Bath ; Dorothy Wilding and Beck & MacGregor, London.

SPENCER (Miss), Victoria; operatic dancer and general teacher. Intermediate Member Association of Operatic Dancing of Great Britain. Member Imperial Society of Teachers of Dancing (Ballroom and Operatic).
Address : 29 Warwick Road, Ealing, London, W.5.
Best photos : Neame, London.

SPESSIVA, Olga (Olga Spessitzeva), " Etoile " dancer at the Paris Opera. Was trained at the Imperial Theatre School, St. Petersburg, and danced at the Marinsky Theatre. In 1915 was *première danseuse* with Nijinsky in North America, and in 1922 made her *debut* in London as *première danseuse* in " The Sleeping Princess " at the Alhambra. Afterwards toured with the Diaghileff Company. In 1924 was invited by the Opera, Paris, to join them as *etoile* dancer, and is still with them. Has appeared in all the roles of the classical repertoire. In 1931 visited Buenos Aires, and appeared at the Colon Theatre.
Address : 39 Boulevard St. Jacques, Paris XIV, France.

SPURGEON, Jack. Trained at the Italia Conti Stage School. In 1931 won the 100 Guinea Trophy of the National Association of Teachers of Dancing for solo operatic dancing. Dancing in " White Horse Inn " at the London Coliseum.
Address : c/o The Italia Conti School, 14 Lamb's Conduit Street, London, W.C.1.

STACK (Mrs.), Bagot; Principal of the Bagot-Stack Health School ; Fellow of the Conn Institute ; Certificated Teacher of Mrs. Josef Conn's Health Exercises. Founder of the Women's League of Health and Beauty, which has met with conspicuous success. Produced demonstration by members in Hyde Park in June, 1930, before the Rt. Hon. George Lansbury and an audience of 10,000 people. Mrs. Bagot-Stack has written articles on Physical Culture for most of the leading periodicals, including *The Dancing Times*, and also for *The Daily Mail*. Has produced a series of five films for the Gaumont Co., and has broadcast a series of four talks for the B.B.C. Has judged the Health and Strength £100 Physical Excellence Competition.
Author of " Building the Body Beautiful."
Address : The Bagot-Stack Health School, Mortimer Hall, Great Portland Street, London, W.1.

STANLEY (Miss), Phyllis; operatic dancer. Trained principally by Mdme. Egorova, Mdme. Karsavina and M. Legat. Appeared with the Balanchine Company at the Alhambra, and in many Camargo productions. Appeared as " First Attendant " on the "Abbess" in " The Miracle," at the Lyceum, and was also first understudy to Tilly Losch in that production.
Address : 25 West Kensington Mansions, London, W.14.

STEIN (Mdme.), Yvonne Daunt; operatic dancer. *Première danseuse* at Étoile Opéra, Paris ; Vice-President of the Operatic Association. Has created parts in *Salome, Frivolau, Thais, Samson et Delila, Lègende St. Christophe, Les Troyens, Castor et Pollux*, etc., etc., appearing in well-known theatres on the continent ; Coliseum, London, etc.
Address : 23 Avenue de la Celle St. Cloud, Garches, S. et. O., France.
Best Photos : Sabourin, Paris.

STERN, Sydney; ballroom dancer and teacher. Examiner of London Academy. Winner of "Star" Champion-

ship 1928 and 1929 ; European Championship 1930 ; Grand Prix d'Elégance ; and World's Championship 1930.
Address : 147 Anson Road, Cricklewood, London, N.W.
Best Photos : Le Dernier Cri, London.

STEWART, Maxwell; ballroom teacher. Fellow Imperial Society of Teachers of Dancing, and Examiner ; Member Syndicat Nationale des Professeurs de Danse. Began dancing at Colour Schemes Studio in 1922 ; later at Queen's Hall Roof Garden. Winner with Barbara Miles of World's Dancing Championship, 1924 and 1925 ; with Pat Sykes, 1926, 1928 and 1930 ; European Championship, International Championships, 1930 ; Professional Championship of Great Britain, 1928 and again in 1931 ; Tango Championship, 1926 ; " Star " New Dance Competition (the Skater's Waltz), 1929. Originator with Pat Sykes of the Sugar Step, Skater's Waltz and Kerb Step. Recorded for Parlophone Co., 1930. Filmed by Pathé Freres, Gaumont, Ltd., Fox Movietone News, etc., 1924-1930. Adjudicated at " Star " All England Championships, 1926-1929 ; Columbia Amateur Championships, 1926-1927 ; International Championship, 1929, etc., etc. Danced by special request at Command Performance before T.M. The King and Queen of Norway, 1928. Has appeared at Alhambra, Coliseum, London, Murray's Club, etc. First partner was Sylvia Hawkes (Lady Ashley), with whom competition was won in 1922.
Author of " Modern Dancing " (W. Foulsham & Co.) ; " Dance Instructor " (W. Foulsham & Co.).
Address : 11 Granville Place, London, N.W.1 ; and School of Dancing, Mostyn Hotel, London, W.1.
Best Photos : Lenare ; Sasha, London.

STOKES, William Michael. Originator and Founder of the Ancient Order of Fox-trotters in 1927. Life Governor of the Royal Northern Hospital in consequence of financial aid given to it by the above organization.
Address : 213 Piccadilly, London, W.1.

STONE (Miss), Suzanne; teacher of mime and natural movement. Licentiate Imperial Society of Teachers of Dancing ; Member of Natural Movement Committee. Trained at Madge Atkinson School, Manchester. Instructor of Mime at the Royal Academy of Dramatic Art, and of Mime and Dancing at the Ben Greet Dramatic Company. Has visited U.S.A. three times as organizer of Dramatics at a Summer School.
Author of Mime Plays (French, Ltd.).
Address : Dormers, Stoke Poges, Bucks.

STRAUSS (Miss), Sara Mildred; modern concert dance artiste. Treasurer and Board Member of the Concert Dancers' League. Director of the Strauss School of the Dance in Carnegie Hall. Was the first to give an entire performance without music. Miss Strauss and her group have visited some of the most noted schools of the dance in Berlin, Dresden, Vienna and Salzburg, where she directs her European Summer School. The Strauss dancers have given several performances in New York and abroad during the seasons of 1929 and 1930.
Author of " The Dance in Life."
Address : Studio 825, Carnegie Hall, 57th St. and 7th Avenue, New York City.
Best photos : Arnold Genthe and Lejaren Hiller, New York.

STRUDWICK (Miss), Gipsy; ballroom teacher. Trained by and has taught for Miss Vacani. Is now Principal of the Empress Rooms Dancing Staff—since 1921.
Address : C/o the Empress Rooms, Royal Palace Hotel, Kensington, London, W.8.
Best photos : Dorothy Wilding, London.

STUART (Miss), Molly; teacher of all branches of dancing. Member of the Operatic Association, and of the

Imperial Society. Has a School of Dancing in Rhodesia, and specialises in children's work.

Address: P.O. Box 223, Bulawayo, Rhodesia.

STURGIESS (Miss), Murielle; ballroom dancer and teacher. Member of the Imperial Society. Studied operatic dancing as a child, but took up ballroom dancing at the age of 16, and in less than a year had passed the ballroom examination of the Imperial Society. Has won a number of competitions in Lancashire, including the " Allied North of England Dancing Championship." Has been trained by Miss Josephine Bradley, and is now partner to Mr. Frank Ford at the Empress Rooms, London.

Has contributed articles to the *Manchester Chronicle*, etc.

Address: c/o The Empress Rooms, Kensington, London, W.8., and Oakdene, Scarisbrick New Road, Southport, Lancs.

SUFFIELD (Miss), Mollie; general teacher. Member of Association of Operatic Dancing. Is in partnership with Miss Madge Atkinson, and has for over ten years controlled the operatic, ballroom, musical comedy and cabaret work of their school. Trained originally by Miss Madge Atkinson, she subsequently gained considerable professional stage experience and further special training. Specializes in work required for training of teachers and in special dance productions for stage and cabaret work; also for teachers' competitive work. With her partner has five times won the *Dancing Times* Cup at the Blackpool and Scarborough Dance Festivals, and with her has several times been runner-up at the finals of the Sunshine All England Competitions in London. Has judged many important competitions. Has presented her dancers at the Manchester Beecham Opera Festivals, principal Manchester theatres, etc. Is local Secretary for Children's Examinations of the Operatic Association.

Address: 259 Deansgate, Manchester.

Best Photos: Schmitt, and W. S. Kay, Manchester.

SUTTON (Miss), Sylvia; ballroom teacher. Was Principal Instructress at the Langham Studio of Dancing, Henrietta Street, London, and in 1928 acted as hostess and teacher at the " Owner Driver's Club," Piccadilly; is now teaching at Sydenham.

Address: 3 Lawrie Park Road, Sydenham, London, S.E.26.

SUTTON (Miss), Vera; general teacher. Is Co-Principal with the Misses Young and Ward of the Sutton School of Dancing, Brighton. Holders of the Intermediate Certificate of the Operatic Association, and Members of the Imperial Society's Operatic, Greek and Ballroom Branches. School has been successful in local competitions.

Address: Sutton School of Dancing, 1 Upper North Street, Brighton.

SVETLOFF, Valerian; art and dancing critic; member of the Association de la Presse Etrangère in Paris. Born in St. Petersburg and received a professional military education. For many years attended to choregraphic criticism. Has written in several newspapers and important art magazines. Possessed in St. Petersburg a big ballet museum and a library of theatrical and choregraphical works, which disappeared after the Bolshevic revolution. Fought for two years in the war (on the Galician front). Now living in Paris where he continues his literary work.

Author of the following books: " The Contemporary Ballet," in French and Russian (M. de Brunoff, Paris); " Anna Pavlova," Monograph, in English and French (M. de Brunoff, Paris); " Les Programmes des Ballets Russes," in French (M. de Brunoff, Paris); " Terpsichore," in Russian (A. Marks, St. Petersburg); " The Sources of Greek Dancing," in Russian. (The two last named are out of print.) Also " Anna Pavlova," " Artists of the Dance Series " (British-Continental Press).

Address: Cayre's Hotel, 4 Boulevard Raspail, Paris, VIIe.

SWAN (Miss), Winifred; teacher of natural movement. Holder of the Annea Spong Certificate and Diploma. Trained by Mary Evans, of Nottingham, in Natural Movement Dancing, and Elocution. Gained two certificates in elocution from the Guildhall School of Music ; also one in Pianoforte from the Associated Board. Has a Studio for Natural Movement Dancing, Elocution and Pianoforte at 18 The Arcade, Letchworth.
Address: 142 Wilbury Road, Letchworth, Herts.

SYKES (Miss), Pat; ballroom dancer and teacher. Fellow and Examiner of Imperial Society of Teachers of Dancing. Trained with Madame Astafieva and Henry Cooper ; worked at Carlton Hotel and Empress Rooms, London. With Maxwell Stewart, winner of World's Dancing Championship, 1924, 1925, 1926, 1928 and 1930 ; European Championship, 1930 ; International Championship, 1930 ; International Competition, 1930 ; " Star " New Dance Competition, 1929 ; Professional Championship of Great Britain, 1928 and 1931 ; Tango Championship, 1926. With Maxwell Stewart was originator of Sugar Step, Skaters' Waltz, Kerb Step, Adjudicator for " Star " and Columbia Championships ; International Championships, etc., etc. Filmed by Pathé Freres, Gaumont, Ltd., Fox Movietone News, and recorded for Parlophone Company.
Co-Author of " Modern Dancing " (Foulsham & Co.). Co-Principal of School of Dancing at the Mostyn Hotel.
Address: 15 Oval Road, Regent's Park, N.W.1.
Best Photos: Lenare ; Pollard Crowther, London ; Walden Hammond, Leamington Spa.

SYLVIA (*see* ALBERTO AND SYLVIA), of Alberto and Sylvia, juvenile ballroom exhibition dancers.

T

TACEY, W. Thornton; ballroom dancer and teacher. Three times winner of " Star " Tango Championships ; third in British Professional Championship of England (Slow Foxtrot) in 1928. Now teacher on the staff at the Empress Rooms.
Address: Empress Rooms, Kensington High Street, London, W.

TALBOT, Leon; teacher of ballroom dancing. Member Universal Association of Teachers of Dancing, and was Vice-President and on the Examining Board 1927-1929. Member International Dancing Masters' Association. Holds Saturday evening dances at the Albert Hall, Derby, and has own dance band—the Leon Dance Band.
Address: Leon School of Dancing, London Road, Derby.

TALBOT (Mrs.), Leon; teacher of ballroom dancing. Member Universal Association Teachers of Dancing ; Member International Dancing Masters' Association. (*See also* LEON TALBOT.)
Address: Leon School of Dancing, London Road, Derby.

TAPERELL (Miss), Eileen; general teacher and exhibition dancer. Advanced Member of the Association of Operatic Dancing, and holder of their Solo Seal. Trained by Espinosa (operatic), Max Rivers (tap) and Santos Casani (ballroom). Was engaged to instruct the film artists in the Tango for the British film, " City of Song," made at the Wembley Studios. Acts as Dance Hostess at the Majestic Ballroom, Wembley. Has four successful schools, at Golders Green, Edgware, Wembley and Hastings.
Address: 52 St. Augustine's Avenue, Wembley Park, Middlesex.

TARRANT, Bert; ballroom teacher. Member Midland Association. First Prize Diploma at Birmingham Conference, 1924. Proprietor and Licensee of the Salisbury Dance Hall, Queen's Park, N.W., 1922-1927. Principal of Dancing Academy.
Address: Dancing Academy, College Hall, 230 Great College Street, London, N.W.1.

TAYLOR (Major), Cecil H.; ballroom teacher. President of the Imperial Society of Teachers of Dancing since 1908. Has acted as Judge in the Finals of the Worlds Championships, " Star " Championships, Scottish and Irish Championships, and the International Championships (Continental) and other important competitions. The inventor of the " Yale Blues " and many other successful dances. Director of dancing at the Royal Hotel, Scarborough. Served with the Devonshire Regiment for eleven years, and during the War was Commandant on a section of the North East Coast.
Author of " The Modern Dancer's Guide " (1910) (Jennings, Leeds).
Best Photos: Walker, Scarborough.

TAYLOR, G. Douglas; teacher of Scottish and ballroom dancing. Member and Treasurer Imperial Society of Teachers of Dancing.
Author of " Some Traditional Scottish Dances " (C. W. Beaumont).
Address: 3 Furnival St., Holborn, London, E.C.4.

TAYLOR (Miss), Mollie; ballroom teacher. Teacher's Advanced Certificate (Incorporated London Academy of Music). Has written articles for *Dancing and the Ballroom*, etc.
Address: 60 Avondale Road, South Croydon, Surrey.

TCHERKAS, Constantin; operatic dancer. Trained by Cecchetti, Nijinska, Legat, Egorova. Member of Diaghileff's Russian Ballet Company 1923-1929, appearing in *Les Sylphides, Zephyre and Flora, Les Biches, La Boutique Fantasque, Cimarosiana*, etc., etc. Appeared in Cochran's 1930 Revue. Is now at Théatre National de l' Opéra, Paris.
Address: Théatre de l'Opera, Paris.
Best Photos: Lenare, London ; Tanqueray, London ; Dimitrieff, Paris.

TCHERNICHEVA (Madame), Lubov (Madame Lubov Grigorieff) ; first dancer of Serge Diaghileff's Russian Ballet. Professor of Classical and Ballet Dancing (Method Cecchetti). On completing her studies at the Petrograd Imperial School entered the company of the Imperial Ballet of the Marinsky Opera House, where she danced for two years. She then accepted an engagement to join M. Diaghileff's Company and left Petrograd for Western Europe. On the completion of her studies at the Petrograd Imperial School she continued studying under the guidance of Cecchetti. Her *repertoire* is extremely diverse, comprising both purely dancing parts and character dances and also numerous dramatic mime parts where plastics play an important feature. To the first category belong such parts as danced in *Sylphides, Carnaval, Children's Tales, Good-humoured Ladies, Apollo Musagetes, The Gods Go a'begging, The Three-Cornered Hat, Les Facheux, The Fire-Bird*. To the second category the parts of *Cleopatra, Scheherazade, Thamar, L' Après-midi d'un Faun*. During the past three years she gave classes to all the dancers of the Russian Ballet, which were entrusted to her by M. Serge de Diaghileff after Cecchetti's death.
Books: Mentioned in all the leading works on the Diaghileff Ballet.
Address: 16 Boulevard d'Italie, Monte-Carlo, Principauté de Monaco.
Best photos: V. Dimitrieff, Paris.

TERPIS, Max; ballet master. Principal of the Terpis School, Berlin. Born in Zürich, Switzerland. Ballet Master Staatsoper, Berlin, 1924-1930, and at Scala, Milan, and Staatoper, Vienna, 1930-1931. Created many ballets including *Der Letzte Prinot, Don Morte, Die Nachtlichen, Prometheus*, and is well known as a teacher of classical and modern dancing.
Address: Berlin : Charlottenburg, Nene Kantstrasse 21.
Best Photos: Robertson, Berlin.

THOMAS (Miss), Mollie; general teacher. Member of the Association of Teachers of the Revived Greek Dance. Co-Principal with Miss May

Hare of the May Hare and Mollie Thomas School of Dancing, London.
Address: The Studio, 209 Archway Road, Highgate, London, N.6.

THOMPSON (Miss), Eileen; operatic dancer. Advanced Member Association of Operatic Dancing of Great Britain. Holder of a number of medals and certificates for stage dancing competitions. Trained by the Atkinson-Suffield School, Manchester.
Address: 20 Poplar Avenue, Levenshulme, Manchester.
Best photos: W. K. Thompson, Manchester.

THORNE (Miss), Dorothy; teacher of stage dancing. Was principal dancer at Prince's, Ambassadors and Court Theatres. Is Co-Principal with her sister, Miss Madge Thorne, of the Thorne Academy.
Address: 10 Henrietta Street, Cavendish Square, London, W.1.

THORNE (Miss), Madge; teacher of stage dancing. Is Co-Principal with her sister, Miss Dorothy Thorne, of the Thorne Academy.
Address: 10 Henrietta Street, Cavendish Square, London, W.1.

THORNTON (Miss), Norah; Intermediate Member of the Operatic Association. Member of the Ballroom Branch of the Imperial Society (Elementary), and has obtained a Certificate for Advanced Country Dancing. Is an assistant at the Violet Allen School of Dancing, Wolverhampton.
Address: 55 Darlington Street, Wolverhampton, Staffs.

TILLIO (*see* MITTY AND TILLIO).
Address: 162 Rue Ordener, Paris.

TIMMINS, Ronald; exhibition dancer and teacher of ballroom and tap dancing. Member Imperial Society of Teachers of Dancing. Winner World's Championship (Exhibition Dancing) and of Referee Cup Open Waltz Competition in 1924, and finalist in other important competitions. Managing Director of Norman and Saxon School of Dancing, Bournemouth; judge of dancing competitions; writer on dancing for the B.B.C. Tours extensively in England and on the continent as an exhibition dancer and demonstrator. London studio at 95 New Bond Street, W.1.
Address: Lloyd's Bank, Messrs. Cox's Branch, 6 Pall Mall, S.W.1.
Best Photos: Hirstbrunner, Lucerne.

TOMS, Frank R.; ballroom teacher. Member of the National Association of Teachers of Dancing. Has organised and officiated at a number of local dances.
Address: 64 Acacia Road, Leytonstone, London, E.11.

TONGE, Avis, B.A. (Miss); teacher of operatic, Greek, ballroom, step and Highland dancing. Intermediate Member Operatic Association; Licentiate Imperial Society of Teachers of Dancing (Operatic and Greek branches); Member of General Branch. Has School of Dancing at 12 St. George Gate, Doncaster, with branches at Barnsley, Worksop, Sheffield and Wath.
Address: 12 St. George Gate, Doncaster.

TORDIS (Madame), Elinor; well-known dancer and teacher in Vienna. Has her own school.
Address: Grunangerasse, 2 Vienna, 1.

TORRENS - DIXON (Miss), O; teacher of ballroom dancing. Began teaching in London in 1924, later teaching in private houses in Pembrokeshire. Revised and brought up to date "Ballroom Dancing" (Geographia, Ltd.).
Address: 6 Lexham Gardens, W.8.

TOSH, Esme; musical comedy dancer. Trained in Melbourne, Australia. Appeared with Audrey Tosh as the Tosh Twins in "Shake Your Feet," "Oh Kay" at London theatres; at Moulin Rouge, Paris; in cabarets at London hotels; also touring Europe. First engagement alone in

the "Love Race" at the Gaiety Theatre, London.
Address: 74 Gloucester Road, London, S.W.7.
Best Photos: Sobot, Paris.

TOYE (Miss), Wendy; operatic, step, Greek and character dancer. First appearance at the Albert Hall in January, 1922, in a polka when 4 years old. Runner-up for the Junior Cup, "All England Solo Competition" in 1924 and 1925, and winner of that competition in 1926 and 1930. Winner of the European Championship Solo Charleston (Amateur) Competition at Charles B. Cochran's Charleston Ball, at the Albert Hall in 1926. In 1927 produced her first ballet, *And Their Colours go to make the Rainbow*, at the Palladium when only 10 years of age. In 1929 produced *Mother Earth* at the Savoy Theatre, and in 1930 *The Legend of the Willow Pattern*, and was first in Pedlars' Fair ballet production competition. Child lead in "Toad of Toad Hall" at the Lyric Theatre in 1930. Appeared in "Hiawatha" at the Royal Albert Hall, 1931, and in "The Miracle" at the Lyceum.
Address: 13 Warwick Road, Upper Clapton, London, N.E.
Best photos: Douglas, Lenare, London.

TRAILL, Jean; general teacher.
Address: 42 Amesbury Avenue, Streatham Hill, London, S.W.2.

TRAVANOVA (Miss), Pamli; operatic and character dancer and teacher. Studied under Nicolas Legat, Anton Dolin, Alfred Griffin, and others.
Address: 20 St. Quentin Avenue, London, W.10.
Best photos: Raphael; Claude Harris, London.

TREFILOVA, Vera (Mdme. Vera Solovieva). Prima Ballerina Imperial Theatre, St. Petersburg—appointed on the same day as Anna Pavlova. Educated at the Imperial Schools, and studied under Gerdt, Johanssen, etc. Appeared in the leading rôles of the classical repertoire: *Paquita, Casse-Noisette, Le Petit Cheval Bossu, Bayadere*, etc. Left the stage after thirteen years to marry M. Solovieff, director of an important literary review. Rejoined the stage to appear with the Diaghileff Company in London as the Princess Aurora in *The Sleeping Beauty*; in Monte Carlo in *The Swan Lake*; and in Paris in *The Spectre of the Rose* with Idzikowsky. Has created such divertissements as *The Black Swan* (Sibelius), and *The Japanese Dance*. Now possesses her own large School in Paris. André Levinson says of her :—
"The purity of her dancing is such that I am frightened to express it in words. It is absolute dancing. A simple preparation of hers, a fifth position in its motionless equilibrium moves us by its perfect and effortless composition, by the simple and logical harmonies of her curves and straight lines."
Portrait by Constantine Korovin.
Busts by de Boulogne.
Books on Trefilova: in English by Arnold L. Haskell (Artists of the Dance Series—Vol. I, British-Continental Press)—the same author's "Some Studies in Ballet" is dedicated to her: in Russian by André Levinson. Is also mentioned in all the leading works on the subject. An important chapter, fully illustrated, appears in Levinson's "La Danse d'Aujourdhui."
Address: Savoy Hotel, Rue de Rivoli, Paris.
Best photos:

TREMAYNE (Miss), Ida (Ida Randles); operatic, Greek and ballroom teacher. Diploma of Jean McKay and Charles de Cerjat School of Dancing. Was a pupil of Kathleen Jepson, of the Ginner-Mawer School, and opened own School of Dancing in Exeter in 1927. Winner of Waltz Championship of Devon in 1926.
Address: 46 St. David's Hill, Exeter, Devon.
Best Photos: G. & N. Hawkwell, Exeter.

TRUCHÉ (Miss), Nini; general teacher and demonstrator. Principal of The Shirley Park School of Dancing, Croydon. Pupil of Santos Casani.

Dance Hostess at Davis Theatre, Croydon.
Address: 1 Shirley Park Road, Croydon.
Best Photos: Reprograph, London.

TSOUKALAS, Nicholas; operatic, Greek, Spanish and character dancer and teacher. Member and teacher of Dancing Masters of America; Vice-President and Teacher for Chicago Association of Dancing Masters. Born in Athens, where all types of dancing were studied at an early age. Toured extensively in Greece. Opened a School of Dancing in Chicago, for all types of dancing, where he is well known as an authority on Greek Dancing. Writes and lectures on various subjects connected with dancing and produces ballets, recitals, etc., for Chicago theatres. Editor and publisher of "Self Expression Magazine." Author of booklets on "Greek Classic Dancing" and "Spanish Dancing."
Address: 218 So. Wabash Avenue, Chicago.

TUDOR, Anthony; operatic dancer and choreographer. Secretary of the Ballet Club, and also Assistant Stage Manager. Pupil of Mdme. Marie Rambert. Has appeared at the Ballet Club performances as "The Bowler" in *Cricket*, etc.; also at the Lyric, Hammersmith, in June, 1931. Danced in *Façade* for the Camargo Society's third performance. Created and danced in *Cross-Gartered* (Frescobaldi), 1931 and "*Lysistrata*" at the Ballet Club.
Address: C/o The Ballet Club, 2a Ladbroke Road, London, W.11.

TURNER, Harold; *premièr danseur*. Associate Imperial Society of Teachers of Dancing. Holder of Intermediate Certificate Cecchetti Society. First studied with Mr. Alfred Haines, of Manchester, when 16 years of age, and remained with him for two years, and attracted general attention by his success at the "All For Dancing" Festival in that city. Through the influence of Leonide Massine, came to London to study under Madame Rambert; was also helped by Mr. Anton Dolin, who gave him an engagement in his company at the Coliseum, and on tour in 1927. Appeared in Haine's English Ballet at the Royal Opera House, Covent Garden; Old Vic., and in "Jew Suss," at the Duke of York's Theatre. At the age of 20 partnered Mme. Karsavina in *Spectre de la Rose* for a season at the Art's Theatre, London; also for a season at the Lyric Theatre, Hammersmith; also toured with her in Germany. Partnered Lydia Lopokova at the Arts Theatre. Was *premièr danseur* in Karsavina-Rambert season, Lyric Theatre, Hammersmith (June, 1930). Soloist in "Bow Bells," London Hippodrome, 1932.
Books.—A special chapter on Harold Turner appears in "The Marie Rambert Ballet" by A. L. Haskell (British Continental Press).
Address: 17 Bracken Avenue, Nightingale Lane, Balham, London, S.W.12.
Best photos by Van Chandos; Swaine, London.

TURNER, J. T. Blundell; ballroom teacher. Member of the Imperial Society. One of the Principals of the Nottingham Academy of Dancing.
Address: Bretby House, Burns Street, Nottingham.

TURNER (Miss), Margaret; operatic teacher and tap dancer. Advanced Member of the Operatic Association; also Advanced Member of the British Ballet Association; Associate of the Imperial Society (Operatic and Ballroom Branches). One of the Principals of the Nottingham Academy of Dancing.
Address: Bretby House, Burns Street, Nottingham.

TWEEDY (Miss), Muriel. Advanced Member of the Operatic Association. Has recently been taken into partnership by Miss Madge Atkinson and Miss Mollie Suffield in their well-known School at Manchester.
Address: c/o The Atkinson-Suffield School of Dancing, 259 Deansgate, Manchester.

TYNEGATE-SMITH (Miss), Eve; ballroom teacher. Fellow, Examiner and Hon. Secretary of the Imperial Society's Ballroom Branch. Member of the Official Board. Originally trained with Madame Vandyck. Opened her own school in 1921. School covers all classes of dancing. Judge of the " World " and " Star " Championships since their inception. Inventor of Ballroom " Baltimore." Has written many articles on Ballroom Dancing for the *Dancing Times*, the Imperial Society's *Dance Journal*, and other publications. Her school won the Gold Medal for the senior Group Dance in the " All England Competition " in 1930.

Address: Hotel Russell, Russell Square, London, W.C.1.

Best photos: Navana, London.

TYSSER, Alfred St. Hilaire, LL.B.; First Hon. Treasurer of Camargo Society; Director of British-Continental Press, Ltd. (Publishers of books on dancing. Born in Vienna. Studied dancing as a " detached observer " there, in Italy, Germany, Switzerland, Holland, France and Great Britain, where resident since 1924. Pet ambition to aid in eventual realisation of a World Dance Congress, meeting periodically.

Address: British-Continental Press, Ltd., 40 Fleet Street, London, E.C.4.

V

VALERIE (Mdme.), Marcelle; creative dancer; teacher of Dalcroze, Eurythmics, Greek and Expressive dancing. Member of the Imperial Society (Cecchetti Branch). Member of the International Union of Dalcroze Teachers. Has a thorough knowledge of Swedish Gymnastics, Music and its Composition, and has qualified at the Jacques-Dalcroze School of Eurythmics. Was for three years with Cecchetti at his Russian Ballet School in London, afterwards opening her own school in London. Has given frequent recitals at the Rudolf Steiner Hall.

Address: Studio D, 29 High Street, Nottingham Hill Gate, London, W.11.

Best photos: Sawara, London.

VANDYCK, Clifford Gordon; late ballroom teacher; now hall manager. Eldest son of Madame Vandyck, of London. Started teaching at the age of 15 during the Tango boom of 1913. Served throughout the War, at first in the Royal Field Artillery, and later in the Royal Flying Corps. After demobilization did not immediately return to the dancing profession, but in September, 1921, became Assistant Manager at Billy's Club, Newman Street, London. In November, 1922, was appointed Manager at a new hall in Bournemouth, the King's Hall Rooms at the Royal Bath Hotel, and he has been solely responsible for its management ever since, with the exception of a period between 1925 and 1928, when he temporarily left the dancing profession. Has been mainly responsible for making Bournemouth one of the leading dancing centres. Takes a great interest in anything likely to further the cause of dancing generally.

Address: The Grove, Grove Road, Bournemouth, Hants.

VANDYCK (Madame); teacher of all branches. Principal of the Vandyck School of Dancing, one of the oldest established and best known academies. Commenced her teaching career 36 years ago. Her school is one of the most up to date in the kingdom, covering every branch of dancing, both from the pupils' and the teachers' angle. It is from the Vandyck School that many of the best known of the younger generation of teachers have graduated into their own spheres. The school has always exerted a good influence over dancing, and has done much to preserve its best traditions and to stamp out too much exoticism. Madame Vandyck was the first teacher to evolve the low, slow fox-trot from the jerky, cumbrous dance that first arrived in London.

Address: Vandyck School of Dancing, 95 Finchley Road, London, N.W.8.

VANEL (Mademoiselle), Helene; danseuse and mime. Trained by Raymond Duncan, Margaret Morris and Stowitts. Appeared in Paris with Lois Hutton, and founded a School for Greek Dancing, décor, etc., at Saint-Paul, Cannes and Paris in 1924. Toured in Europe with ballets *Rhythm et Conleur* in 1929 ; opened theatre of this name at Saint-Paul with "Mardis de la Danse." Recitals of the latter are given in Paris, Brussels, etc., each year.
Address: Saint-Paul (Alpes Maritimes), France.
Best Photos: Marant, Paris ; Salerni, Nice.

VINCENT, Ernest; teacher of ballroom and tap dancing. Specializes in ballroom. Has a well-known School in South London.
Address: 30 Brixton Road, London, S.W.9.

VISCHER, Jo (G. Joachim Vischer-Klamt) ; teacher of dancing. Co-Principal of the Jutta-Klamt School in Berlin. Director of the Jutta Klamt-Gemeinschaft E.V. Originally teacher of agriculture and political economy. Took up gymnastics and dancing in 1918. Married Jutta Klamt and joined the Jutta-Klamt School as co-principal. Invented own system of dance-writing which was acknowledged at the Dance Congress in Essen, 1928.
Address: Berlin-Grunewald, Gillstr, 10.
Best Photos: Robertson, Berlin.

VITAK, Albertina; operatic dancer. Studied under Cecchetti, Fokine, Adolph Bohm, Chester Hale. In 1922 danced as soloist with Fokine at Hippodrome, New York, and in the same year appeared with Ziegfeld Follies in London and New York, including Howard Short's "Ritz Review." Became *prima ballerina* at Capitol Theatre, New York, in 1926, and since then has danced in Ziegfeld's "Palm Beach Nights," Cochran's "This Year of Grace," etc.; also appearing in films for Metro-Goldwyn-Mayer at Hollywood.

Address: 4730 Woodlawn, Chicago, Illinois, U.S.A.
Best Photos: Nicholas Murray; Maurice Goldberg, New York.

VIZAY, R. W.; teacher of ballroom dancing and deportment. Member of the American Society of Teachers of Dancing, New York, and the Wisconsin Society of Teachers of Dancing, and President of both of these Societies, 1931. Has been Instructor of Dancing at the United States Military Academy at West Point, N.Y., since 1884. Joined the American Society of Teachers of Dancing in 1882.
Address: 2039 W., Wisconsin Av., Milwaukee, Wis., U.S.A.

VLADIMIROFF, Pierre; ballet dancer. Trained at the Imperial Schools, St. Petersburg, and made his *debut* there. Danced with Karsavina in *Lac des Cygnes*, etc., and appeared in all the leading roles of the classical repertoire. Danced in the Diaghileff Company for a few seasons, notably in the revival of *Lac des Cygnes* and *Les Sylphides*.

VOLININE, Alexander; ballet dancer. Trained at the Imperial School, Moscow, under Tichimiroff, and made his *debut* there. Has appeared in all the roles of the classical ballet—*Swan Lake*, etc. Danced in London with Madame Genée. Was *premier danseur* with Pavlova during many of her tours, appearing with her in "Christmas," etc. Has opened a dancing school in Paris.
Address: 9 Avenue de Montespan, Paris.

VON LABAN, Rudolf; leader of the modern dance in Central Europe. Studied art and ballet in Munich, Paris and Vienna. 1910 founded his first school and dance-group on modern ideas in Munich, which was later moved to Ascona (Lago Maggiore), and visited by most important international dancers and artists. Remained in Switzerland during the War; returned to Germany 1919 and founded the "Tanzbühne Laban." 1921, appointed ballet master of the "Mannheimer

National Theatre" and later the "Landestheater Stuttgart." 1923, headquarters moved to Hamburg; first productions of dance-dramas, ballets, movement-chorus works on larger scale. Establishment of the first Amateur Movement Chorus. 1924-1926, foundation of the "Kammertanztheater," and toured with this small group all over Germany and abroad. 1926, first visit to America. 1927, organised the Dance Congress at the theatrical exhibition in Magdeburg, and the professional association of the modern dancers' "Deutscher Tànzerbund" in co-operation with the ballet association. 1929, organised the Procession of Industries in Vienna with 10,000 people taking part, and Alltag Und Fest (chorus-work) in Mannheim with 500 people. 1930, Choreographer for "Tannhauser" at the Wagner Festival in Bayreuth. Appointed ballet master of the State Theatres in Berlin. Invented a system of dance-writing and laid the foundation for a new theory of movement harmony.

Published the following books : " Die Welt des Tänzers," " Choregraphie," " Gymnastik und Tanz," " Des Kindes Gymnastik und Tanz," " Methodik der Tanzschrift," and numerous articles and essays on dancing, theatre and related subjects.

Address : State Opera, Berlin, Unter den Linden.

W

WALKER, Billy and Marjorie (Mr. and Mrs. W. Walker); ballroom teachers. The only Irish couple to reach the semi-finals of the "Star" Championship at the Albert Hall, London, in 1929. They are now Host and Hostess at Clery's Ballroom, Dublin. Billy Walker won the Irish Championship in 1930.

Address: 61 Blessington Street, Dublin.

WALKER, H. K.; ballroom teacher. Vice-President of the Manchester Association of Teachers of Dancing. Holds the position of Amusement Manager to the Belle Vue Gardens, Manchester, and is the originator of the North of England Dance Band Contest, which has been held each year since 1924.

Address: 22 Guildford Road, Levenshulme, Manchester.

WALKER, Madam (Mrs. Walker-Peters); general teacher. Gold and Silver Medal (Dancing), Bronze Medal (Singing) Society of Arts. Opened Victoria Academy, Southsea, in 1899, for dancing, singing, stagecraft and elocution. Produced the Walker Juveniles, an act which toured Great Britain, 1914-1922, under Moss Empires, Stolls, London theatres of Variety, including Coliseum, Palladium and Holborn Empires ; later toured Europe as Madame Walker's Famous Academy Girls, from which title roles have been chosen for European productions of " The Desert Song," " Rose Marie," etc. Companies of Juvenile Dancers toured provinces, 1918-1929, during pantomime seasons ; Ballet Mistress for 11 years at Theatre Royal, Portsmouth.

Address : 2 Portland Road, Southsea, Portsmouth.

WALKER (Miss), Mary; ballroom teacher. Member Imperial Society. On the staff of the Audley School of Dancing.

Address : C/o The Audley School of Dancing, 449 Oxford Street, London, W.1.

WALLMANN (Fraulein), Margarete; choregraphic director of the Salzburg Festivals Plays ; dancer and dance producer. Leader of the Wallmann Dance Group. Teacher and Director at the Mary Wigman School in Berlin. Member of the Deutsche Tanzgemeinschaft and Singchor and Tanz. For a period of twelve years received training in ballet work at the Berlin and Munich Opera Houses and under Russian teachers. Then for fifteen years toured Germany, Holland and Switzerland with her own Recitals, after which she joined the Mary Wigman School in Dresden, and appeared with Mary Wigman in her Dance Group. Founded the Berlin branch of the Wigman School, and was responsible for several big productions, including the dance-dramas of "Orpheus Dyonisos" and "The Last Judgment." During the past three seasons has toured the United States giving lecture-demonstrations. When in Berlin gives weekly lessons and lectures from the Broadcasting Station Deutsche Welle. Has recently ceased to represent Miss Wigman.

Author of " Der Neue Kunstlerische Tanz."

Address: Paulsbornerstrasse 74, Berlin-Halensee, Germany.

Best Photos: Charlotte Rudolph, Dresden; Backer and Maas, Berlin.

WALMSLEY (Miss), Mae; ballroom dancer and teacher. Partnered by Mr. Sydney Stern, was winner of the "Star" Professional Championship in 1928 and 1929, and runner-up in 1930. Winner of the Grand Prix d'Elegance at the Worlds Championships 1930, and runner-up for the European Professional Championship, 1930.

Address: Carlton Hotel, Haymarket, London, W.1.

WALTON (Miss), Louie (Mrs. Silas Palmer); general teacher. Member of the Association of Operatic Dancing. Life Member and Fellow of the Imperial Society. Has served on the Council. Is the proprietress of Walton's School of Dancing, which was founded in 1843 by her grandfather, and was afterwards carried on by her father Mr. James Merscy Walton. Mr. James Walton was one of the founders of the Imperial Society of Teachers of Dancing, and at the time of his death in 1909 was Examiner and Vice-President of the Society. In conjunction with her late husband, Mr. Silas Palmer, Miss Walton has been responsible for many excellent productions by the Margate Amateur Operatic Society, and her annual Dancing Matinées have been the means of raising considerable sums for the Margate Hospital.

Address: Walton's School of Dancing, Ivy Cottage, Booth Place, Dane Hill, Margate.

WANTLING, Arthur; ballroom teacher. Examiner and Past President of the Manchester Association of Teachers of Dancing. Member of the National Association of Teachers of Dancing; Member Official Board of Ballroom Dancing.

Address: 7 Cranmere Avenue, Levenshulme, Manchester.

WARBURTON (Miss), Nina (Mrs. Alfred Haines); operatic dancer and general teacher. Principal dancer of the "Haines English Ballet." Made first professional appearance at the London Coliseum in 1915. Is still touring with the Ballet. Was trained by Mr. Alfred Haines.

Address: Westwood, Upper Chorlton Road, Manchester.

Best photos: F. Ash; F. Ingham: Manchester.

WARREN, Alex. S.; teacher of ballroom dancing. Member Imperial Society. Technical Instructor to the International Dancing Masters' Association. Was born into the dancing profession, his father and mother having been teachers before him. Has done a great deal to foster the high standard of ballroom dancing in Scotland. In 1924-5 he promoted the West of Scotland Championships, which have been held each following year very successfully. Was for some years M.C. at the Blackpool Winter Gardens, and is now Manager of the Albert Palais de Danse, Glasgow, and Co-Principal with his brother, Mr. John G. Warren, of the Warren School of Dancing. His personal competition successes include: 1925, Winner 100 guineas Shield, Blackpool; Winner North of England Championship; Finalist, "World's Championship" (partnered by Miss Nellie Lees). 1926: Finalist "World's Championship; Winner All England Championship, organized by "Allied Newspapers, Ltd." at Manchester (partnered by Miss N. Lees). 1927: Finalist "Star" Championship; Finalist Yale Blues Championship (Miss N. Lees). 1928: Winner first Scottish Dancing Championship, and Finalist "Star" Championship (fifth), dancing with

Miss Celia Bristowe. 1929: Winner Scottish Championship (with Miss Betty McGregor); Finalist "Star" Championship (with Miss Freda Haylor); Winner North of England Championship (with Miss Betty McGregor). 1930: Finalist "Star" Championship (with Miss Betty McGregor). 1931: Finalist "Star" Tango Championship (with Miss Betty McGregor). Was third in British Professional Championship (partnered by Miss Betty McGregor), and with Edna Roscoe was again third in 1932.
Address: 285 Bath Street, Charing Cross, Glasgow.
Best Photos: F. A. Locke, Glasgow.

WARREN, John G. Member Imperial Society. Co-Principal with his brother, Mr. Alex. S. Warren, of the Warren School of Dancing. Amongst recent competition successes he was a Finalist in the "Star" Championship Fox-trot Competition, 1931.
Address: 285 Bath Street, Charing Cross, Glasgow.

WATKINS (Miss), Dorothy; teacher of operatic, character, national and ballroom dancing. Member Imperial Society of Teachers of Dancing (Classical Ballet Branch). Member Operatic Association. Has a large teaching connection of her own, and is also on the staff of and teaches operatic dancing at the Ruby Peeler School, London.
Address: Collingsbourne, Addlestone, Surrey.
Best photos: Navana; Reprograph, London.

WATSON, George; exhibition ballroom and tap dancer. Began dancing career in South Africa, where he was trained by Miss Phoebe Harris, afterwards partnering her in successful demonstrations. On his return to England visited Mdme Lea Espinosa for tuition in exhibition dancing. Then, together with Miss Phoebe Harris (also in England at the time), formed partnership with Ray and Geoffrey Espinosa, and started cabaret act which met with considerable success. Miss Harris left for engagements abroad, and the three remaining dancers now carry on with that capital dancing act known as "The Two Espinosas and Watson."
Address: C/o Mdme. Lea Espinosa, 26 West Street, Cambridge Circus, London, W.C.2.

WEBB, Arthur E.; ballroom and national dancer. President of the National Association of Teachers of Dancing, 1914-15, and of the Midland Association 1927-28. For some years was on Executive Council of the British Association. Has been teaching dancing for over 30 years. Has organized Saturday night dances at the Wandsworth Town Hall for the last 27 years.
Address: Geraldine Academy of Dancing, East Hill, Wandsworth, London.

WEBB, Cyril W.; ballroom teacher. Began teaching in 1919 and established the Elite School of Ballroom Dancing in Romford in 1925, where students are trained and couples coached for competitions. Judges competitions and demonstrates with Miss Franklyn Harris.
Address: 27 Como Street, Romford, Essex.

WEBB (Miss), Doris Elizabeth; general teacher. Member Imperial Society Teachers of Dancing (Ballroom Branch). Has had experience as dance hostess in England and abroad.
Address: 6a Ye Corner, Bushey, Herts.

WELLS, John G.; amateur ballroom dancer. Vice-President of the Amateur Dancers' Association. With his sister, Miss Julia Elsie Wells, has won the "Star" Amateur Championship for 1930 and 1931, and the European Amateur Championship for those two years. Also a number of other International Championships held in Germany and Switzerland. With René Sissons won the "British Amateur Championship" at Blackpool in 1932.
Address: 22a Grove Road, Sutton, Surrey.

WELLS (Miss), Julia Elsie; ballroom dancer. Partnered by her brother, Mr. John G. Wells, has won a number of competitions, including the "Star" Amateur Championship 1930 and 1931, and the European Amateur Championship, 1930 and 1931. Also other International Championships held in Germany and Switzerland. Recently became a professional and partnered Sidney Stern.
Address: 22a Grove Road, Sutton, Surrey.
Best photos: Bertram Park, London.

WESTON (Mademoiselle), Eunice (Eunice Payne Weston); general teacher. Advanced Member Operatic Association, and their Official Representative in Australia; Fellow Imperial Society of Teachers of Dancing. Was one of the original members of the Operatic Association, and played "Dandy" in revival of "The Dancing Master" at their first matinée. Trained at Battersea Polytechnic, London, and opened Academy of Dancing in Melbourne, Australia, in 1927. Ballet Mistress and solo dancer in revival of "The Quaker Girl" by Victoria Operatic Society, and Ballet Mistress at Regent Theatre, Melbourne, 1929. Since then annual Summer Schools have been held, public performances given for charities, and children and students trained from all parts of Australia and New Zealand.
Address: 1st Floor, Hygeia House, 236 Elizabeth Street, Melbourne, Australia.

WESTON (Miss), Irene; teacher of the Revived Greek Dance and general teacher. Holds First Class Certificate Ginner-Mawer School. Received three years' training at the Ginner-Mawer School, London. Also trained at the Ruby Peeler School (Ballroom) and Max Rivers School (Musical Comedy and Tap Dancing). Has teaching connections at Leicester and Nuneaton, and in addition is in charge of the Greek Dancing at the Swedish Gymnasium and School of Dancing, Friargate, Derby.
Address: The Homestead, London Road, Leicester.

Best photos by Lenare, Leicester; and Navana, London.

WHITELEY (Miss), Peggy; general and operatic teacher. Intermediate Member of the Association of Operatic Dancing of Great Britain; Licentiate Imperial Society of Teachers of Dancing (Operatic Branch), and Local Organiser for the Children's Examinations. Is herself a pupil of Nicolas Legat, Judith Espinosa and Carlotta Mossetti.
Address: 29 Palmerston Road, Southsea, Hants.
Best Photos: Hana (now Navana), London.

WHITTARD (Miss), Aline; teacher of operatic, tap, and ballroom dancing, and of music and singing. Member Imperial Society of Teachers of Dancing (Ballroom). Trained by the late Charles d'Albert, and by Miss Belle Harding and Miss Josephine Bradley. Has had stage experience in Grand Opera, Musical Comedy and Revue, and founded her School of Dancing in 1920. Was responsible for the dancers in the recent Gloucester Pageant.
Address: Spa School of Music and Dancing, Gloucester.
Best photos: Richard Hall, Gloucester.

WIESENTHAL, Grete; one of the first representatives of the modern epoch. Trained at the ballet school of the Vienna State Opera. After leaving there gave numerous recitals together with her sisters, Elsa and Bertha, all over Austria and Germany. Most famous as representative of Viennese waltzes.
Author of "Der Aupsieg" (her own biography).

WIGMAN, Mary. One of the foremost German dancers and teachers. Received her first training at the Dalcroze School, Hellerau, and later became a pupil and assistant of Rudolf von Laban. Started her career as a solo dancer in the spring of 1919 in Switzerland and Germany, since when she has from time to time made

extensive tours with outstanding success. Founded the Wigman School in Dresden in 1920, and exercises a very considerable influence over the Modern Central European dancing. She has her own group of dancers, who have toured with her. Introduced to England through the medium of *The Dancing Times* in 1928, when she appeared in London at a "Sunshine" matinee. Produced "Totenmal" in Munich in 1930. In 1931 toured the United States, and opened a branch of her School in New York. Appeared in a series of Recitals in London early in 1932.
Address: Dresden, N., Bautzenerstrasse 107.

WILDEBLOOD (Miss), Joan; general teacher. Elementary Member of Operatic Association, and a Member of the Imperial Society (Operatic, Revived Greek, and Ballroom Branches). Holder of the Advanced Certificate of the A.T.R.G.D. Was trained by Mrs. Freda Grant. Is teaching in Farnham and district, and has a connection in Haselmere.
Address: Eversley, Great Austins, Farnham, Surrey.

WILENSKY, Edith; teacher of modern ballet dancing, and ballet mistress. Trained by Mrs. Ellen Tells in Vienna, and is the daughter of a famous opera singer who died in America in 1914. Has created many dances for which she has had the music specially composed. First appeared on the stage at the age of 5 years. When 18 was Ballet Mistress at the Theatre in Linz, and later at Lodz, and is now again at Linz, her native town. Has composed some successful ballets.
Address: Eisenhandstr 29, Linz, Austria.
Best Photos: Alt. Linz.

WILLIAMS (Miss), Beth (with Dolly Williams "The Williams Sisters"); teacher and demonstrator of ballroom dancing. Associate Imperial Society of Teachers of Dancing (Ballroom branch); holder of Casani Certificate. Trained at Casani School in 1929, and with Dolly Williams judged and demonstrated in Richmond, Twickenham, Kingston, etc., and also in London. Principal of large School of Dancing in Richmond, at Cambridge House Hotel.
Address: 14 Riverdale Road, Twickenham Park, Middlesex.
Best Photos: Swaine, London.

WILLS, Eric; ballroom teacher. Member Imperial Society. On the staff of the Audley School of Dancing.
Address: C/o Audley School of Dancing, 449 Oxford Street, London, W.1.

WILSON, Laura (Mrs. Eric M. Agnew); operatic dancer and teacher. Fellow of Imperial Society; holder of their Advanced Certificate for Cecchetti Method; Examiner in Classical Ballet, and Member of Committee. Was a member of the Diaghileff Company from August, 1918, to July, 1919, rejoining again in 1921, having in the meantime been in charge of the Glastonbury Festival School's dance productions. Was solo dancer at Covent Garden Opera House, the Savoy Theatre and the Lyric Theatre. Arranged dances for Sir Nigel Playfair in "The Beaux Stratagem" and 'Tantivy Towers."
Address: Richmond Studio, Fulham Place, W.2.
Best Photos: Basil and Claude Harris, London.

WILSON (Miss), Linley; operatic and ballroom teacher. Intermediate Member Operatic Association; Licentiate Imperial Society and holder of Certificate (Operatic and Ballroom Branches). Member English Folk Dance Society (Country Dance Certificate. Was born in Western Australia, and came to England in 1921, studying dancing under Espinosa, Miss Muriel Simmons, at the Cone School, and under Miss Ruth French. Danced in the ballet of "Hiawatha" at the Albert Hall in 1925. Established as Teacher of Dancing at Perth, Western Australia, since 1926.
Address: 1024 Hay Street, Perth, Western Australia.

Best Photos: Hay Wrightson, London.

WINTERTON (Miss), Eileen; operatic dancer and teacher. Advanced Member of the Operatic Association. Trained principally under Mdme. Judith Espinosa, but has also received tuition from Monsieur Legat, and was for a few months at the School of Dancing connected with the Paris Opera, under the direction of Monsieur Staats. Has been principal dancer of the Carl Rosa Opera Co.; solo dancer with Mdme. Lydia Kyasht's Co.; has danced in pantomime, revue and ballet at the Royal Opera House, etc. Has also appeared in a solo act in London and the provinces. Danced before H.M. the Queen of Greece at a private engagement in 1928.
Address: 13 Conan Mansions, West Kensington, London, W.14.

WOIZIKOVSKI, Leon; ballet and character dancer. Trained at Warsaw, and made his *debut* at the "Big Theatre" there. At the age of 6 he and Pola Negri led a mazurka. Joined the Diaghileff Ballet, and at the departure of Massine undertook many of his roles such as Can-Can dancer (*Boutique Fantasque*), Prince (*Thamar*), Miller (*Three-cornered Hat*), etc. Created many roles of importance—The Card Player (*Les Facheux*), Sailor (*Les Matelots*), and the leader of the Three Ivans (*The Sleeping Princess*). His last creation for Diaghileff was "The Fox" in Lifar's ballet of that name, the very last Diaghileff production. He has since appeared with Anna Pavlova; as guest dancer of the Rambert Ballet at the Lyric Theatre, Hammersmith, and the New Theatre; and also in *Petrouchka* during the Beecham season of Opera and Ballet at the Lyceum Theatre, 1931.

WOLKONSKY, Prince Serge; theatrical critic of the *Dernières Nouvelles* in Paris; teacher of expressive movement, mime. Born 1860. Studied philology at the St. Petersburg University. Occupied in art criticism. Went to America in 1896 with a course of lectures on Russian History and Literature. Director of the Imperial Theatres of Petersburg and Moscow (1900-1902). Has since been engaged in literary work as ballet critic, also drama and cinema. Author of books in Russian on the theatre, and especially theatrical education (elocution and mime).
Address: 'Dernières Nouvelles,' 15 Rue Turbigo, Paris.

WOOD (Miss), Melusine; specialist in historical dancing. Has spent twenty years in travelling all over the world. Has made a special study and research into early dancing and deportment, and is an authority on that. Is Principal of the Court Players' School. Is at present engaged on a book on deportment.
Address: 3 Stanford Road, London, W.8.

WOODMAN (Miss), Marianne; general teacher. Member of the Operatic Association and of the Imperial Society. Principal of the Lincoln School of Dancing.
Address: Lincoln School of Dancing, Castle Square, Lincoln.

WOODWARD (Miss), Alice; general teacher. Member and Local Organiser of the Operatic Association of Great Britain (Intermediate Certificate). Is teaching at the Norman and Saxon School.
Address: Belfast House, Gervis Place, Bournemouth.

WOODWARD (Miss), Edith; general teacher. Hon. Vice-President, Fellow, Life Member and Member of Administrative Council of Imperial Society of Teachers of Dancing, and Examiner for General Branch. Principal of Academy of Dancing and School of Physical Culture, Cheltenham Spa, established in 1907, where all branches of dancing are taught; also gymnastics, fencing and remedial exercises.
Address: 12 Royal Crescent, Cheltenham Spa.

WRYCROFT (Miss), Mabel; dancer and teacher of all branches of dancing.

Holds Advanced Certificate of the Operatic Association. Was trained by Mr. Felix Demery, later being his Head Assistant at his Academy at Bedford, and in charge of his Academy at Northampton, and partnered him in demonstrations of ballroom dancing. Has had stage engagements in London and the Provinces. Is now teaching dancing at the Guildhall School of Music, London.
Address: C/o Guildhall School of Music, Victoria Embankment, London, E.C.4.
Best Photos: Navana, London.

WYATT (Miss), Nora; general teacher. Intermediate Member Operatic Association; Licentiate Imperial Society of Teachers of Dancing. Principal of large Schools of Dancing in Teddington and Twickenham, with branches in Surbiton, Hampton, Shepperton and London. Has appeared with the Beecham Opera Company, Russian Ballet, etc., and now runs own cabaret, which fulfils engagements at the Savoy Hotel, Holborn Restaurant and other well-known London hotels and restaurants. The training of young children is a speciality of the School.
Address : Bredon, Avenue Road, Teddington, Middlesex.

WYMAN (Mrs.), Lilla Viles; general teacher. Member of the Imperial Society; Member of the New York Society of Teachers of Dancing; Founder and First President of the Boston Club of Dance Teachers. Has been a student of dancing in all its forms, Historical, National and Technical, and has travelled to many countries and out-of-the-way places to see dancing in its native element. Has been teaching dancing for nearly fifty years, and been a resident teacher in Boston, U.S.A., for forty-three years. Is the author of a book, " In Quest of Dance-Lore " now in preparation.
Address: 739 Boylston Street, Boston, U.S.A.

Y

YEO, Jocelyn; operatic, musical comedy and tap dancer. Holder of Advanced Cecchetti Certificate. Has studied under Stanislas Idzikowski and Margaret Craske. Was a member of the Diaghileff Russian Ballet and a soloist with Anton Dolin's company. Has recently taken up musical comedy and has been principal dancer at the Lyceum Theatre, London, in pantomime, and also principal girl at the Lyceum Theatre, Sheffield, 1931-32.
Address: 23 Regent's Park Road, London, N.W.1.
Best Photos: Joan Craven, and Reprograph, London.

Z

ZANFRETTA, Francesca (Mrs. Charles Lauri); operatic dancer and teacher. Now retired. Born in Mantua in 1862. Studied at Milan with Ernestine Vautier. First appearance as *prima ballerina* for the Opera Season in 1878 at the Deutches Theatre, Prague, and afterwards at Monnaie Theatre, Brussels, etc. Appeared in England, at Covent Garden in 1880, etc. Took the part of " Phrynette " in original production of *L'Enfant Prodigue* at the Prince of Wales Theatre; " Mephistopheles " in the ballet *Faust* at the Empire Theatre in 1895, and thereafter was Premiere Mime for twelve consecutive years at the Empire.
Address: 24 Yew Tree Court, Bridge Lane, London, N.W.11.

Navana's
threefold ★ service to the profession

★ 1 — 12 prints assorted from 3 positions...15/-

★ 2 — Large studio for ensembles, etc.

★ 3 — Facilities for dances receptions, etc.

You see many Navana portraits on the playboards or in the Press... striking photographs that have caught the subject in the most favourable light and that compel a pause... and admiration. That's a Navana portrait, at your best naturally... photography that effectively "puts you across" and helps so much when jobs are going. Navana's offer to artistes... 12 glossy prints 10" × 8" (assorted from 3 positions) for agents' offices and casting files 15/-. Do you know, also, that the Navana Studio in Leicester Square, probably the largest in town, and certainly the best equipped as regards lighting and scenic effects, permits us to photograph ensembles and large troupes in action? Charges, of course, are moderate. Furthermore, do you know that this spacious, well-lit studio (60' × 30') is available for holding private dances, whist drives, receptions, etc., in fact for anything that demands a central position, a perfect floor, the fullest facilities and reasonable charges?

Write for full particulars to :—

Navana Ltd
(Late Hana)

15 LEICESTER SQUARE, W.1
(*Two doors from Daly's Theatre*)
'Phone: Gerrard 6115

Price £1 1s. net, postage 6d. to any part of the world.

A BIBLIOGRAPHY OF DANCING

Compiled and Annotated by
CYRIL W. BEAUMONT

The Bibliography contains a concise description of the contents of over 400 books relative to dancing—works on all branches of technique, biographies of dancers, histories of dancing, keys to stenochoregraphic charts, stories of ballets, and so on. The books are arranged in alphabetical order under authors, and there is a full index of subjects occupying 28 pages and comprising nearly 2,000 references.

Such a work has long been wanted. How often dancers and teachers of dancing find themselves in need of some special information vital to the arrangement of a film prologue, a dance, or a ballet? A reference to the index of the Bibliography will tell you which book contains the desired information. In many cases it will cite the actual page. All these books are contained in the British Museum Library, and that no time may be lost the reference number of each is given. Those unable to consult the British Museum will quite likely find many of the books in the nearest Central Public Library. Apart from this, much useful information may be gained by a mere perusal of the Bibliography. The price of the book is one guinea—the cost of a single private lesson. Can you afford to be without this key to knowledge?

SOLE PUBLISHERS

THE DANCING TIMES LTD.

25 Wellington Street, London, W.C.2

Some Opinions of the Press and the Dancing Profession.

¶ "Listing some hundreds of titles, the field of dance literature is covered with considerable comprehensiveness. . . . Perhaps the most valuable feature of the present bibliography is its annotation. After every title there is some information as to its content, in many cases running into a description of some length and detail. Often the author has added evaluations and information as to the authoritativeness and reliability of the book in question. The reading of these notes alone constitute a considerable education in dance literature."—*The American Dancer.*

¶ "Your book 'A Bibliography of Dancing' comes as a great help for all interested in the problems of that art. A book like this was very much needed. It is written with knowledge, with neatness, and impartiality, and will be of great use and assistance to many ballet-masters, dancers, historians and dance-critics.

"I heartily congratulate you on your successful completion of this great task."—MICHEL FOKINE.

¶ "In the preface to his 'Bibliography of Dancing,' Mr. Beaumont states the chief object of his work, namely, to help producers in need of documentation by referring them to first-hand information; his book achieves its purpose, and more. In itself the 'Bibliography of Dancing' is an irrefutable argument against the fallacy of common belief in the extreme scarcity of literature on Dancing. This fallacy has been at the bottom of frequent mishandling of the dances of past periods. But, now that there is a reliable guide to research, no excuse remains for the inspiration for a period to be derived from a chocolate box. The Bibliography is as much up to date as the growing literature on the subject will permit. The description of each book is precise and enhances the value of Mr. Beaumont's work. The 'Bibliography of Dancing' should become a handbook for every student of our art."—THAMAR KARSAVINA.

¶ "I have read your excellent volume, 'A Bibliography of Dancing,' and I must say that you are a real expert on dancing. Your book will be very useful not only to *maîtres de ballet*, but to all those who love the Dance.

"As for myself, this book is like having a telephone in one's hand to connect one with past times."—SERGE LIFAR.

¶ "I have read your work with interest and regard it of great importance and most useful, not only to students, but to anyone interested in the Art of the Ballet."—THE LATE MME. ANNA PAVLOVA.

www.ingramcontent.com/pod-product-compliance
Lightning Source LLC
Chambersburg PA
CBHW060048230426
43661CB00004B/708